THE OPPOSITE OF WOE

THE OPPOSITE OF WOE

My Life in Beer and Politics

JOHN HICKENLOOPER

with Maximillian Potter

PENGUIN PRESS

New York

2016

PENGUIN PRESS
An imprint of Penguin Random House LLC
375 Hudson Street
New York, New York 10014
penguin.com

Photographs courtesy of John Hickenlooper unless otherwise indicated.

ISBN: 978-1-101-98167-2
E-book ISBN: 978-1-101-98168-9

Printed in the United States of America
1   3   5   7   9   10   8   6   4   2

Designed by Nicole LaRoche

Penguin is committed to publishing works of quality and integrity. In that spirit, we are proud to offer this book to our readers; however, the story, the experiences, and the words are the author's alone.

To Teddy and Robin with all my love

CONTENTS

One

A NIGHT TO REMEMBER

If you had come up to me when I was in college, in the early 1970s, and told me that I would go to work as a geologist for an oil and gas company, I probably would have tucked my shoulder-length hair behind my ears and said something like, "No way, man, you are out of your mind." In the early 1980s, when I was in fact working as an oil and gas geologist, if you had told me that I would become an entrepreneur and open a string of successful brewpub restaurants across the West, I might have joked that you must have rocks in your head. In the 1990s, if you had walked into one of my brewpub restaurants and tried to get me to so much as consider the possibility that I would go into politics; that I would be twice elected mayor of Denver and then be twice elected governor of Colorado; and that one day the president of the United States would invite me to Washington, D.C., for a fancy gala, I *definitely* would have had the bartender cut you off.

And if you had been with me on the evening of December 4, 2011, a year into my first term as governor of Colorado, when I entered the White House as President Obama's guest, and you asked me to explain

1

how all of this had happened, I'm fairly certain I would have said something along the lines of, "Well, to tell you the truth, it's a pretty unbelievable story. Come to think of it, it's a bunch of unbelievable stories, but I'll
have to fill you in later." At that moment I was preoccupied with trying to
smuggle what I thought would make a fine gift for the president by the
Secret Service. And, as has often been the case throughout my life, my
prospects for success were not looking good.

My wife, Helen, and I were in a line of guests all in black tie and evening gowns, just inside the security gate of the White House. We were
there for a cocktail reception before attending the Kennedy Center Honors with the president and the first lady—or, at least, we were under the
impression we were there to attend the event with the president and the
first lady. Truth was, we weren't entirely sure what the evening had in
store. The invitation for the affair had come on short notice and was
worded rather cryptically.

Five days earlier, a White House representative contacted my scheduler in the governor's office and said the president would like to invite
Helen and me to join him at the Kennedy Center Honors. After talking
with Helen, I declined. It was the holidays; we were busy, and considering the event was only days away, with the seasonal hustle and bustle, we
knew finding a sitter to watch our nine-year-old son, Teddy, would be a
challenge. We figured we were among dozens of guests the president had
invited, and while we were flattered, we didn't think the president of the
United States would miss us.

A day after I declined, the White House again called my office. According to my scheduler, the White House wanted to make sure I understood
that the president himself was extending the invitation to the governor
and the first lady of Colorado. We weren't exactly sure what that meant,
but it appeared to be an offer we ought not refuse. Evidently, the president of the United States indeed would miss us if we did not attend.

Helen and I managed to a find a sitter—well, Helen managed to find a sitter. We flew into Washington on the morning of December 4 and by early afternoon we were checked into our hotel. Neither of us had thought to request a room with two double beds, and so our room had a standard queen. As we put our bags down on the bed, I felt awkward. At home, we had not slept in the same bed for some time.

Our relationship had long had its challenges. We were two strong-willed people who wanted different things. I am an off-the-charts extrovert, while Helen is a classic introvert. And we had chosen to enter public life, which would add stress to any marriage. Two years earlier, Colorado governor Bill Ritter had decided not to run for reelection. I was then in my second term as mayor of Denver, and Helen and I had agreed I would run to fill Governor Ritter's seat, but I—we—would do it in a different way. We would prioritize family time while still running a grueling campaign. No obligatory appearances for Helen. I would not bring the campaign back to our home. As had always been my policy, we would not run any negative campaign ads. And we would still win.

We did all this and more. Unbeknownst to any of our friends, Helen and I had been in marriage counseling and we continued counseling throughout the gubernatorial campaign. Because we didn't want our personal lives to become fodder for political mudslinging, Helen and I devised an arrangement that made it possible for us to meet with a therapist without having to walk into a therapist's office and possibly trigger gossip in a waiting room. Once a week for more than two years, we met with a therapist in the basement of a Quaker meeting house.

Therapy being therapy, we had spent innumerable hours poking and prodding me about my childhood, specifically, how my father died and how my mother lived in response to it. The therapist would parrot back the summary of what I had shared during our sessions: *So you're seven years old; your dad is the most fun person in the whole universe, you worship him. And no one explains to you, not even your mother, that the life is going out of him and that's why he can't play with you anymore. And that's why your mom doesn't attend your school plays or baseball games. All you know is what you see—your mom going up and down the stairs several times a day with sheets stained with sweat and spots of blood.*

Then the therapist would ask me in that therapist sort of way if I thought I might have issues with abandonment and intimacy. Had those issues perhaps made it hard for me to be close to Helen? My wife had her own flaws, but emotional accessibility was not among them. I suppose it was a legitimate question. Still, I couldn't help thinking how surreal such sessions were, especially as they came shoehorned into a spare hour at the end of a grueling day spent solving present-day, wonderfully concrete challenges facing the state. The idea that I was being asked if I had unresolved daddy issues . . .

"Is it possible?" I would say. "Sure."

I'd heard that theory before, but that didn't mean I liked hearing it again.

Not giving my childhood much thought, the therapist gently speculated, might be part of the problem. I'd seen a different therapist more than a decade before, while I was struggling with another relationship, and with commitment issues. Then, too, I waded through my childhood, the random outbursts of white-hot anger, my hypersensitivity to authority or even mild criticism, my general immaturity into my adult years. I think therapists can be useful, though sometimes they seem to rely on only a few cards in the deck.

This time was different.

I had someone in the room with me who knew me and loved me, who held me accountable to myself, whom I trusted to not let me rationalize the uncomfortable parts of my past. We also had a nine-year-old son. As

4

a latecomer to politics—I was fifty years old when I ran for mayor of Denver in 2003—I wasn't so ambitious that I missed too many of Teddy's soccer or baseball games. I took him to movies, to the Tattered Cover to buy books, attended my share of parent-teacher conferences. Still, I left a disproportionate amount of parenting to Helen, who had her own career as a nationally recognized reporter and author.

Raising a son, I could see all the ways he was getting what I never even knew I had missed, the moments of joy or reassurance that I never experienced. I was doing what I thought fathers were supposed to do, and I was finding my way. If most men become the husbands and the fathers they are either because of or despite their own dads, or a mixture of the two, well, I had grown up without either a fatherly foundation or foil.

I'm not naturally inclined toward introspection. Whether due to nature, nurture, or self-defense mechanism, I'm not backward-looking. For most of my life I kept myself too busy to spend much time fussing about things like my past.

However, the more I was made to think about all of what happened and, I guess, all of what did not happen in my youth, I began to see with clarity that my father's untimely death, when he was only forty and I had just turned eight, influenced my whole life—every risk, every decision, every success, every failure, every relationship, both personal and professional alike. As the psychology joke goes, my issues had issues.

Helen and I would eventually separate and then divorce. We still love each other dearly. We still try to do whatever we can to make each other happy. Although we now live in separate homes, they are only a block apart. We still consider ourselves essential partners in the task of raising a healthy child. Teddy will always be our joint joy and priority. Indeed, he is my primary reason for writing this book, to make sure he has a healthy store of his father's youthful wanderlust and a record of my serious endeavors to be of service and make a difference.

My life in politics hasn't been hard only on Helen; it has been a sacrifice for our son, perhaps most of all. For as much as I have been be there for Teddy, I have not been there for him as much as I have wanted. Certainly, I have not been there for him as much as he deserves. My responsibilities as mayor and then governor have made that impossible. I hope reading this memoir will enable him to feel that during the time I have been in elected office, *his* sacrifice was worthwhile. I hope that after reading this record, as imperfect as it may be, Teddy will understand my history, *his* history, and he will think that although I took what has to be one of the most unlikely and circuitous routes imaginable into elected office, once I got there, I actually did a decent job; that I helped make his city, his state, and his future better; and that my many hours away from him were well spent.

Maybe one day, Teddy, all grown up, a father himself, can toss this book into his own child's lap and say, "You know, your grandfather was elected mayor of Denver at a time when the city government was on the verge of economic collapse, when many people had lost faith in the police department, and he worked to fix that and more. He led our state out of an economic recession while shepherding the state through incredibly devastating fires, a historic flood, horrific violence and bloodshed; while fighting for gay marriage, for sensible gun laws, for immigrants, and for regulations that helped keep our environment safe and clean. He did this while making the state one of the most vibrant economies in the country. Your grandfather brought people together to get things done." In the movie version of this moment, Teddy would finish by saying, "And, you know what, he still managed to be a pretty good dad."

I always thought what I most wanted was for my father to be proud of me, but what I want most is for my son to be proud of me. I want Teddy to know how much I have loved our democracy, our city, our state, his mom, and most of all, how much I have loved him, and how he inspired me.

―――――――

BACK IN THAT December of 2011, the hard truth was that Helen and I both sensed our marriage crumbling, but Helen knew that I still felt a bit more of a swing in my step when she was by my side. And I knew, given that Helen is an author and a passionate fan of the arts, that at the Kennedy Center Honors she would feel as if she were standing on the moon. We didn't give a second thought to attending the event together. Regardless of our marriage problems, I think we both took solace in believing we had helped each other become who we were.

"What is that?" a law enforcement officer at the security gate asked me. He nodded at the belt buckle in my hand. It was my gift for President Obama. Not that I was planning on telling security this.

Helen looked my way. The twinkle in her eyes conveyed, *Oh, here we go.*

"Just a belt buckle," I said. The security officer shot me a look. He didn't need me to tell him it was a belt buckle.

Governors don't typically have to go through metal detectors, not even at the White House. I wasn't expecting to have to go through one this night. Answering the security officer's questions, I was irritated and I tried to be vague, figuring if I told him it was a gift for the president my buckle would be confiscated. I had taken the buckle out of my pocket as soon as I spotted the metal detector. As there was no way I could sneak the buckle through the metal detector, I thought I might have a better chance of getting the thing inside if I held the buckle in my hand and tried to make my case to security. The officer took the buckle from my hand and turned it over and over, inspecting it. The buckle was a large silver piece inscribed with the carving of a donkey in a ring of gears, and the phrase "Get your ass in gear."

I like the story of how the donkey became the symbol of the party. During the 1828 presidential campaign, Andrew Jackson was regarded as a stubborn populist. His slogan was "let the people rule." His opponents labeled him a "jackass," saying if he was elected and the people ruled it would amount to a bunch of jackasses running the country. Jackson, a decorated hero of the War of 1812, recognized a strategic opportunity when it was handed to him. He embraced his populism and the jackass. He highlighted the virtues of the donkey: persistent, loyal, able to carry a heavy load. He put the image on his campaign posters and rode the jackass right into the Oval Office, becoming the first Democratic president of the United States. Despite Jackson's truly disgraceful treatment of Native Americans, the donkey remained a likable symbol of the Democratic Party.

"*Why* do you have a belt buckle?" the security officer asked. He looked down at the cummerbund around my waist and then looked back up at me.

"It's important," I said. "I didn't feel comfortable leaving it in the hotel room."

The agent remained unpersuaded. Finally, I came clean and told him I wanted to give it to the president. Sure enough, my buckle went bye-bye. As we walked away from security, I told Helen the president would now never see the damn thing; it would end up stored in that warehouse where they put the Ark of the Covenant at the end of that Indiana Jones movie.

It wasn't just that I paid more than $300 for the thing and that it was made by a Colorado artist. I had what I thought was a pretty clever reason for wanting to gift it to President Obama in this particular moment. What's more, I was nervous and I was counting on the buckle to be an icebreaker.

Once we were through security, a United States Marine escorted us up some stairs and into the East Room. It was stunning, just like the holiday White House you see on television. Several Christmas trees decorated with white lights, garland meticulously hung. The room was filled with people and alive with the murmur of conversation. Guests were pretending not to be discreetly sizing up one another.

Helen and I recognized very few people and suspected no one recognized us. There was a marvelous buffet and a bar and a large-screen TV. The Marine informed us that in this room guests would be watching the Kennedy Center Honors live on TV. Helen and I exchanged a puzzled look. I suggested to the Marine that perhaps there had been a mistake. I explained that the president himself had invited us.

First the confiscated buckle, I thought; now this.

The Marine politely explained that he had directed us to the proper spot and with an apologetic smile added that whatever else would or would not occur were decisions that had been made above his rank. Perfect pivot, off he went. "Crap," I said to Helen. "Let's get a drink." As Rodney Dangerfield put it: no respect. I know, I know, I was the governor of Colorado at the White House, and I should have been honored and thrilled—and I was—but I've had a chip on my shoulder for as long as I can remember.

Growing up, I was the skinny dork with acne and the Coke-bottle-thick eyeglasses. I was a petulant loudmouth, perpetually teased by my classmates. At home, I was the youngest of four kids: my oldest sibling, my sister Betsy, was the brilliant one; my older brother, Sydney, was the star wrestler; my sister Deborah, aka Tad, was the poet and artist; and me, I was the baby. With such competition, I never got the attention—or the respect—I wanted. More than anything, I wanted my voice to be heard.

During our family's dinner-table conversation I couldn't get a word in edgewise. I was constantly hip-checked to last in line for the bathroom and, for that matter, pretty much everything. On my high school's championship baseball team, I was the second-string pitcher, and off the field wasn't exactly the socially graceful Casanova. And college, well, during my ten years there, I was told I didn't have what it takes to pursue my dream of becoming a writer, and time and again I watched the girl I pined for walk off with somebody cooler. You know, I was your typical geek.

So it went for my careers in business and politics: forever pegged as the goof with a snowball's chance. Even my own mother wouldn't invest in my first business. Now, here I was, the governor of Colorado who had hoped to show his long-suffering soon-to-be-ex-wife a night to remember by taking her to the Kennedy Center Honors where we'd be seated in the same audience as the president of the United States, and instead I was having a gin and tonic, watching poor Helen tolerate her heels, as we stood around and waited to watch the real action on TV. Though I should have been happy with where I was, I was not—the story of my life.

Just as I was motioning to the bartender for a second G-and-T, another Marine appeared and asked us to follow him. An exquisitely orchestrated whirlwind of movement ensued: We were led outside the White House and joined a handful of guests onboard a black shuttle bus. Moments later, at the Kennedy Center, we were led this way and that, up some stairs, more stairs, through double doors, and finally, Helen and I were led to a balcony box, front and center of the stage. The front row of our box had only four seats—the other two seats were empty. I pointed out to Helen that our box was labeled *No. 1*. "What do you think that means?" she asked. I said I didn't know, but probably something good. Seeing Helen smile made me smile.

IN THE BOXES to our right were the honorees for the evening: actress Meryl Streep, cellist Yo-Yo Ma, saxophonist Sonny Rollins, Broadway singer Barbara Cook, and singer Neil Diamond. We nodded and smiled in their direction, and figured they must have all been wondering who the hell we were. It was only as the lights dimmed and the show began that President Obama and Michelle slipped into the seats immediately to our right. We shook hands, quickly said hello, and thanked them for the invitation, but not much more. The show was under way and the president seemed intent on relaxing while someone else took the stage.

Helen whispered in my ear that the president had probably been shaking hands all night. Yes, I thought, and he had spent all day extracting troops from Iraq and Afghanistan, fixing the country's lagging economy and debt crisis (Wall Street mismanagement and Occupy Wall Street outrage), implementing the Affordable Care Act, and attempting to negotiate with a bitterly divided legislature with Republicans in control of Congress—not to mention that he was ramping up his reelection campaign.

The 2012 race, Helen and I agreed, was why the president had invited us. Polling didn't look great for his reelection. Even though he had presided over the intelligence and military operation that had finally taken out Osama bin Laden only months earlier, the president was wildly unpopular with Republicans. Seventy percent of the country believed the nation was headed in the wrong direction. Analysts put his chances of winning at an iffy 50-50 at best. The optics of being seen with the governor of Colorado was a subtle yet very public way of projecting an alignment with the West and a state he would need to win the election.

Immigration, fracking, capital punishment, guns, water, budget deficit, the Affordable Care Act, Common Core, same-sex marriage, legalized recreational marijuana: you name it, all of the nation's most vexing and volatile issues, which Washington politicians had done a stellar job of avoiding or otherwise mucking up, were unfolding all at once in Colorado, a state where registered voters were almost equally divided among Republicans, Democrats, and independents, and where rural and urban communities were often at odds—all of which, by the way, was emblematic of national trends. Also like Washington, Colorado had a divided legislature. On a visit to our state, a national political operative had told a couple of my senior aides, "Right now, Colorado is more America than America."

With a critical difference.

According to virtually every political analysis of the state, the consensus was that during that first year of my first term we had accomplished what no one in D.C. and very few state governments could seem to do: we'd persuaded ideologically opposed constituencies to agree on a middle path and we had nudged progress on nearly all of the issues we tackled. Most notably, we passed a balanced budget with overwhelming bipartisan support. Our plan to implement the Affordable Care Act also passed with support from both parties. We were growing our state's economy, and we'd just gotten representatives of the oil and gas industry and leaders from the environmental community to stand shoulder to shoulder and support the most transparent frack-fluid disclosure policy in the country. Along the way, we endured the worst drought in seventy-five years and fought the flames of a series of devastating wildfires.

As the media often noted in 2011, while D.C. seemed broken and the politics in other purple states around the country seemed to be fracturing the electorate and generally further eroding Americans' confidence in democracy, Colorado offered evidence that democracy can work and was a reason for the nation to have, as the president had put it in his last campaign, hope.

Having Helen and me in the box wasn't just an opportunity for the Democratic president to cozy up to the shiny Democratic state bauble of the moment. Colorado had emerged as a strategically valuable battleground state in presidential politics. For the last twenty-five years, voting trends in presidential elections have remained virtually unchanged, with the vast majority of states voting the same way in the last six elections. These races have been decided by a few swing states, one of the most influential of them being Colorado.

One of the country's leading political statisticians, Nate Silver, had pointed out that in the last two elections, Colorado was the new Ohio—the tipping-point state. It was no coincidence that the selection committee for the 2008 Democratic National Convention chose Denver as the host city and Barack Obama accepted his party's nomination standing in the Denver Broncos' stadium, against the backdrop of the Rocky Mountains. And so it wasn't likely a coincidence that President Obama had invited the governor of Colorado to join him for a high-profile event just as the incumbent began the campaign to win his second term.

THE SHOW ON THE STAGE at the Kennedy Center Honors was remarkable. In tribute to Neil Diamond, Smokey Robinson sang "Sweet Caroline" backed by a choir dressed in Boston Red Sox gear—a wonderfully surprising touch as the song is the unofficial theme of Fenway. The entire Kennedy Center audience stood and clapped and sang along like we were all in a cozy bar on Boylston Street. How could we not? Caroline Kennedy, who had inspired Diamond to write the song, joined Smokey onstage and sang along with Lionel Richie. But the highlight of the evening for Helen and me came at the intermission.

We joined the president and the first lady, and all of the honorees and a handful of other balcony guests, in a room behind the boxes. I talked with Meryl Streep about the challenges of raising a child and having a demanding career. She gave advice I won't forget: when talking with your child, never make it about you or what you're doing; make the conversation about them and what is going on in their lives. Helen chatted with one of her idols, Yo-Yo Ma. It's hard to say whether her face or his lit up more when she told him she had written her first book, *Just Like*

Us, while listening to and inspired by his music. I talked with Neil Diamond about his mountain ranch in Colorado: yes, occasionally, cars filled with kids drive by his place late at night singing "Sweet Caroline."

I was hopeful I could make an impression on the president. I wanted to make him laugh. I have long relied on humor as a calling card, as a way to connect. When I was the baby of the Hickenlooper kids at our family's dinner table, telling a funny story was often the only way for me to earn stage time. When the grade-school kids would tease or bully me, I would try to joke myself out of harm's way. One of the few bits of advice I remember my dad giving me is, "If you can't talk your way out of a fight, you deserve to get whupped." When dating, when I was in the business world, even when I was a fifty-year-old "beer man" running for mayor of Denver, I always first turned to humor, often making myself the butt of the joke. Over the years, I'd learned that if you're a gangly, insecure nerd out in the world, if you embrace that, if you—to paraphrase Chris Matthews— hang a lantern on your perceived weakness, it can become a strength. Not unlike Jackson and the jackass.

I told the president about how I had brought the belt buckle to give to him because I thought he might choose to wear it when he visited Colorado during the campaign. A big old cowboy buckle inscribed with the donkey and "Get your ass in gear" is just the kind of humor we like in our state. But, I informed him, alas, security had taken my threatening buckle and spirited it off to the bowels of someplace that probably requires a top secret security clearance to access. He laughed out loud. I quietly declared victory and decided to change the subject before I wore out my welcome.

After the show, the president was whisked away with almost no time for good-byes, and Helen and I exited in a sea of people. In our cab on the way back to the hotel, we were exhilarated and spoke excitedly about the evening. By the time we returned to the hotel room, the air was gone from our sails. Helen curled up in the far corner on her side of the bed near the lamp on the end table and read a book. I sat down on the edge of my side of the bed and watched the highlights of that evening's Broncos game. The Broncos had faced the Vikings in a crucial late-season matchup.

I had adopted the Broncos as my team upon my move to Denver three decades earlier. Like many sports fans, my allegiance to my team was about more than the game itself. For me, the Broncos were emblematic of the story of modern Denver and of my own Colorado story. Only two years after I came to town the Broncos landed a kid from Stanford by the name of John Elway. In 1983, Elway had been the number-one draft pick of the Baltimore Colts, but he refused to go to the Colts. Elway said he would be a garbage collector before he'd go to Baltimore. Quickly traded to Denver, Elway had a couple of rough seasons, but ended up leading the team to a Super Bowl in 1987, and four more after that, including back-to-back Super Bowl wins in 1998 and 1999. The Denver Broncos went from being one of the most unremarkable teams in the NFL to becoming one of the most exciting and successful franchises in football.

So it went for Denver. During that era, the city began to shake the stigma of a flyover cow town and matured into a destination city. Gleaming high-rises sprouted into an expanding skyline that competed with the Rocky Mountains for the eye's attention. Capitalizing on its rugged western history and aerospace industry, the city that had a reputation for oil and gas booms and busts birthed a promising tech sector. In 1993, Denver even got its own professional baseball team and two years later opened the first major U.S. airport in a generation.

Similarly, it was also during that period that I experienced my own series of booms and busts in Colorado. Ultimately, I found success while I helped shape the rise of the new Denver, both in the private sector, opening brewpub restaurants, and when I found myself in the public sector, as the mayor of Denver, a move that was itself directly tied to the Broncos.

I felt a unique kinship with that 2011 Bronco team because of its head coach, John Fox. He was in his first season with the team, just as I was in my first season in the governor's office. We both got off to shaky starts and then found our grooves. As he had managed his team into the play-offs, I had navigated my first legislative session.

Seated at the foot of the hotel bed, leaning into the blue light of the television, I watched highlights of our Broncos' come-from-behind win over the Vikings. I clicked off the TV, delighted. Filled with optimism about what was next for Coach Fox and the Broncos, I felt optimistic about my own future as governor and what we could achieve for the state. Pulling back the covers and slipping into bed, I tried not to disturb Helen. She was lost in one of the many children's novels she read from time to time, stories about child wizards and innocents, generally to ensure they were suitable for a nine-year-old. That these fantasies per-haps provided her with some refuge from the disappointments of our marriage wasn't lost on me.

While we were in counseling I began to feel that I had failed her, our family, and myself. I had not made good on all of my promises to be fully present for her and Teddy. I hadn't always made it home for dinner. I'd sometimes been distracted by the duties and preoccupations of being governor. Helen being Helen, she told me not to be so hard on myself. The way she saw it, when my father died, half of my heart cauterized; and, she said, while the half that was left was wonderful and lovely, it simply didn't pump all of the emotion sometimes needed. That was why, as she put it, I saw the world from a more dispassionate, analytical per-spective; it was why, for me, occasionally facts tended to trump feelings. Helen said that while that did not make me the ideal partner for her, it made me an ideal, pragmatic governor for the state.

As I lay in bed, I replayed highlights from the Broncos' win, from the wonderful evening we had at the Kennedy Center, and from my first year on the job as governor. My drowsy head filled with all sorts of boy-oh-boy plans for the future. However, glancing at Helen, her back turned to me, was a reminder that, moving forward, I would be alone; a reminder that the best-laid dreams can be upended by heartbreaking realities you never see coming, although perhaps you *should* see coming; a reminder that I would be embarking on an uncertain future while still trying to make sense of the past and just how exactly all of this had happened.

Two

THE NEARNESS OF FARAWAY INCIDENTS

When it comes to taking stock of our lives, Clarence Oddbody may have said it best. You remember Clarence. He's the guardian angel out to earn his wings in the classic movie *It's a Wonderful Life*. George Bailey and his savings and loan are in such dire straits that George wishes he'd never been born, and good old Clarence appears and shows George just how different the world would have been without him in it. There's that moment when Clarence is watching the visibly shaken George reflect on the alternate universe he has just seen, and in his sweet, wise way, Clarence says: "Strange, isn't it? Each man's life touches so many other lives. When he isn't around he leaves an awful hole, doesn't he?"

When I was a kid in the late 1950s that movie was beginning to air on television and became a family favorite. At the time, I didn't appreciate the wisdom in Clarence's words. I didn't see, or maybe I didn't *want* to see, my obvious connection to that part of the story. It just didn't occur to me to think about the guy who wasn't around in my life and the awful hole left behind. What the boy in me liked about the film was that George's family and friends, really the whole town, rallies around him like one big family and the evil Mr. Potter doesn't win. The movie reassured me that in the end, despite whatever heartbreak and setbacks we face, life is wonderful.

But I have long since realized how insightful Clarence's observation is. When you stop and think about it, it is indeed strange: how one person makes a decision in his own life, in the moment, and that bold choice or seemingly simple act affects the lives of the people around him, and what's more, affects the lives of people born years, even centuries later. But that's how it goes; one thing can influence so many others. In my case, my life was shaped by generations of fate and family long before I was born. However, two moments, as the geologist in me would put it, were seismic.

The first occurred in the fall of 1682.

A twenty-nine-year-old Englishman by the name of Anthony Morris escorted his wife, Mary, through the hustle and bustle of London's waterfront. Mary, who I imagine was probably rather anxious, held the couple's son, who was only a little over a year old and named after his father and grandfather. Anthony led Mary and baby Anthony to a pier where they stood at the start of a long plank that stretched to a large ship, and ultimately, the young couple hoped, to a new life. The ship was bound for America.

Anthony knew a long voyage presents risk. His father was a mariner who had made many trips between London and Barbados, and on one such journey, in 1656, was lost at sea. Anthony was only two years old when the ocean took his father; he never even got the chance to know his dad. Anthony's mother died four years later, leaving him an orphan at six. More or less on his own, Anthony lived through both the Great Plague and the Great Fire of London, which it appears he accepted as acts of divine intervention that convinced him to join the Society of Friends, the Quakers.

Now, here was Anthony, along with his wife and son of his own, boarding a ship to travel a distance farther than his seaman father had ever dared. Being the devout Quaker Anthony was, he had prayed for safe passage to the colonies. By the grace of God, Anthony hoped that he and his family would arrive at William Penn's "Holy Experiment."

The other critical moment came two and a half centuries later, in the summer of 1945.

A twenty-three-year-old Army pilot on base in Stuttgart, Arkansas, strapped himself into the cockpit of a small plane. Samuel Bowman Kennedy was back in the States a bona fide hero after two tours in Europe fighting the Nazis. Over There, "Bow" flew a P-47 Thunderbolt; of the twenty-five pilots in his 406th Fighter Squadron, he was one of only two who survived all of the group's 120 missions.

On D-Day alone, Bow flew six missions low over Normandy, strafing the beaches, providing cover for the U.S. invasion. During one of those dive attacks Bow's plane, the "Annabelle," which he had named after his wife, took enemy fire; oil blacked out his cockpit windscreen. Flying virtually blind, Bow finished the mission and reached England safely, a feat that earned him the Air Corps' highest honor: the Distinguished Flying Cross.

Now on base in Arkansas awaiting his discharge paperwork, Bow decided he would take off on a much more pleasant mission. His plan was to fly to nearby Norman, Oklahoma, where he would have dinner with friends and then fly right back to Arkansas. He expected to be in his bunk in Stuttgart before midnight. He expected that within a matter of days he would be home in Philadelphia, with his wife and two small children.

If either of these two faraway incidents had turned out differently—if one of these two men had not survived his trip, or if the other one had—I never would have been born.

MY MOTHER WAS Anne Doughten Morris Kennedy Hickenlooper, but those who knew the suburban Philadelphia girl best didn't bother with all that. To them, she was "Shrimpy." Shrimpy, because although she was athletic and curvaceous, she was barely five feet tall. My father, a thin-framed fellow of average height and build from Cincinnati, was John Wright Hickenlooper, but everyone called him "Hick." "Hick" because, well, let's face it, "Hickenlooper" is a goofy mouthful of a thing to say. You don't need to tell a Hickenlooper that his name sounds like an amusement park ride or a brand of kazoo—or, as I learned firsthand, reminds people of an eccentric chocolatier.

When my partners and I were trying to decide what we would call our first brewpub restaurant in Denver, we ran ideas by informal focus groups. By informal focus groups, I mean we spent many nights in Denver pubs. I would belly up to the bar and strike up a conversation with the sort of clientele we were hoping our place would attract. I'd tell them we were opening a pub and considering what to call it. Inevitably, people would ask, Well, what are some of the names? There were eight names in contention; I had them all scribbled on multiple sheets of paper I carried in my back pocket. I'd unfold one of the lists, slide it over and ask what they thought. "Hickenlooper's" was on the list. Too often, I would get reactions like, *No way, that's too silly and made up, sounds like the hamburger chain Fuddruckers.* Or, *Really?! Hickenlooper's?! Why not go with Willy Wonka's Beer Factory?*

"Hickenlooper" also presented challenges when I got into politics. Shortly after I was elected mayor of Denver some decisions I made didn't sit well with the police department. During one particular dustup a huge formation of off-duty police officers gathered outside my office window and chanted "Chickenlooper!" It was catchy, I'll give them that. The media loved it. Though it wasn't particularly original; I'd heard that one quite a bit from kids when I was in elementary school, usually right after "Poopenscooper" or "Chickencooper," which if you ask me are far more inspired.

During my first term as governor of Colorado, *Men's Journal* sent a writer to do a profile of me. The opening sentence went like this: "John Wright Hickenlooper Junior. It doesn't melt on your tongue as much as it gets lodged like a wishbone in the windpipe. (Twenty-eight letters!) It sounds made up—a character from one of Kurt Vonnegut's lesser books, which it sort of is."

But more about Denver cops and Vonnegut later.

When I say everyone called my father "Hick," I mean literally *everyone*, including me and my siblings. Mom was "Mom," but the four of us kids— Betsy, Sydney, Deborah, and I—we never called our father "Dad," always "Hick." I understand that may sound strange, children calling their father by a nickname, but in our home "Hick" was a unique term of endearment, emblematic of just how loving and thoughtful our parents were in the midst of the bittersweet circumstances that had brought them together.

Mom was born just outside of Philadelphia in 1921, the eldest of Sydney Morris and Helen Doughten's five children, all girls. They lived in the "country" suburbs west of the city, as had generations of Morrises before them. Their home was in Daylesford, at the western edge of a string of communities that together formed an area famously known as the "Main Line." During Mom's youth, horse-drawn buggies and new motorcars traveled on the quiet roads lined with big, old leafy trees and big, old stately mansions. Generally speaking, the Main Line enclave as a whole was lined with big, old money.

Early in the nineteenth century, the Pennsylvania Railroad laid a "main line" of track that connected Philadelphia to the pastoral suburbs west of the city along the way to points farther west, like Chicago and Cleveland. Many of Philadelphia's most established families moved from the city to what formerly had been their country homes out *on* the Main Line. Business and banking dynasties with names like Mellon, Cassatt, Biddle, DuPont, and Montgomery Scott would lunch at the Merion Cricket Club, fox hunt in Radnor, and gather in Devon for the annual horse show. They enrolled their fortunate daughters in Bryn Mawr, and sent the male heirs, at least those who didn't opt for one of the Ivies, to Villanova and Haverford; all were colleges on the Main Line and in many cases founded by the wealthy residents' ancestors.

If you're thinking this all sounds pretty Waspy, it was. And this next little bit is to be read in your best country club voice—indeed, quite, rather, just that—Waspy. For a glimpse of the Main Line culture that surrounded my mom during the early twentieth century, you could watch another movie that was popular on TV during my youth: the 1940 Academy Award–winning film *The Philadelphia Story*. In the black-and-white classic directed by George Cukor, Katharine Hepburn stars as Main Line socialite Tracy Lord, torn between suitors played by Cary Grant and Jimmy Stewart.

The film, based on the Broadway play of the same name, was inspired by the real-life escapades of Helen Hope Montgomery Scott, the daughter of a Philadelphia financier who married the scion of a Pennsylvania Railroad family. Helen Hope was the type of bon vivant who had the financial and psychic wherewithal to jaunt off to Paris and dance the Charleston with Josephine Baker. She was an accomplished equestrian, and the organizer who persuaded everyone they absolutely must trot over to Devon and support the horse show. To the world at large that cares about such things, she was the poster child for the early twentieth century Main Line. *Vanity Fair* described her as "the unofficial queen of Philadelphia's WASP oligarchy."

While Mother knew of Helen Hope and grew up on the Main Line, she was raised in a very different, far less exciting world, where such pricey pursuits were about as far off as a Hollywood movie lot. Syd and Helen's home wasn't anything like the Main Line mansions. It was a modest, white, clapboard colonial near the Daylesford train station. Syd and Helen couldn't afford to send their daughters off to a tony boarding school. Heck, they couldn't afford the tuition for the local girls' school. Shrimpy was able to attend the Agnes Irwin School only because she won a scholarship.

Strangers who visited Syd and Helen's home and saw the team of live-in domestics might have gotten the idea that Shrimpy's parents were living in clover, but the "staff" were a husband-and-wife team who worked in exchange for room and board. It was the Great Depression, and my grandparents couldn't bear the idea of this couple possibly going homeless and standing on the bread lines. Fact was, if Helen and Syd weren't lucky enough to have ties to a long-standing family business, they themselves might not have been able to make ends meet.

You see, Syd had launched a distillery, the Old Orchard Distillery, and the Old Orchard collapsed for a variety of reasons. The explanations I got as a kid depended on whom I asked and how much leftover Conestoga Brandy they'd had to drink. Regardless, when the business went under it was a blow to my grandfather, financially and emotionally. "Boppa," as we grandkids called our grandfather thanks to Betsy's baby pronunciation of "grandpa," was forced to take a job at Morris, Wheeler & Co., an iron business that had been in the family for generations. Boppa could have gone to work there, but he had wanted to be his own man, an entrepreneur. That's why Old Orchard's failure hit him so hard, personally, and hit his family. My mother learned to sew so expertly that throughout her life she almost never purchased a dress.

While going to work at Morris, Wheeler & Co. put salt in the wound of my grandfather's pride, he recognized that the salary put food on his family's table and kept the roof over their heads. It turned out to be fortuitous that their home was near the Daylesford train station, as Morris, Wheeler & Co. was in Philadelphia. The firm's location hadn't changed since it was founded in 1828 by Syd's great-great-grandfather, Israel Morris, a direct descendant of the very same Anthony Morris who boarded that ship in London back in 1682.

ANTHONY MORRIS'S PRAYERS were answered. He and Mary and baby Anthony all made it safely to the colonies the same year their ship departed England. Very little information exists about that voyage. But thanks to the research efforts of one of my great-uncles, I can tell you that Anthony's ship was one of about a dozen ships filled with Quakers that over a period of months followed William Penn's ship, the *Welcome*, to America. Anthony's vessel set sail two months behind Penn, and it took Anthony's ship fifty-seven days to reach shore, which was double the "typical" travel time for a journey from England to the New World.

I don't know why it took Anthony's ship so much longer, but if his crossing was anything like Penn's, and it likely was, the prolonged voyage was a mighty unpleasant one. Passengers were tightly packed in quarters below deck, and many of them got seriously ill. About a third of the Quakers who traveled with Penn on the *Welcome* contracted disease and died. Those onboard the *Welcome* often would gather on deck, with heads bowed in prayer as yet another corpse of a Friend was dropped overboard into the sea.

Not only did Anthony and his family all make it safely to the American colonies, but by the late 1680s, Anthony had made a nice life for them all in Philadelphia, laying the foundation for the generations of Morrises that would follow, including my mother, and of course, me.

Anthony built a comfortable home—red brick with white shutters—in the center of town. He became one of Philadelphia's best known and most popular figures. A street was named after him, Morris Lane, or, as it's known today in Olde City Philadelphia, Morris Alley. He was equally chummy with everyone from the blacksmiths to the business class and civic leaders, including William Penn. In fact, Anthony himself was on his way to a career in politics.

And all of it flowed from beer.

When Penn and his Quakers arrived in the Philadelphia area they had a considerable to-do list. The territory that England's King Charles II granted Penn in 1681 was a deal made to settle a debt with Penn's father, an admiral whom the king greatly respected. Because of that great respect, Penn walked away with a great deal of land, all of what would become Pennsylvania, and part of New Jersey and Delaware. In that sprawling territory, the Quakers set about establishing a civil society of law and commerce rooted, as we all learned in school, in religious freedom, where people of all faiths, or no faith, would be welcome. Penn's Quakers were just the sort of God-fearing, hardworking people to roll up their sleeves and build Penn's "Holy Experiment." And they quenched their thirst with beer.

Although the Quakers frowned upon drinking spirits, beer was a different story. In the Quakers' homeland of England, water more often than not was unfit to drink. Beer was the much safer alternative. One had to boil the water to make beer, and even low concentrations of alcohol in weak beer killed off the bacteria that could cause dysentery. And beer would keep. When Penn's Quakers sailed to America they made sure barrels of beer were stocked among the supplies, and once on land as those barrels emptied they began to brew more. Lots more. In no time, the Quakers were home brewing here, there, and everywhere, and those with the means to do so were erecting their own personal breweries.

William Penn made certain a malt house was built on his estate just north of Philadelphia.

The Quakers were not the first immigrants to brew beer in the New World. As early as 1587, Virginia colonists were fermenting ale from corn. In 1612, a couple of guys from Amsterdam, who settled in what would become Manhattan, established the first known brewery in the United States. Then there's the *Mayflower* story, which I think is fantastic: The Pilgrims did not choose to anchor at Plymouth Rock, nor was there any grand plan behind the decision to do so. Beer supply onboard the *Mayflower* had run low and the crew insisted the ship anchor when and where it did so they would still have supply for their return to England. As William Bradford recorded in his diary, "We could not now take time for further search or consideration, our victuals being much spent, especially our beere." Essentially, the Pilgrims were dropped off at the Rock so the crew wouldn't run dry.

However, there is a case to be made, and I guess I'll make it here, that a century before the Founding Fathers would craft the Declaration of Independence, in that same city, Penn's Quakers distinguished themselves as the Founding Fathers of America's craft brew industry. By 1683, there was enough variety in town that an immigrant to Philadelphia noted in letters to family back in England: "I have bought good beer. . . . Here is very good Rye . . . also Barly of 2 sorts, as Winter and Summer . . . also Oats, and 3 sorts of Indian Corne, (two of which sorts they can malt and make good beer as Barley)."

Penn himself, in a 1685 account of progress in his colony, made a point of highlighting the advances in beer:

"Our drink has been Beer and Punch, made of Rum and Water: Our Beer was mostly made of Molasses, which well boyld, with Sassafras or Pine infused into it, makes very tolerable drink; but now they make Mault, and Mault Drink begins to be common, especially at the Ordinaries and the Houses of the more substantial People. In our great Town there is an able Man, that has set up a large Brew House, in order to furnish the People with good Drink, both there and up and down the River."

I didn't learn of this historical entry until after I was out of the brewpub business; otherwise, I assure you, we would have tried whipping up a batch with some of these ingredients. It would have made for some terrific marketing opportunities. We could have called it "Holy Experiment" ale and served it when we ran the pigs through the streets of downtown Denver to commemorate the anniversary of our opening. But I'm getting ahead of myself again.

As I was saying.

The "able Man" Penn referenced was William Frampton. In 1683, Frampton built what is believed to be the first brewery in Pennsylvania, what Penn referred to as a "great brewhouse." It was on the eastern edge of Philadelphia, near the docks on the Delaware River. It didn't last long, as Frampton died in 1686. A year later—I would like to think because he saw an opportunity in the marketplace—Anthony Morris opened a brewery just a stone's throw from where Frampton's operation had been. Serving his signature beers to Philadelphians was how Anthony became a wealthy merchant and a central figure in the city.

There's no historical record of this, but the Morris Brewery almost certainly was an unofficial and perhaps moderately unholy meeting place for many Quakers. I imagine the townsfolk gathering at his establishment, backslapping, hoisting toasts, exchanging information and debating the issues of the day. What is undeniable is that the Morris Brewery gave Anthony a popular profile and community respect such that he was appointed to a number of positions in the city and provincial government. He became the second mayor of Philadelphia. As much as I would like to say that I was the first in my family to brew a life in beer and politics, alas, that honor goes to Anthony Morris.

As Anthony grew into old age, he turned his attention more to the Society of Friends and the effort to build Quaker schools, but he made sure his son was well trained to take over the beer business. In 1696, he arranged for his boy, Anthony Morris III, to apprentice under a Philadelphia brewer. During the seven years of his apprenticeship, Anthony III agreed he would "not disclose or discover to any person or persons during ye sd term . . . the art & mystery of brewing" learned from brewer Henry Babcock.

The investments Anthony the elder made in his start-up brewery and in his son's training would pay big dividends. For well over a century, the Morris Brewery endured as one of the nation's longest-running family businesses. Although the brewery was taken over by the Perot family in 1836, through a Morris-Perot marriage the Morris family remained involved in the brewery for nearly 220 years, until it closed its doors in 1902.

Anthony the elder did far more than brew a legacy of beer and politics, he sired a family line that included a patriot who led the charge in the fight for America's independence, and another notable figure, an entrepreneur who would provide the steel backbone for our nation's first capital city.

Anthony the elder was lucky in business and politics, but he was not so lucky in love, or, depending on your perspective, maybe he was repeatedly lucky in love. His first wife, Mary, who had made the journey to America with him, died five years after they arrived. A year later, in 1689, the widower married Agnes Bom, who, as my sister Betsy once put it, must have had quite a story to tell, as Anthony was her *fourth* husband. Not long after Anthony and Agnes married, she died in 1692. The following year, Anthony took a third wife, another Mary. Mary number two gave birth to four children during their six-year marriage and died in 1699. Betsy also once joked that Mary number two probably died of fatigue. Old frisky Anthony wasn't done yet. He married a fourth and final time, to Elizabeth Watson.

One of Anthony's grandchildren from his series of marriages was Samuel Morris. Sam did well as a merchant and earned himself a life of leisure. He was an excellent horseman who delighted in hunting. He was the founding president of the Gloucester Fox Hunting Club. But Sam was no dandy aristocrat. In 1774, he joined in the simmering preparations for revolution. As the first Continental Congress assembled in Philadelphia, Sam was ahead of the curve on the Second Amendment and formed a well-regulated militia in the form of America's very first mounted cavalry, the Light Horse of the City of Philadelphia. Twenty-one of the twenty-five members who saddled up for this unit were members of Sam's Fox Hunting Club.

When George Washington was appointed commander-in-chief of the Continental Army in June 1775, Sam was given the rank of captain. He and his Light Horse Troop served General Washington in many capacities. They were Washington's personal security detail, escorting him to distant points throughout the colonies. In addition, the troop transported prisoners and spies and delivered top secret messages between outposts and battlefields.

In late December 1776, Captain Sam and the Light Horse reported to General Washington in Trenton for what may have been their greatest contribution to America's Revolution. The troop covered the rear of Washington's Continental Army as it retreated across the Delaware pursued by Lord Cornwallis and his British and Hessian troops. Then, on Christmas night, 1776, when the Continental Army recrossed the Delaware in the dead of night, the troop went along. Because of the icy river conditions, the craft that carried the Light Horse could not reach the shore and Captain Sam and his mounties were forced to take to the water, making their way across the floating ice with their horses in the dark. The Continental forces approached Trenton at dawn. Escorting General Washington during the Battle of Trenton, the troop joined a Continental

Army detachment engaged in a firefight with a company of Hessians hunkered down in a barn. The battle lasted forty-five minutes, and when the last of the musket smoke had dissipated into the sky, the troop had captured about a thousand Hessians. Captain Sam and the Light Horse kept at it, serving as the army's rear guard as it recrossed the Delaware, patrolling the roads until dark.

While Captain Samuel Morris served alongside General Washington, another Sam, this one a Samuel Wheeler, a blacksmith from Philadelphia, did his part to defeat the British. Wheeler built cannons for the Continental Army and then joined in the fight himself. That is until General Washington ordered Wheeler back to Philadelphia for what many believed was an impossible task. Wheeler hammered, forged, and joined the links that formed a massive webbing of iron chains that General Washington's forces stretched across the Hudson River to block the descent of British warships from the north.

Decades after Captain Samuel Morris and blacksmith Samuel Wheeler were joined together in the fight for America's independence, their descendants came together in the iron business of Morris, Wheeler & Co. The firm supplied steel that helped build our nation's first capital city, including steel supports for the twenty-six-ton statue of William Penn atop Philadelphia's City Hall.

Thanks to such a thriving business the man in charge of that iron firm, Israel Morris, became wealthy, with money enough to build one of the greatest mansions of its time on the Main Line. After Israel's death, that fortune slowly diluted. Israel had a number of children, and one of them, my great-grandfather Theodore, had sixteen children and he crafted his will so that the majority of his fortune went to his unmarried offspring. Thus my grandfather Sydney was by no means a wealthy man, which is why when his Old Orchard Distillery went under he and my grandmother were fortunate he could turn to a job at Morris, Wheeler &

Co. He had to pay off his debts and take care of my mother and her four sisters.

MOM HAD ALWAYS been an excellent student. Just as she won a scholarship to the Agnes Irwin School, a scholarship also was her ticket to Vassar College. She relished the adventure of leaving home and heading off to the campus in Poughkeepsie, New York, not to mention escaping her four little sisters. Her Shrimpy nickname had started when Mom was at Irwin. There were three Annes in her class and each of them was given a nickname. At Vassar, Mom hoped to ditch the nickname at last, but one of her Irwin classmates also joined her on campus, so no such luck. Long live "Shrimpy."

It was while she was home on summer break before her senior year that Shrimpy met and fell in love with local boy Samuel Bowman Kennedy. "Bow" was home on break from the University of North Carolina. Right about that summer of 1941 when Shrimpy and Bow began dating, Bow was a Phi Delta fraternity man eager to enlist if the nation went to war. As his romance with Shrimpy blossomed, Japan bombed Pearl Harbor. Bow dropped out of UNC and enlisted in the Army Air Corps. Promptly thereafter, he dropped to one knee and proposed to Shrimpy. Thus began the long run of what would be the best of times and the worst of times for my mother.

Within months, in October 1942, Bow and Shrimpy married. Because the war was on there was no time for a honeymoon. Instead, the couple headed off to Napier Field in Dothan, Alabama, where Bow had recently completed flight school and was to be a flight instructor. On their way out of Philadelphia after the nuptial celebration the couple spent their wedding night at the Hershey Hotel in Hershey, Pennsylvania. Years later, when Mom would talk of that trip, she would say how the town smelled of chocolate.

To say that Shrimpy felt "settled" on base in Alabama would be a generous and inaccurate interpretation of events. While Bow loved flying and had a blast taking off and teaching, Shrimpy's days were grounded in grim realities. Bow's pay was a meager $38 per month, and with rents jacked up around the airfield the best the couple could do was half a house without heat or hot running water. In the year they lived there, in order to save money, Mom never purchased curtains. She used her college dorm drapes for the living room and the newlyweds dressed and undressed in the bathroom. I remember Mom saying that the worst of it all was the cockroaches. To hear her tell it, the large southern variety of roaches were immune to all roach powders. When she turned off the lights at night, the walls seemed to move.

Because Bow was an officer, according to military rules, he and Mother could only socialize with other officers and their families, which left Shrimpy with a small pool of friends. None of the other officers' wives had attended college. In order to fit in, Shrimpy, the proud Vassar graduate, never spoke of her degree. Mostly, she spent the day trying to kill cockroaches, doing her routine of chores, and waiting for Bow to get home. Shrimpy got so bored she would iron her bras and Bow's boxer shorts.

A typical wartime bride, Shrimpy wanted a baby, and in October 1943 she gave birth to my sister Betsy. Two months later, Bow was reassigned to another base in Richmond, Virginia, and then another, and then he was informed he was going overseas to fly a fighter plane in the real thing. Just before Bow left in the spring of 1944 he and Shrimpy spent a week together. Shrimpy then returned to Daylesford and began anxiously waiting out the war. While she waited, on January 4, 1945, she gave birth to my brother, Sydney, named after her father. As mom would later joke, that weeklong visit she had with Bow before he went overseas was plenty of time to make a baby.

Bow served the rest of the war in Europe. In addition to flying in the

D-Day invasion, he flew dozens of missions to liberate Germany. Many commendations and a Distinguished Flying Cross later, he was one of the first pilots sent home after V-E Day. His furlough brought him home to Philadelphia briefly and then on to Stuttgart, Arkansas. During those few days Bow spent at my grandparents' home in Daylesford, he visited with Shrimpy and their daughter, and he held his son, Sydney, for the very first and what would be the very last time.

That day Bow strapped himself into the cockpit for the flight from Stuttgart, Arkansas, to Norman, Oklahoma—June 13, 1945—he was going to visit with Tory and Goody Livingston. Tory had been my mother's roommate at Vassar. According to what Tory would later tell my mom, the Livingstons and Bow had a lovely dinner, and when Bow took off for his return flight to Arkansas weather conditions were fine. The explanation the Army would give to my mother for twenty-three-year-old Bow's fatal crash was that his plane malfunctioned. In time, Mother would have reason to suspect that the plane malfunctioned because it was a plane that should never have been cleared for takeoff. Most of the tip-top aircraft were still overseas; most of what was left in the States were subpar flying heaps.

In Daylesford, a day after the crash, Shrimpy was scrubbing the bathroom floor, happily preparing for Bow's return, when her father walked in and sat on the edge of the tub. Shrimpy saw there was a telegram in his hands, but since Bow was safely in the States she didn't give it a second thought. Then Boppa gave her the news. Years later, when Mom told me about this moment, I asked her how she reacted and she said, "I just continued scrubbing the floor. What else was there to do?"

AS YOU MAY be starting to gather, my mom was not an openly emotional or especially affectionate person. I never questioned her love and devotion to me and to my siblings, but she wasn't one to give any of us a hug or say, "I love you." She didn't talk about her feelings, or, for that matter, anyone's feelings. Throughout my life, there would be times when my mother's stoicism would be one of the things I admired and loved most about her. But on those rare occasions when she hugged me, I mean really hugged me, I would nearly faint for joy. Suffice it to say, my mom never complained. That's the truth: my mother *never* complained. She never felt sorry for herself. She was pretty happy most of the time.

However, I suspect that after Boppa gave her the news and left that bathroom, if my mother really did keep scrubbing, she scrubbed and she wept. I believe she probably sat on that bathroom floor, in the privacy of her pain, and wept while she considered the future. She was only twenty-three years old, a widow with a newborn baby, little Syddo, and a two-year-old, Betsy. I know that Shrimpy believed no man would ever want someone in circumstances like hers, and that she had great anxiety about how she would take care of herself and her two children.

I have thought about this period in Shrimpy's life during my two terms as governor. I have thought about it when I have watched members of our armed forces from Colorado deploy and redeploy to Iraq and Afghanistan, and to volatile missions around the world; when I have attended funerals and memorial services for military members returned home in coffins; when I have visited military bases in our state and talked with families waiting for military-member loved ones to return home—waiting for a father, a mother, a husband, a wife, a son, a daughter; and when I have talked with military families who have a beloved breadwinner serving abroad and listened to how hard these families work to make ends meet. After all, they have their own forts to hold down. I have thought about Shrimpy's anguish and Bow's sacrifice when I see how veterans of these conflicts and of past wars, with wounds visible and concealed, return to civilian life and too often are made to struggle to find an opportunity to rebuild something resembling a normal life.

I have found myself thinking of Bow and Mother living on that base in Dothan, Alabama, in that roach-infested half-a-house on a meager salary. I have thought of Mother getting that telegram, left alone to pick up the pieces of her heart and the pieces of her family, and having to put what was left back together and somehow move on. I am in awe of Bow's heroics and of what my mom endured. Just as I am in awe of the courage and sacrifice that all of our veterans and their families display every day in quiet anonymity.

Like so many U.S. military widows, Shrimpy resiliently soldiered on. Boppa and Granny insisted she and the children stay with them in Daylesford. Mom agreed, but she didn't want to be a burden on her parents. She went to work and paid for a part-time nanny to help her and her parents care for Syd and Betsy.

At Vassar, Shrimpy had majored in English, and now she put that degree to work as a researcher for a Philadelphia-based magazine, *The Country Gentleman*. During the nine to five, Shrimpy checked facts in articles set for publication and wrote a few herself. One of them I still have; it's entitled "How's Housing? Recent Trends in Rural Housing Facilities and Repair." When Shrimpy wasn't at the magazine, she did her best to make sure Betsy and Syddo didn't wreak too much havoc on her parents' rural home.

Although Shrimpy had deemed herself and her children too much of a sad-case undertaking for any sane man and didn't think about dating, that did not keep those around her from trying to pair her up. Sometime in early 1947 one of Mother's Vassar classmates introduced her to a guy with a funny name from Ohio who worked the night shift at the Philco television plant in Philadelphia. John Wright Hickenlooper was a friend of a friend of that classmate.

I remember Mom telling the story of one of her first dates with Hick. He had invited her to dinner at his place, which she described as his "splendid" apartment in Philadelphia. No self-respecting woman of her day could have allowed herself to attend such a rendezvous unchaperoned; Shrimpy enlisted her sister Debbie to go along. When Hick answered the door of his apartment, he saw the two women wearing overcoats that they nonchalantly opened to reveal ridiculously over-the-top ball gowns. In a tone as deadpan as she could muster, Shrimpy said, "I thought we were meant to dress for dinner?" Hick, as Mother would say it in her telling, "nearly passed out in embarrassment." Once let in on the joke, however, Hick thought it was hilarious.

As Mom would soon learn, Hick was from Cincinnati, the youngest of three sons born to Smith Hickenlooper, a federal judge, and Anne Bailey Wright Hickenlooper. Hick graduated from Cornell University with a degree in engineering, and shortly thereafter, with the United States engaged in World War II, he and his two older brothers went to enlist.

It was expected that Hickenlooper boys would do their part. The Hickenloopers had a history of military service in their family that was as storied as the Morris line. During the Civil War, Hick's grandfather Andrew joined an Ohio-based battery of Union troops and was quickly promoted up the ranks. He exhibited such gallantry fighting the Confederates in the battles of Shiloh and Vicksburg, and during Sherman's March to the Sea, that General Ulysses S. Grant endorsed Andrew's promotion to the rank of brevet general. Hick's father, Smith, served in the Army during the First World War. Smith was stationed in Europe and discharged honorably.

Uncle Sam took Hick's brothers, but Hick himself was rejected, deemed unfit because of a variety of physical ailments. Hick's brothers, Smith and Gordon, had always been the handsome and athletic ones, Hick told Shrimpy in the self-deprecating manner she came to learn was his way, while he had pretty much always been something of a reject: thin, awkward, with thick-lensed eyeglasses and stomach issues.

Hick felt ashamed that he had not been accepted to serve his country. Outwardly, he looked to be every bit an able-bodied American man. Going about his daily life, he felt stares, whether real or imagined. He worried that folks on the street pegged him as a coward. He threw himself into his work at the Ohio-based Wright Aeronautical plant. Throughout the war, Hick worked the assembly line for engines that powered planes like the one Bow had flown. Decades later, as one of my dad's brothers would recall, during the three years Hick was on the engine assembly line he never missed a day of work, even refusing to take off holidays and Sundays. Hick was of the mind that if our troops don't get a day off, neither should he. He worked more than a thousand consecutive days.

It was obvious to Shrimpy how much Hick adored her. But she kept trying to discourage him, saying things like, "You don't want a widow and her two children." But he did. When Hick proposed early in 1948, he took her to dinner at the Bellevue Stratford Hotel, the nicest dining room in all of Philadelphia. After the meal, he set out more than a half dozen ring boxes on the table. "Pick one!" he commanded, smiling boldly. At that time, if you put a small deposit on a ring and gave the jeweler sufficient contact information, you could take a ring with the understanding that if your sweetheart didn't care for it—or, I suppose, if you were an unlucky fellow who was turned down—you could bring the cursed ring back. Hick had taken full advantage of that arrangement at *many* of the shops on Jewelers' Row. He figured if he presented such an array of choices to Shrimpy, along with so much romantic drama, she would be swept away.

Hick's trick worked. Mom picked a ring and they wed on September 25, 1948, at All Saints Episcopal Church not far from my grandparents' home in Daylesford, which is where the postceremony celebration was held. Not all that long ago, my sister Betsy compiled an extensive family history, which she neatly assembled in a three-ring binder, complete with photos. In one of the pictures from my parents' wedding day, Mom and Hick are standing together, just the two of them, each holding a cup of punch and smiling away. Mom looks as joyous as any bride I have ever seen.

In another picture, the bride and groom are standing with three-year-old Sydney and five-year-old Betsy. In this shot, neither Mom nor Hick is smiling. Mom has one hand on little Syddo's neck, looking like she wants to wring it—quite possible, as he was always mischievous—and her other hand on angelic Betsy's shoulder. The look on Mom's face screams, *Hurry up and take the damn picture already!* Hick's expression is a blank stare, like he's wondering, My God, what have I gotten myself into? The look is purely for effect. He knew exactly what he'd gotten himself into and he could not have been happier, or more perfectly suited to step into the role of father for Syd and Betsy.

He courted the children as much as he had courted Shrimpy, always sensitive to the fact that they had lost their "real dad." His tender way with the two kids had been one of the things that drew my mother into Hick's arms. That sensitivity was genuine and only continued after Hick and Shrimpy married. Hick was the one who suggested the two children call him by his nickname. Having discussed this with Shrimpy, Hick felt it was the most appropriate, most natural form of address, intimate yet still affording the two small children the opportunity to come to know and define the new man in their lives in their own time.

Meanwhile, my sister Deborah was born on July 26, 1950, and then I hatched on February 7, 1952. (Hick called us his "tadpoles.") This complicated the possible evolution from "Hick" to "Dad." Our parents went to great lengths to ensure that all four children felt equally part of the family, equally loved. There would be no step-sibling difference in the Hickenlooper house. It wouldn't do to have my sister and me refer to our father as "Dad" when Betsy and Syddo called him "Hick." And so Deborah and I were raised to call our dad "Hick" and it just came to pass that we all always called him "Hick."

A big part of the reason my father was so keenly attentive to Sydney and Betsy's plight was because he could empathize in a way few others could. One night, when Hick was fourteen, his parents left their home, each bound to chaperone two separate dances, one for each of their older sons. As his parents were making their way out of the house that night, Hick had been horsing around and must have gone a little too far and angered his father. The stern, imposing judge had told him to stop, "this moment!" In a measured voice, he told Hick, "Don't be such a smart aleck." Without another word, he turned and walked to the car and never returned. That night, he suffered a fatal heart attack.

Not unlike George Bailey, who suddenly experienced what the world was like without him in it, teenage Hick abruptly found himself a kid in a world without his dad, only this was no Clarence Oddbody stunt that could be undone.

Although the death of his father didn't make for such a wonderful childhood for Hick, Syd and Betsy would tell you it helped make him a wonderful father. And indeed that is how they both came to regard him. As Betsy once put it, "We were exceptionally fortunate to spend most of our childhood and early adolescence in his care. He was the best father we could have ever hoped for."

The hell of the irony is that Hick's unique knowledge of what it was like to be a kid who loses your dad made his own prolonged painful death all the more agonizing for him—for Hick knew just what an awful hole he was going to leave behind.

Three

ME AND THE HICKS

For me, there are three Hicks: the father of Betsy and Syddo's stories, whom I never met; the healthy and happy father I hardly knew; and his ghost, which I have spent the better part of my life either seeking or fleeing. From the time I was a boy through my college years, these personas were a blessing and a curse. Mostly, a curse. The one constant for me during this tumultuous period was my remarkably patient mother. If Mom were alive today and had a glass of sherry truth serum in her, she might say the same thing about me: that in my youth I was a blessing and a curse. If Mom had a second glass of sherry in her, she might get even truthier and tell you that when I was growing up I was mostly a curse.

In 1948, the newlywed Hick and Shrimpy returned from their honeymoon in upstate New York and moved into a home they had bought in the town of Narberth. Located on the eastern edge of the Main Line—much closer to the workaday realities of West Philadelphia than it was to the high society of fox hunts and horse shows—Narberth was a mix of blue-collar and white-collar residents. Among Hick and Shrimpy's neighbors were the butcher from the local supermarket, the neighborhood mailman, and a journeyman plumber they called upon from time to time. Not long after Hick and Shrimpy married, Hick left the night shift at the Philco plant and went to work as a supervisor at a Sylvania television factory, on a nine-to-five schedule.

Narberth was a fine place to raise a family: picturesque tree-lined streets, small single-family homes; a quaint town center with a library, a movie house, a five-and-dime, and a lovely park. The home my parents bought on Rockland Road was a fixer-upper, which provided Hick with an excellent excuse to indulge in one of his great joys: estate auctions. As he explained it to my mom, Hick went to the auctions for the bargain hunting. Being the frugal, do-it-yourselfer engineer and first-time home owner that he was, Hick went in search of the nuts and bolts he needed for home repairs, and the chance to pick it all up for a song. At least that's how he sold it to Shrimpy. While that explanation was true, the rest of the truth was that Hick relished the prospect of low-risk treasure hunting. Whenever the auctioneer would say, "Next up for bid, a chest filled with unknown contents," Hick's eyes and imagination would light up.

He brought home at least a half dozen of these mystery trunks. As Mother would watch him pull into their driveway with yet another dusty old wooden box in the back of their white 1952 Plymouth station wagon, she'd wonder where she was going to find the space to put *this* one. Just for delightful spite she'd ask Hick if he had managed to find anything useful for the home repairs. Hick would respond with a mischievous smile and proceed along in his glory, the suburban pirate once again pulling into his home port with a chest of exotic artifacts from some Davy Jones's locker.

In that same spirit of suburban adventure Hick loved to get lost. In those early days, before my older sister Deborah and I were born, on days when Mom just wanted everyone to please get out of the house, especially on rainy weekend days, Hick would pile the tykes, Betsy and Syddo, into the Plymouth and drive off on one of the highways. He'd take an exit ramp that the family rarely if ever had taken before. He'd tell the kids to direct him where and when to turn. The Ohio transplant to the Philly suburbs would then drive and drive, turning here and there on the winding back roads far from the Main Line, the whims of the children as his compass, with the goal of discovering a new place and the challenge of having to find his way home.

Hick was all about mental challenges, always vigilant for an opportunity to test his engineering expertise. He welcomed the phrase "assembly required." Working at the Sylvania television factory he could have bought a Sylvania TV at discount, but nope, Hick being Hick, instead he brought home a box filled with parts from the factory floor, dumped them onto the living room carpet and assembled a television right there, himself. He placed his Frankenstein tube inside a plywood box, a sheet of plastic for the screen.

Hick wasn't at Sylvania long. Boppa, who had risen to an executive position at Morris, Wheeler & Co., determined that the company needed new blood. The way he saw it, M, W & Co. hadn't kept up with the rapidly evolving modernization of the iron and steel industry, and so he recruited his engineer son-in-law. Hick began working at Morris, Wheeler during the day and at night attended Drexel University's Institute of Technology, pursuing a degree in advanced engineering. My sister Betsy remembers that one of his professors described Hick as the brightest student he'd ever taught.

That may have been so, but Hick wasn't much good at assembling a meal. Under normal circumstances, Mom would get up to fix breakfast for him and the two kids, but when she became pregnant with my big sister Deborah, Hick insisted Mom sleep in and leave it to him to whip up breakfast for him and Betsy and Sydney. Which meant pouring Cheerios into a bowl and remembering to add milk.

One morning in the old house on Rockland Road, Hick opened the cereal box and out jumped a mouse. Startled, Hick jumped back, and in what he would insist was a clear case of self-defense, he threw the box at the rodent, fatally slaying the beast in a hail of whole grain O's. Turned out the clobbered mouse had been pregnant, which made for a spectacular mess and filled Hick's head with all sorts of macabre anxiety about his own pregnant wife. But as I've said, Deborah was born in the summer of 1950 and I was born eighteen months later, without complications.

The guy who had boldly presented more than a half dozen engagement rings when he proposed to my mother was romantic and tenderhearted in many ways. Most nights he would be the one to tuck in the kids by reading them a story. He loved the *Wizard of Oz* books. Or he would make up tales of his own, often something mildly spooky that in the end wasn't so spooky after all. He loved a summer storm, the louder the thunder, the more dramatic the lightning, the better. Hick would lead Betsy and Sydney out onto the porch, and with them in his arms, they would watch Mother Nature put on her show. To Hick, the flashing-crashing spectacle, as with the not-so-scary bedtime stories he would tell, presented a teaching moment wherein he could show his children there was really nothing out there to fear.

As Betsy and Syddo got older Hick encouraged them to embrace new experiences of their own. When one of them would do something for the first time, like swim the length of a pool, or dare to open their eyes underwater and retrieve a shiny penny, or even beat him for the first time in chess, Hick would take them both out for a celebratory dinner. The nerdy charm he had used to disarm Shrimpy wasn't the shtick of a suitor, that was who he was. He loved to entertain the family by reciting limericks and singing humorous ditties. There was the one about the beers from his hometown of Cincinnati:

Once there was a Boyce who fell into an Anheuser Busch
and tore two Schlitz in his Pentz.
Was he a sadder Budweiser boy?
Pabst, no. Pabst, yes.

Hick especially liked verses that were risqué for the times. This was one of his favorites:

There was an old farmer who took a young miss
In the back of the barn where he gave her a [long pause]
Lecture on horses and chickens and eggs
And told her that she had the most beautiful [long pause]
Manners. . . .

But I wasn't around for any of those moments. Such blissful days with Hick predated my birth and trickled into the time when I was a baby and a toddler, when I could barely walk, let alone catalogue memories. I only know of that happy-time Hick and those recollections because I eventually heard about them from Betsy and Sydney. I've been fortunate that over the decades they have shared these stories with me, but I confess, when I have heard their lovely anecdotes about what sounds like such an idyllic time with Hick, I've felt a twinge in my chest. Betsy and Syddo got the best of Hick—the father I never knew.

I have very few firsthand memories of my dad. If we're going to put a number on it, I have only three truly distinct memories involving the two of us. All of what little I do remember of us occurred when I was a small boy, between the ages of five and seven. Before that period, as I say, I was too young to recall anything, and then, well, he was gone.

My earliest memory of Hick and me isn't an especially fond one.

About a mile's walk from our house in Narberth there was a drugstore called Doc's. I'm in the store, a skinny kid, a Narberth Elementary first grader of six years old. Bottle-thick eyeglasses, a blond buzz cut, very much the chip off my dad's geeky block. I'm with a handful of older kids. We're playing the pinball machines in the back of the store—my treat. The kids are all eating penny candies, also my treat. In fact, I've been treating them to penny candies and pinball for the last several days. I'm smiling away, basking in my popularity with these older kids, when I feel a steel grip lock on to my arm. I turn and see Hick.

There's a quiet fury in his eyes. "Let's go!" he says. He's so angry he can barely get out the words. He drags me through the store, I'm not even sure my feet are touching the ground, and whisks me right out the front door. The Plymouth station wagon is at the curb. Mom is in the passenger seat. Hick pushes me onto the front seat, next to her, and he goes back inside the store.

"What were you thinking?" Mom growls. "How could you steal from your father's coin collection?" I keep my mouth shut. I know what I've done is wrong, but I don't think it's the crime of the century. Taking silver dollars, nickels, dimes, and pennies from his room—what's the big deal? Hick has so many. Mom tells me what I didn't know: that each of the coins I used to play pinball and buy bubble gum and Swedish Fish were Mercury dimes, Indian-head nickels, nineteenth-century silver dollars— each a piece of valuable complete sets Hick has painstakingly assembled over many years.

"Just be glad you're not Doc," Mom says.

We both look to the store. Through the plate glass windows we see Hick leaning over the counter. He's in Doc's face. Doc is leaning back, and looks awfully uncomfortable. Neither of them is moving a muscle, except for Hick's mouth, which is moving fast indeed. Hick is now speaking much more loudly and clearly. We can hear him lay into Doc clear out to the car. "Just where did you think a six-year-old boy was getting those types of coins? You should be ashamed of yourself taking those from him."

Hick marches back to the car. He heads home. I'm sandwiched between him and Mom. He doesn't say a word the whole ride. He's so disgusted with me he doesn't want to speak to me even to send me to my room. Mom does that.

My second memory of Hick is the one that's nothing but a fun ride.

We're in the Plymouth station wagon, the whole family, on a day that's warm enough for us to have the windows down. We're heading to a cookout at my grandparents' house in Daylesford. We stop at an intersection and a fire engine races by in front of us, siren screaming. In the passenger seat, my mother lowers her head because she knows what's coming next. Hick sticks his head out the driver's window and lets out a shriek, imitating the siren, but sounding more like an elephant in agony. He steps on the gas, pulls a hard right, and chases the fire engine, his head out the window doing his elephant-siren wail over and over. Each time he does it, Betsy, Sydney, Deborah, and I get more and more excited. We bounce on the seats, crawl all over one another, and wail along with him.

Mom just keeps her head down. She is resigned. She has witnessed Hick do this exact thing many times before. He can't resist. He's fascinated by fires and firemen. Hick follows in the engine's slipstream for a couple of miles, through stop signs and traffic lights, like he's some kind of self-deputized Main Line fire marshal. We reach a brick building that's ablaze. It's four, maybe five stories tall. Naturally, the fire engine pulls into the center of the action and, naturally, we glide alongside of the engine. All of us—except Mother, of course—are breathlessly delighted.

That's when the police officer appears at the driver's-side window and asks Hick just what he thinks he's doing. In a tone of well-isn't-it-obvious, Hick explains that we're here to watch the firemen put out the fire. The cop lets us stay just long enough to write up a ticket which he shoves into Hick's chest and orders us to leave, *immediately*. While Hick stammers the *but-but*-buts, Mother assures the officer that Hick will comply. Reluctantly, like a crestfallen child, Hick complies.

My third and final memory of my father involves me and my sister Deborah, whom my father nicknamed "Tadpole," which became shortened to "Tad." This memory of Hick churns up mixed emotions for me.

It's a Sunday morning. I'm about six or seven years old and Tad is around nine. Betsy and Sydney are teenagers still sleeping or doing whatever it is they are doing. As Tad and I do every Sunday morning after we finish the breakfast Mom has made for us, we run from the kitchen, across the old wood floors, up the stairs and down the hallway toward Hick and Mom's room to play our game with Hick. Hearing our charge coming, Hick sits upright in the center of his bed with his eyes closed. Tad and I run into the room and stop cold just inside the doorway. We would like to think we are dead silent, only we're not. We giggle and shush each other.

Tad gets into position on one side of the bed and I move into position on the other. We begin to "sneak" toward Hick. From opposing sides of the bed each of us dives in and pokes him. With his eyes still closed, Hick tries to grab us. We dive, poke, and then try to scurry away before he can catch us. The double bed seems as immense as a football field. For a while, when he nabs one of us the other attacks his flank and tickles him until the captured kid "escapes." Finally, Hick snatches us both in his arms. He pulls us so close to him that I can feel his whiskers scratch against my face, and he says, "These, *these!* Are my jewels." It feels as if he doesn't want to ever let us go, and I don't want him to let go.

Because of Hick's work schedule, I don't see much of him, or at least I feel like I don't see much of him. He leaves early and returns late. And now that we are together and he is holding me, I hold on to him. I nuzzle my head under his chin and lie on his chest. As always, he smells faintly of deodorant. From the corner of my eye, I see Mom leaning against the doorway. She stands with her arms folded. She's smiling, or at least what looks to me like a smile. She stands there for a few seconds gazing at us, not saying a word. Then I see tears in her eyes, on her cheeks. She wipes them from her face and turns and heads back to the kitchen.

I figure Mom's crying because she's happy. I know adults do that sometimes. What I do not know is that Mom is crying because Hick is dying. Mom has known this for a while. Hick has known this for a while. My oldest sister Betsy, who is sixteen, also knows, but only by accident. During one of the multiple times Hick has been in the hospital, Betsy went along with my granny and mom to visit him, and in the car ride Betsy heard them talking. She heard enough from the backseat to lean up and ask: "Hick isn't going to get better, is he?" Mom and Granny paused for a moment, and Mom matter-of-factly told Betsy the truth: "No, he isn't going to get better." Mom instructed Betsy not to tell the other children.

So at this point, Tad and Sydney and I don't have a clue how bad it is. All the three of us know is that Hick is very sick, and that he's been to the hospital a couple of times. But, I figure, lots of people get sick and go to the hospital and get better all the time.

IT TURNED OUT that the medical issues Hick had as a young man, which had kept him from joining his brothers and going off to the war, were nothing to worry about. However, the diagnosis of intestinal cancer was. The diagnosis came in 1958, ten years into my parents' marriage. There was one surgery and then another, each removing more and more of his insides. But these operations were only buying him time. The cancer was at an advanced stage, rapidly chewing through him. Hick set about doing what he could to make sure he left my mom and us kids as well off as he could. At the time, of course, I didn't realize that's what he was doing.

My parents sold the house on Rockland Road and we moved into a home in Wynnewood, a few communities west of Narberth. Wynnewood, my mom and dad believed, had better public schools, and the house they bought on Kent Road had more room. It also put Mom closer to her parents in Daylesford. Wynnewood was a pricier ZIP Code. Working those three years during the war at Wright Aeronautical back in Ohio, with no time off and living at home, Hick had saved up a considerable sum. He'd applied his savings to the purchase of the Narberth house, which sold for a profit. With that and his salary from Morris, Wheeler, Mom and Hick were in a position to buy the Wynnewood place. I remember Kent Road as perfect, lined with elm trees and meticulously groomed hedges.

And I remember our early days fondly. Once in the new home, there was a period of normalcy and even happiness. Tad and I got to run into Hick and Mom's new bedroom on Sunday mornings and play the tickle game. We took a family vacation. But the joy lasted only a few months. Hick's cancer now overwhelmed him. He again went into the hospital. His doctors said there was nothing more they could do. It was during one of those hospital stays that Betsy found out the truth in that car ride with Mom and Granny. Betsy was always one to be prepared. Although I wouldn't know this until years later, Betsy came home that evening and made sure her black dress was cleaned and pressed in the closet.

Hick was now almost always bedridden. No, Mom would tell us, he couldn't play ball or take us out. No, he couldn't take us on a ride to get lost. "I'm sorry," she would say, "I'm afraid he's too tired at the moment." My mother spent most of each day caring for him. In effect, she was now tending to Hick in what was a prolonged hospice that would drag on for nearly a year. Tad and I no longer were allowed to sneak attack Hick on weekend mornings. We couldn't curl up with him and be his "jewels." We were now discouraged from going into their bedroom at all.

Mom didn't want us to disturb Hick, and he didn't want us to see him as he was now, weak and wincing. He was in pain both physically and emotionally. Physically, because the cancer was rotting away his insides. Emotionally, because he was about to leave us, and in particular, leave Tad and me at such young ages. Having been through the death of his own father, Hick had a sense of what was in store for us. He knew we probably would not remember much of him, and that much of what we would remember would be these months of his being sick and absent. Hick knew he was about to leave a hole.

As a parent now myself, I can better imagine some of what must have tortured my father. To know your children are going to endure such loss and pain, and to know that you are going to be the cause, and there is nothing you can do to prevent it; the insidiousness of it all—that he wouldn't be around to help us deal with the hurt he was going to cause us. To be in such agony, to be so aware, to be so loving and so sensitive and so . . . helpless . . . and not to be able to do a damn thing about it.

Throughout his adult life Hick had kept a scrapbook that he filled and updated with funny cartoons and amusing articles he clipped from newspapers and magazines for the purpose of loaning to friends and family when they were ill. Hick always said if you can laugh at something, it can never beat you. Hick would deliver the "Sick Book," as it was dubbed, hoping it would lift an ailing loved one's spirits. He would tell the recipient to hold on to it until he or she was on the mend, and he encouraged them to paste in any cartoons or articles they felt would make a good addition. I still have the Sick Book, its pages tattered and stained. The last page was where "Recupertees" could sign and share comments.

According to the signatures, the Sick Book passed through the hands of at least fifteen people dear to Hick. Among the feedback inscribed: "Patient & nurses enjoyed thoroughly." "Kept me in and out of stitches!" "Feel better already—I really appreciate your sense of humor and your thoughtfulness, Hicky." Yet there was no Sick Book that could have cheered up my father in his final months.

For what he knew would be his last Christmas, in December 1959, Hick insisted he come home from the hospital to be with us. As Mom would tell me years later, as she helped Hick settle in at home she asked him how he was doing; he told her that after his first surgery he thought he had experienced as much pain as a person could endure, but he had been wrong; that pain was a fraction of what he was now experiencing. As a Christmas gift, one of my mother's well-intentioned sisters gave Hick a book. It wasn't anything like Hick's Sick Book. It was a self-help book of the time on how to deal with pain. When Hick removed the wrapping paper and saw the title, he used what strength he could muster to throw it across the bedroom.

The task that consumed most of Mom's time during those final months was changing the sheets on Hick's bed, as they would quickly become covered in his perspiration and sometimes spotted with blood. She'd gently roll Hick to one side of the bed and then to the other in order to remove the soiled sheets and replace them with fresh ones. My mother, remember, was a small woman, and my father was not a small man. Mom would do this chore three, sometimes four times a day.

One day, a truck appeared in our driveway and a delivery man dressed in an impeccably white and pressed uniform appeared at our door with a stack of impeccably white and pressed sheets. He explained to Mother that every few days from that day forward, for as long as she needed the service, he would arrive with fresh linens and he would take away the soiled ones to be laundered. This delivery man who had appeared on our steps like an angel informed Mom he had been sent by Agnes Nixon.

Agnes lived nearby and was a close friend of my mother's. She is one of the most thoughtful, empathetic people I have ever known. A decade later, the media would make a fuss over Barbara Walters as the first woman to earn a million-dollar salary; the media overlooked Agnes, who was earning a million dollars annually in the early 1970s. She was the writer and producer who created the television soap operas *One Life to Live* and *All My Children,* among others. She was also a keen judge of talent of all sorts. She discovered Pierce Brosnan and the future chairman and CEO of the Walt Disney Company, Robert Iger.

Agnes had visited with Mom at our home enough to see what real drama looked like. She saw that changing and cleaning the sheets had become a time-consuming and emotionally draining ordeal for my mother. Agnes took it upon herself to provide the linen service to my mom. She saw a need and she did something. One Christmas holiday, years later, I asked Mom of all the gifts she had ever received, which one had been her favorite; Mom said the linen service Agnes had arranged was "the greatest gift anyone had ever given me. It gave me precious more time with Hick, and with you kids."

But as far I was concerned, whatever time that was, wasn't enough for me. I was seven years old, recently enrolled in a new school, Penn Valley Elementary School, and I had landed what I thought was a plum role in the third-grade play. It was the story of America and I was the narrator. This meant I was in virtually every scene, providing commentary. I wanted Mom to attend. I was probably far more narcissistic and attention starved than your typical seven-year-old. I begged Mom to come and finally she promised me she would.

My big day came and Hick was too ill for Mom to leave him. I'd had enough. When I returned home after the show, Mom appeared just inside the front door to greet me. I now suspect she had been waiting to greet me because she felt terribly guilty she had broken her word to me and was unable to attend. But I was not remotely as thoughtful in the moment. I ignored her kindly delivered question, "How was the play?" I stormed up the stairs from our first floor and headed to my bedroom. Just outside my bedroom door, I stopped, leaned over the railing and screamed at her, "What about me? You guys never come to any of my stuff. What about me? Don't you care about me?"

Just then, a force hit me from out of nowhere, pinning me up against the wall. It was my big brother, Sydney. He was then fourteen years old, well on his way to becoming an undefeated high school state wrestling champion. When I say Sydney pinned me up against the wall—I mean *up*. He lifted me by my shoulders and put his face inches from mine and with spittle flying from his mouth, angrily whispered, "Don't you think Mom and Hick *want* to be at your baseball games and big play? Hick is sick and Mom is taking care of him. How do you think it makes Hick feel when he hears you say that? Do you ever think how he feels?"

Syd then tossed me onto my bed. I lay there crying, feeling sorry for myself, but for the first time was aware that I wasn't the only one with feelings. I hadn't seen Hick for days, but I knew that he was wracked with pain, and now I considered that he had almost certainly heard everyword I'd shouted and I ached that I had made his pain worse.

I'd like to say on that afternoon I had an epiphany that lasted. I'd like to be able to tell you that Syd shook lasting sense into me; that I heard what he said and from that moment on I began to see the sheets spotted with sweat and blood, that I began to see the quiet heroics of Mom and Hick and Agnes, and that I began to recognize there was something far more important going on around me than my childish wants and needs, but that was not the case.

I was a kid who continued to think only about himself. In hindsight, I realize maybe I ought to be grateful to my parents for that. Mom and Hick mercifully kept me shielded from the bleak truth of what was unfolding in an effort to preserve my childhood innocence, and along with that, my childish ignorance. Mom and Hick made it possible for me to live those days in the bubble of childhood, unburdened by the reality that my dad was dying; they kept their misery and sadness to themselves, and gave me the luxury of being self-absorbed.

There would come a time, however, when I would reflect on the self-lessness of my mom and Hick and Agnes Nixon, and I would have an awakening of sorts. I would think of the three of them during my time as governor of Colorado, when our state was in the midst of a seemingly endless series of tragedies: a string of fatal shootings and destructive wildfires, and a devastating flood.

Our state would endure destruction and bloodshed and senseless violence I could never have imagined. Homes would burn and wash away, lives would be upended. As governor, as a human being, I would feel overwhelmed and wonder what I should do, what I could do to help. And I would find myself thinking of Agnes and Mom and Hick. Revisiting those memories would give me strength and guidance, alter my view of what it means to be an elected official, and make clear to me what public "service" means. But that was all several decades and many more life lessons away.

WHEN WE MADE that move to Wynnewood, I didn't get off to a great start at Penn Valley Elementary. I entered the school as a third grader and had an impossible time making friends. I looked like a dork—rail thin with the 1950s Poindexter eyeglasses—and I acted like a jerk. In the class-room, I was always eager to show I knew the right answer, which in and of itself annoyed my classmates. And I was a good student who often *did* know the right answer, which only annoyed my classmates even more. I would make fun of other kids and interrupt them. Out on the playground, whether it was kickball or baseball, you name it, I had to win. I was competitive to the point where I would argue rules that didn't go my way. All in all, none of this was exactly a winning strategy for making friends. Instead, the kids gave me pretty much what I had coming. I was made fun of, I was isolated. Every day I ate lunch alone and was taunted at recess.

After I came home enough times in tears, Mom devised a plan she hoped would improve my behavior and social skills. She clearly knew how to manage me: Mom appealed to my competitive nature. On a piece of paper she drew a chart of columns; the columns were labeled with things like "Offer someone a compliment," "Listen before you speak," "Don't interrupt," "Don't answer every question." Maybe this wasn't the exact wording of the categories, but that was the gist. Each day I would come home from school and Mom would go over the categories on the chart with me.

Upon reviewing the events of the day, if we agreed I had achieved success in one of the behavior categories, I'd get a gold star sticker. If I had shown improvement, a silver star. If I slipped, I got a purple star. After several weeks of an effort that seemed to require more work from me than any math or reading exercise, I reached coveted gold and silver status across the board. Never all gold stars, for no one can be perfect. There was *always* going to be room for improvement in my behavior. The real reward, however, was that little by little I made friends.

In retrospect, I wonder if seeing my attitude and behavior improve provided my mom with some joy and hope, for while she was having great success saving me from myself, there was nothing she could do to save Hick.

I do have one more distinct firsthand memory of Hick and me.

In January 1960, he's in Bryn Mawr Hospital. He's been there for a few days. One night, Mom drives all of us kids over to see him. A nurse meets us at the front door. She tells us that it is after visiting hours and instructs us all to be quiet. She leads us down long dark hallways, by many dimly lit rooms that I try to peek into. I'm thinking it's weird that we are sneaking into a hospital at night, and I'm wondering why. The answer, of course, is that Mom believes Hick is about to die. Finally, the nurse escorts us into Hick's room. He's in his bed, clearly out of it, no doubt sedated, with morphine seeping into his blood. The nurse leaves and we stand around the bed in an awkward, somber quiet. After a while, Mom nods and we file out of the room.

Within days, he came home from Bryn Mawr, but only a couple of weeks later he was back in the hospital for what would indeed be the last time.

On February 7, 1960, I turned eight years old. There was a birthday cake and I blew out the candles surrounded by a few friends and my family, with the exception of Hick. He was once again back in my parents' bedroom. Was he alert enough up there to hear everyone sing "Happy Birthday" to me? If so, did it make him smile or cause him to cry? I'll never know, and perhaps that is for the best.

Ten days later, on February 17, my next-door neighbor, Stuart Searing, was having his birthday party over at his house. I was running down the stairs from the second floor of our house, on my way out the front door, when Mom called me and said she had something she needed to tell me. No, she said, it could not wait. We sat down next to each other. I must have sat a step or two above her, because I remember our eyes were at the same level. I remember looking into her eyes, because I remember how wet they were. And that's when she told me Hick was dead. He was forty years old.

I don't recall the precise words Mom used. I do remember that her voice cracked and her eyes welled up. But she did not cry. I remember that I was anxious for her to finish because I wanted to get to my pal's party. I remember that when Mom was done I got up and ran out the front door to Stuart's house as if what she had told me was just another version of "Hick won't be able to make it to your next school play."

Maybe I reacted that way because in my mind that's what I heard her say, that's how I processed the news. And maybe that's how I processed the news because over that year I'd grown accustomed to Hick's being absent and I thought this wouldn't be any different. Maybe somewhere along the way, like that night we all went to the hospital, I'd sensed Hick was dying and I'd convinced myself that I was fine with it. What I knew for sure was that I was numb and I wondered what was wrong with me, as I wasn't crying like the kids I'd seen in the movies.

Maybe Mom made the right decision or the wrong decision in letting me run off to Stuart's party. Maybe she thought celebrating a friend's birthday was much better for me in that moment than confronting my father's death day. Maybe she was too grief-stricken to think at all. Maybe she let me go to the party for the same reason she had kept on scrubbing the bathroom floor when Boppa told her Bow's plane had crashed— because, once again, she figured, "What else was there to do?"

I don't know.

But Mom did let me run out our front door to Stuart's party, with all the anger and anguish and fear and confusion and sad love I didn't realize I had inside me. And in a way, I have never stopped running with all of that inside me—only now I'm aware of it, or rather, over and over again, I have been made aware that I should be aware of it.

I don't know.

I do know that I regret not having more memories of my father and that so many of the ones I do have occurred under such dark clouds, with so few moments of sunshine. And I regret how little I remember about the day we buried him.

Hick's funeral was at All Saints Church, where my parents had married twelve years earlier. I remember the church being very full, standing room only. All of the guys from Morris, Wheeler turned out. One of the guys was Johnny Fillippi. Johnny worked on the factory floor and Hick had been his foreman, but they were about the same age and I knew they were good friends. I remember Johnny walked up to me in All Saints, his face red and wet with tears. It was the first time I had ever seen a man cry who was not on TV. I remember Johnny hugged me so hard I almost couldn't breathe, then he let me go and walked away.

And that's all I've got from that day.

Well, that and Hick's ghost.

Four

HICKENLOOP-HOLES

All of the daily activity that went into caring for Hick—the changing of his sheets, acquiring and administering his meds, preparing and serving his meals, his coming and going from doctors and the hospital, visitors visiting, the simple wondering if today might be a day when Hick would feel strong enough to come down the stairs and spend a few moments with us—all of that had filled our home with an energy, an anticipation. Our life had been built around his dying. That now was gone, replaced by an empty stillness that became my mother's new life. Or rather, as a widow for the second time in fifteen years, her new old life, only this time with four kids: Betsy, seventeen years old; Sydney, fifteen; Tad, nine; and me, only eight. Without Hick and the routine of him, Mom once again faced the question, *Now what?*

Thanks to Mom's intervention and her ingenious behavioral modification chart, my social skills continued to improve. Throughout the rest of my time at Penn Valley I developed friendships at school and with kids in my neighborhood. I was still me, though. Still competitive. Still argued. Still wanted to win and prove I had the right answers. With Hick gone, maybe even more so. No chart could cure me of me.

One of my closest pals by the time I hit the sixth grade was Henry Baird. His family lived on the other side of Kent Road, seven houses down. Henry and I were in the same grade at Penn Valley and we were teammates on the local Little League team, the Wynnewood Warriors. When Henry and I were in baseball season, just about every day, weather permitting, we'd play some version of baseball in the Bairds' backyard.

He was our catcher and I was a shortstop and second baseman. But after a couple of seasons it became apparent to any and all that I would never be much of a hitter. My Coke-bottle-thick eyeglasses would wobble on my nose when I swung, and it seemed that every bat was too heavy for me. If I was to have any future in baseball, I decided, I needed to be a pitcher. I truly loved the game. Trouble was, pitchers were either the big, confident kids or the sons of coaches. Not to mention that I had one of the weaker arms on the team. Henry was the only person who didn't think the idea of my pitching was a joke. He became my secret ally.

In season, out of season, he and I would practice for an hour or more almost every day, me pitching and him catching, simulating real-game scenarios. Of course, we always put ourselves in the most nail-biting of circumstances: *Two outs, bases loaded, bottom of the ninth. Warriors are up by one. The Ardmore Aces have their best hitter at the plate.* Henry flashes me one finger, signaling for my fastball. I shake off that call, not feeling it. Henry flashes me the two fingers. I nod affirmatively and go into my windup for what we called the "Big Bender," or the "Hickenlooper Curve." I couldn't throw heat, but the curve . . . *that* was my bread and butter.

The first couple of years there wasn't much of a bend in the Big Bend, but we believed there was a curve in there. And then, eventually, darned if that dang ball didn't begin to curve. And drop. Sports psychologists talk a lot about the power of visualization; if you envision a winning outcome, if you believe it, you increase the odds of making it happen. Making the Hickenlooper Curve actually curve was my first lesson in the power of believing. We put in a lot of hard work. With more and more practice, I began to put the ball wherever I wanted, and to control the ratio of the drop to curve. I won't deny that it was the slowest curve in the country, but in time it became a precision instrument.

The coaches didn't let me pitch until we had moved up to the next age level, the Cadet League, and I didn't pitch against another team until I was in my second year there. I might have been fifteen years old. But I wasn't going to quit. Persistence.

Almost every game, players from the opposing team would stand around the cage behind home plate during pregame warmups and watch me throw that curve. Me looking like the Hickenlooper dork I was on the mound, and that pitch—the way it came looping in, so slow and fat in the air—the other team would be drooling, literally laughing at me, talking about how they were going to smack my "junk ball" over the fence. Henry and I would smile at each other and keep practicing that pitch.

I released the curve with what I must say was a wicked flick of the wrist, less angled for more drop, which thanks to Henry I had practiced over and over and over again. The ball would indeed lollygag toward the plate, spinning fast, though moving as if in slow motion, aching to be hit, but then right as it reached the plate—right when the batter would swing with visions of himself rounding third toward his team waiting at the plate to greet him and celebrate his home run—that ball curved and dropped like a rock; he would swing and wonder what in the world just happened.

And then the ump would tell him: *You're out!*

I was learning about more than just the power of believing and hard work and persistence. It was then I started to become aware that my outward appearance gave me an advantage. It was a great thing when I would step on the mound during warmups and our opponents would focus on the gawky geek I was and the slow, nonthreatening arc of my pitch. For while their eyes and egos focused on goofy me and the slow looping trajectory, they would underestimate the curve right before their eyes, the curve that would shortly be coming their way. They would never notice the wrist flick that set it in motion. Decades later, I would learn that this sort of theatrical strategy is part of what political operatives call "optics," when I would ride into my first mayoral campaign on a moped.

Henry and I also played a lot of Wiffle ball and touch football and all manner of games in his backyard. Henry's brother, Douglas, who was two years younger than us, would often be pressed into action to keep score. Of course, like all self-respecting boys playing Wiffle ball, we established ground rules tailored to the unique characteristics of our playing field. If the batter hit the ball into the left-field bushes, it was ruled a single, or in the air, a double. If the ball was hit in the air all the way to the hedge in "center field," automatic triple. If you hit a foul ball into the neighbor's driveway, you were out and for a few minutes despised. We hated climbing that fence. Anyhow, you get the idea.

These ground rules and countless others were first agreed upon and codified in our brains back in the fourth grade. In the months and years that followed, Henry and I grew. We got smarter. We learned more about the game, about life, and about ourselves. Also the field changed. Sometimes the grass in the yard was freshly cut and a ground ball traveled faster. Sometimes the Baird boys skipped the chore of mowing the lawn and the turf got pretty high and slowed down a ball that otherwise could have been a ground-rule double. By the time we reached sixth grade, Henry and I were bigger and stronger; what had seemed like a reasonable distance for a ground-rule double didn't seem like such a reasonable distance anymore. Or at least these were the sorts of arguments I would make. No one challenged more calls than I did.

If you asked Henry, he would tell you that I wasn't trying to cheat or gain unfair advantage; rather, he would say I sincerely believed I was right. He would also tell you that he didn't always agree with me and there were times when I was wrong and annoyed the living hell out of him. During debates, where one of us—okay, me—became intransigent, we would appeal to the Supreme Court of his parents. Mr. and Mrs. Baird were both doctors. Usually, Mrs. Baird was our level-headed Lady Justice. She had infinite patience and a sharp sense of humor. As we would file into her kitchen for a ruling, she would say, "What sort of Hickenloophole are we going to rule on today?"

Many years later I would meet a young lawyer in our new craft-brewpub restaurant. He repeated my name and asked if I knew a Douglas Baird. It turned out that Douglas had risen to become dean of the University of Chicago's law school. However, he also taught an introductory contract law class to first-year students. His first lecture was on the malleability of language. He began that class with a description of backyard Wiffle ball and his brother's friend Hickenlooper and his Hickenloop-holes.

In my defense—here I am, as I often do to my own political detriment, making my case about why I made my case—I feel compelled to say I have never been one who believes rules are meant to be broken or for that matter amended rashly. However, as evidenced by Wiffle ball in "Baird Park," I have long believed that when circumstances demand it, rules ought to be revisited and potentially amended, and possibly, undone.

Rules, like our nation's laws, which arguably began with Penn's provincial "Frame of Government," are unquestionably a good and necessary thing. We rightly hold our constitutional truths that my ancestors fought to defend as sacred and self-evident. But rules, regulations, and laws are crafted and enforced to ensure fairness, accountability, responsibility, and equality. When rules, regulations, and laws that have been created in a certain time and with the best of intentions fail to do that, or even get in the way of that, well, that is the sort of thing that when I ran for mayor I called the "fundamental nonsense of government."

Debating our Wiffle ball ground rules with Henry, I was simply trying to address the reality that we were playing with a new set of facts and in the context of these new facts the rules as we had originally conceived them were not as fair as we intended. This is the philosophy and perspective that would drive what would turn out to be some of my most controversial decisions as governor, like supporting gun legislation and gay marriage, and when I refused to execute a mass murderer on death row. Just as the playing conditions and the facts we faced in the Baird backyard evolved and changed over time, so it goes with the world. As William Penn himself put it, "truth never lost ground by inquiry."

The thing is, as Henry not all that long ago pointed out to me, when we're kids, once we settle our disagreements, our camaraderie and play resume. We finish our games, say, "See ya tomorrow," and look forward to our next day together, as friends who care for one another and give one another the benefit of the doubt. It's when we become adults that we tend to hold on to frustration and anger, and we can't seem to get past our narrow self-interest. Ironically, we adults call that sort of behavior "childish."

Henry also reminded me that I had some amazing luck. As he put it, I had "an incredible facility to win at games of chance." When the weather made it impossible for us to play ball in Henry's backyard we'd go inside and often play dice or a baseball board game wherein the action was determined by flicking one of those spinning arrows. And we spent a ridiculous amount of time playing electric football.

For those of you who have the good fortune of being too young to have ever heard of the game, electric football was played on a football field game board made of a thin sheet of metal that plugged into an outlet. Players arranged their teams on the field in formations modeled on real-game X's and O's. Then you turned on the board and the vibrations bounced the two teams into the "play." Each of the tiny player pieces was on a base of toothbrushlike bristles. Allegedly, if you adjusted the bristles you could assert some control over that piece's movement. I say "allegedly" because that was absolute baloney.

Henry and I would spend forever between "downs" painstakingly adjusting the bristles, arranging the teams into carefully considered formations, but no matter what we did to the damn little player pieces and their bristles, when we turned on the board they bounced all to hell every which way. More often than not, the offensive player piece holding the itty-bitty foam football ended up heading backward into his own team's end zone. A "play" was powered off when the little player piece with the itty-bitty foam football was either touched by a piece from the opposing team or scored, or ended up in his own end zone. If you were looking for a near surefire way to incite a fistfight between eleven-year-olds, here was the game.

Henry and I, however, never came to blows over it. I credit that to his Zen-like demeanor. Henry possessed a maturity and patience well beyond his years. Never mind electric football, how else to explain his putting up with me? Regardless, when it came to this game with a bunch of little plastic player pieces, which had the illusion of requiring skill and preparation but really was dictated by nothing more than random electrically charged vibrations, I won every time, which may very well have been the best preparation I ever received for my time in politics.

I kid. I kid.

Sort of.

———————

HENRY'S LITTLE BROTHER, Douglas, wasn't merely our Wiffle ball scorekeeper. He was an amateur filmmaker. With his nifty eight-millimeter camera he made several movies that he wrote and directed, featuring kids in the neighborhood. I had a starring role in one Douglas Baird production—probably because I insisted on starring in it. Probably because I felt I was put on earth to play the role. In fairness, this was one instance where I did have unique experience and motivation I could channel into the character.

The film was called *The Chase for the Silver Dollar.* You can probably guess where this is going. The film was about the theft of a valuable coin and the series of madcap chases that ensued to track it down and secure its recovery. Neither Douglas nor Henry had any knowledge of my job on Hick's coin collection, as it predated my friendship with them. Douglas's script was merely a coincidence. I could make no claim that my likeness had been unlawfully appropriated and attempt to sue for a percentage of the film's profits. But clearly, I was perfect for the leading role of the dastardly coin thief.

Fortunately, Douglas didn't fancy himself a documentarian, or else he might have caught on film how poorly I treated my mother. Henry and Douglas, along with just about all of my friends from this period of my life, witnessed plenty of examples of what a relentlessly hard time I gave my mom. No matter what she asked me to do—cut the grass, clean my room—I'd throw tantrums and argue and often refuse to do it. No matter what Mom did or how hard she tried, it was never good enough for me. I had the audacity to complain about what she would prepare for dinner or that the meal was ready too late. Whether it was the cereal or ketchup or socks she bought for me, I would complain that she had bought the wrong thing. *Whatever* was going on, in my eyes, my mom could do no right.

Incredibly, Mom didn't take any of my petulance personally. She recognized that I had a storm of anger raging within me. I knew it, too. Even then I was conscious of it. I distinctly remember a time when I was about twelve years old. I was home from school on a sick day. I went into my mother's bedroom and lay on her bed to watch her portable television. Across the room, next to my dead father's desk, there was a small, round, metal wastebasket. I noticed a piece of letter paper on the bed. Lying in bed, I created a game for myself. I crumpled up the piece of paper into a ball and tried to see how many times I could shoot the paper ball into the basket. I made two in a row. So I went for three in a row. I made three. I got to the goal of making five consecutive baskets from the bed.

I couldn't get to five in a row.

I tried three, four, five, perhaps a half dozen times, but each time, along the way I missed a shot. On one attempt, I at last made it all the way to four of the five. However, my final shot hit the rim of the wastebasket and bounced to the floor. I walked over to the basket and kicked it. I kicked it against the desk, against the wall. I kicked it over and over and over again. When I was done kicking it, I saw that the wall around the wastebasket was badly chipped and I'd even gouged divots. Later in the day Mom noticed and asked me if I had any idea what had happened. I said I didn't know. Probably seeing through me, but not wanting to force the issue, she raised an eyebrow and said that she didn't think our dog was capable of doing such damage. I shrugged and maintained that I had no idea what happened.

I started to shoplift. After my inside job of taking Dad's coins and playing the role of a thief, I attempted to steal from local stores. On several occasions, I actually got away with shoving some 45 records down the front of my pants. But I was nabbed trying to pocket a candy bar from Mapes' drugstore, and the police were summoned when I was caught stealing a sponge, of all things. One of my chores that my terrible mother imposed upon me was washing the dishes. One day in the Penn Fruit grocery store, I got it in my head that if I had a sponge it would make the job easier. Each time I got caught, a store clerk called home and Mom came to get me.

Not once did Mom lose her temper. Not when I back-talked to her, not when I blew off doing my chores, not when I kicked the hell out of the wastebasket and chipped the paint in her bedroom, not even when I got caught stealing. What she did do was take me to talk with our former neighbor Victor Hansen. He seemed like a nice enough guy; I'd always liked him and his kids. I had gone to Sunday school with his three children, but I wasn't sure why Mom was taking me to see him. We entered his office through a basement door, which I noted was odd. We waited in a sitting area, and then Mom took me into an office where Mr. Hansen was seated behind a desk; he invited Mom and me to take a seat and asked Mom to tell him what was happening. I kept thinking, *What is going on? Why are we here with Mr. Hansen?*

After Mom filled him in, Mr. Hansen talked with me alone for a while. I wish I could tell you what we discussed, but I don't recall. I suspect, based upon what I would learn later from Mom, that I gave Mr. Hansen my version of recent events. Then Mr. Hansen sent me to the sitting area and he and Mom talked privately again for a while. Then we left. It was as Mom and I exited, with my curiosity feverishly piqued, that I noticed the small sign outside, on the lawn beside that basement door. Mr. Hansen was Dr. Victor Hansen, a psychiatrist. *Oh, boy,* I thought, *Mom thinks I'm nuts.*

Years later, I asked Mom about this visit. She said Dr. Hansen's diagnosis was that I wasn't a bad kid; rather, I had been acting out at school, at home, and with the thefts because I was hurting and because I wanted attention and validation. In retrospect, it doesn't seem like one needed to be a board-certified psychiatrist to come to that conclusion. I was a transparent cliché of a case study. Sure enough, Mom had been thinking all along exactly what Dr. Hansen had concluded, but since I'd been such a handful she was relieved to hear a professional come to the same finding.

So this was the mess of me who finished Penn Valley Elementary and started seventh grade at the local Ardmore Junior High School. At Ardmore, I had even more of a difficult time making friends than I did at Penn Valley. Adolescents can be a tough crowd. With so many new students from the area's feeder schools forming cliques, in no time Ardmore, for me, was like *Lord of the Flies*. Not surprisingly, I managed to irritate a fair number of classmates just as I had first done at Penn Valley. One kid, George, took such a disliking to me that it seemed he was threatening to beat me up once a week. He and a buddy would wait for me on my walk home from school. I tried to avoid him by switching up my route, going so far as to walk blocks out of my way, but this son of a gun was on to me. I would often come home in tears.

Considering the way I had been treating my mom, I can't say I would now fault her if she had stood by while this George kid kicked my ass and I struggled at Ardmore Junior High. My mom, of course, did not do that. She did everything she could to assist me. Rightly sensing I was in a phase—at least she hoped it was a phase—of rebelling against everything she did or said, and that I would have resisted any more of her attempts to directly help me get my act together, she pulled me out of Ardmore after that year. Which was fine by me. She enrolled me in the nearby Haverford School.

FOUNDED BY THE QUAKERS in 1884, Haverford is an all-boys K–12 academy that still requires jackets and ties and good behavior. Though Mom never said as much to me, I have no doubt she hoped the predominantly male faculty would keep the tie tight around my neck and instill some discipline and respect in me. Mom believed in the transformative power of education. She felt a lifetime of indebtedness to Vassar. Hick had left Mom in financial circumstances such that with frugal living she could handle the Haverford tuition.

Hick's grandfather, Andrew Hickenlooper, had been a Civil War hero. Enlisting in Cincinnati, he became a general in the U.S. Army when he was only twenty-eight years old, making him the second-youngest general in the U.S. military. Andrew was the architect and on-site in-the-trenches foreman for the tunnel-and-explosive tactic that ended the siege of Vicksburg. He also led the team of 180 men who built the bridges and swamp boardwalks during Sherman's March to the Sea.

When the war was over, Andrew worked his way up the civilian ranks and became president of what eventually became the Cincinnati Gas Company. At the time he entered the energy business each community had its own utility company. That changed as bigger companies began to acquire or "roll up" smaller local providers. Andrew was a primary architect of the Cincinnati Gas Company's roll-up strategy. He became an expert in the field, authoring a book about the marketplace, *Competition in the Manufacture and Delivery of Gas*. Andrew was no robber baron, but he did well for himself, amassing a small fortune. He had many children—my grandfather, Smith Hickenlooper, the judge, being one of them—and thus their inheritance was diluted. Still, there was enough of the "general's money" that came through to Hick and then to Mom.

After Hick died, if Mom kept driving old cars and sewing her own clothes (and most of ours), she could raise four kids without returning to work again. Under Mom's direction, ours was a household of hand-me-downs and leftovers. She canceled our subscription to the local newspaper; she washed and reused aluminum foil. The high-end sherry she kept handy to serve guests was merely a high-end sherry bottle that she filled with the cheap stuff. Our twice-widowed mother often reminded us kids of the motto she'd adopted during the Great Depression: "Use it up, wear it out, make it do, or do without." But education—if she thought I was a clear and present danger to myself and humanity, and that this Haverford School was the last best hope to save us all, it would be so. She would spend money on that.

And she was right about Haverford. My mom really did know best—though I never admitted this to her at the time. Well, to be fair, she didn't know best about *everything*. When I told her my idea of opening a brewpub restaurant in Denver, she declined. More about that in a bit. But that her opinion would matter so much to me in my late thirties, and that she would offer me such a bluntly discouraging response, is a good reflection of how we sometimes frustrated each other, often when it mattered most. Point is, my mom was right about *most* things, and she was definitely correct about Haverford.

As had been and always would be the trend in my life, I got off to a rough start at the Haverford School. In this instance, there were reasons—I mean reasons beyond me being me. First, because Haverford was K–12 I wasn't just entering a junior high class of kids who had been together since the sixth grade; this group for the most part had been together for seven years, since kindergarten. So I felt all the more of an outsider. Second, because I was a slow reader, indicative of my mild dyslexia, Mom mandated that I repeat the seventh grade. I felt both like the new-kid outsider and somehow less than my classmates.

My first couple of years there, in seventh and eighth grade, I was bullied by not one, but two kids. One of my two nemeses was a city kid who ate suburban dweebs like me for lunch. I developed a friendship with a boy in my class who lived near me, Jed Rulon-Miller. Although I was not thoughtful enough at the time to describe Jed in such terms, there was a tenderness about him. Unlike me, he didn't care about who was and was not among the in crowd. He was perfectly content to be who he was—"uncool"—and so we were uncool together.

I loved going to Jed's home. He had two older brothers, Sam and his oldest brother, Billy. Billy taught me how to play backgammon and got me to lose quite a bit of money to him along the way. I very much liked their father, Sam. He loomed large in my life. Mr. Rulon-Miller was the head of marketing for a pharmaceutical company in Philly. He oversaw ad campaigns and often would tell us stories about the "big name" stars hired to sing the jingles. Mr. Rulon-Miller was charismatic, larger than life—what my adolescent self regarded as a man's man. He went out of his way to make room for me in his family's life, and I came to view him as one of my many surrogate fathers. With my brother, Syd, off at college by then, and my father dead for several years, over at Jed's place I felt welcomed into a pride of cubs under a benevolent Lion King. However, Jed was in school with me for only my first two years at Haverford; he left after seventh grade. Like his elder brother, he went off to St. Paul's.

I had no social circle, and was now without the one good friend I had. Naturally, I thought, Mom was partly to blame. I found myself drifting through cliques of other outsiders—artsy types, math nerds, theater geeks—developing a kinship and an appreciation for those on the fringe. I wish I could tell you I was mature enough that being "cool" didn't matter to me, but it did.

The summer before tenth grade, I had an experience that gave me a new perspective, one that enabled me to truly enjoy and make the most of the rest of my years at Haverford and, for that matter, to enjoy and make the most of my life ever since. I owe this experience to my mother as well.

One of my mom's sisters was sending her two boys off for eight weeks at Camp Kieve in Maine. Mom decided to send me along. I imagine the conversation between my mom and my aunt was a version of Mom saying

THE OPPOSITE OF WOE

that I was an ungrateful pain in the ass, always angry and complaining, and that because of my attitude I was once again having a hard time making close friends, and that she was concerned about what I was going to do with myself over the summer. My aunt then suggested, why not send me off to camp with her two boys? One way or another, that would fix me.

I WAS FIFTEEN. My cousins Sam and Charlie Cantrell, sixteen and fourteen, were much more mature than I was in every way. I would be assigned to Sam's bunkhouse, with the oldest kids at camp, meaning I wouldn't be spending my time playing capture the flag and telling ghost stories and roasting marshmallows. For the first days of camp my bunkhouse trained on how to handle a canoe on lakes and in rough water. We learned how to pack food securely in cooler-size crates called "wannigans," and how to pitch four-man tents in the dark. We then embarked on a six-day excursion on the Machias Lakes. Machias is a name derived from an American Indian word that translates into "bad run of water" or "bad little falls." Suffice it to say, as we put in on the first Machias Lake, I thought Mom's idea of sending me off with my cousins to ride the "bad run of water" was a positively terrible idea. I tried poorly to hide it, but I was scared.

On this first canoe trip, the falls weren't so bad, nor the rapids too rough. As we developed experience on the water, our trips got increasingly gnarly. We spent a week on the Penobscot River learning to negotiate rapids. In rapids, the stern paddler, always the strong hand, barks orders to his bow-man. In order to navigate around the boulders and the giant haystacks of water that smash against them, the stern-man will shout, "Pull right! Pull right!" or "Paddle hard left!" Lots of adrenaline. I was almost liking it.

Next came the "big trip." Oh, man.

I was one of eleven kids shipped off to a sister camp, a ten-hour drive north, into Quebec, on Lake Capitachouane. No, I'd done nothing wrong and this was not some banished-to-Siberia deployment. This was for a twenty-two-day advanced canoe trip down a series of rivers and curling back through a series of lakes. We were led by three experienced counselors. The lead was Chat Weatherall, a college senior. He was a skilled and rugged outdoorsman. Weatherall, indeed. I also remember Chat's right-hand man was George Merrow. He was only a few years older than us, but a generation more mature. We called him "Dairy Anne," after his hometown of Darien, Connecticut. We readied our backpacks and boxed up our rations, which were a variety of food items that did not require refrigeration: bags of potatoes, oranges, rice, chicken stock, Velveeta cheese. We would see no person and have no opportunity to restock for the full three weeks. The next morning, off we went. We were divided into seven boats, with the weakest paddlers in a boat with a counselor paddling stern. Not long after we put in, a low-pressure front took over the sky and it started to rain. Those clouds stayed above our heads and pissed on us for the next eleven days.

The trip required a great deal of portage. Each crew member was responsible for carrying his own backpack and also lugging additional supplies and oars. Sometimes I was tasked with carrying the sixty-pound box of rations, sometimes one of the sodden tents, which weighed more, but not as much as the Old Town canoes. I was a weakling to begin with, and after hours of paddling my arms were numb. Paddling into the headwinds was brutal. We'd paddle, portage, paddle, portage. One portage was two miles, with long hikes through the dreaded muskeg, a goop of moss and mud; in places it was like quicksand. Your footing would slip off a root and you'd be up to your hip in muskeg, your backpack half submerged as well. At the end of each day we'd set up camp. Because of the rain, by the third day, everything was soaked. At night, we'd hang all the wet clothes that we could by the campfire.

I bitched and moaned. I hated it. All of it.

On the fifth day, we headed down a long series of treacherous rapids. Still raining, by the way.

On rapids, you have to paddle faster or slower than the current, otherwise you can't steer. As with life, if you go with the flow, it's harder to get to where you want to go. When the rapids became too dangerous, we'd portage. At the top of one of the worst rapids, Chat and Dairy Anne had us kids portage everything so they could paddle the empty canoe and try shooting the rapids. These were no millstream rapids. We're talking about four-foot drops, mini falls, boulders everywhere. They made it less than halfway, flipped, and broke sixteen ribs of the canoe on the way down. For a few moments I was filled with glee, thinking we might be forced to signal for rescue and return to the main camp. But alas, these counselors knew what they were doing. They cut branches from birch trees, fashioned new ribs, and patched up the canoe. Onward.

Paddle, portage, paddle, portage. Set up camp, sleep, wake up and do it again.

Still raining.

At a certain point on a trip like this it's virtually inevitable that either you absolutely break and absolutely refuse to go any farther, *or* you recalibrate your expectations and wants and needs. You learn to be grateful—for the orange you have for lunch and for the gumbo you heat up over the campfire at night. That mixture of rice, potatoes, and big chunks of Velveeta in a chicken-stock and Dinty Moore beef stew base was some of the best food I ever tasted.

You realize complaining doesn't do any good, whining doesn't do any good. You realize the not-so-secret secret is that what is required is to do your part, keep on, and keep at it—persist. For if you do your part and persist, you may be rewarded with a moment like the one we enjoyed on the morning of the twelfth day when those clouds broke apart and the sun streamed through, little by little, until it was all there in its round blazing glory.

Although I didn't realize it at the time, Mom had done it again: that canoe trip she had sent me on served a similar purpose as her behavior chart, albeit far more exhausting. On the "bad run of water" I matured a bit more, I paddled and portaged my way a little farther along into adulthood. With my attitude adjusted, having learned to persevere, I began to adjust at Haverford.

REALLY, NOW THAT I began to look around, I mean really look around and take notice of Haverford, I was lucky to be there. Classes were half the size they were at Ardmore. Teachers had more time to provide students with more individual attention and validation. The same held true on the playing fields. All Haverford students were required to play sports. Naturally, I played baseball and also joined the soccer team. And again, because of the smaller student population, coaches were able to provide more personalized instruction and give the sort of "attaboys" Hick wasn't around to give me, or for that matter, that I would ever get from Mom. Everyone got to play.

But: no girls! This was good and bad. I didn't need to stress about trying to impress the opposite sex while acting like I wasn't trying to impress the opposite sex. If I wanted to pick my nose, I could pick my nose. Without girls around, I felt less pressure to be something other than who I was, while I was beginning to figure out who I was. On the other hand, no girls meant I didn't have the chance to learn how to act around the fairer sex. In short, girls terrified me. This would have repercussions, as you'll see. All in all, I suspect Dr. Hansen would have said that my mother had made all the right moves for me: the canoe trip and the Haverford environment were just the sort of treatment I needed.

After my summer on the rough waters of the North Woods, the rapids of high school back at Haverford didn't seem so bad. There were still plenty of times when I felt as if those clouds had rolled in over my head and the sky was pissing on me. But I didn't complain or whine—well, I did, but not nearly as much. I worked hard to keep paddling and stay faster than the current.

I worked hard to make friends and indeed found a place in the social order where I no longer was bullied, but I was still very much a nerd. On the field many of my baseball teammates were friendly, but off the field, we didn't interact as friends. I was still on the periphery of the in crowd. As much as I wish I could tell you that sort of thing didn't matter to me, it did. I desperately wanted to be cool, but I wasn't.

That would change my junior year. All because I smoked a little pot.

THE SUMMER BEFORE my junior year at Haverford was the summer of 1968. The war in Vietnam was reaching its disastrous peak. Antiwar protests were everywhere. Robert F. Kennedy and Martin Luther King Jr. had just been assassinated. Richard M. Nixon was the Republican front-runner for president. Feminist Valerie Solanas had shot Andy Warhol. The Beatles' "Hey Jude" would hit number one on the charts early that fall. Weed and war. Peace and love. Flower power. All of this was in the air as my family traveled to Middletown, Connecticut, for a weekend to attend my brother Syd's graduation from Wesleyan University.

My mom and aunts stayed in a motel, all squeezed into a single room with two singles and a cot. At my brother's suggestion—God bless him—I stayed with him at his off-campus house, where he lived with his girl-friend, Susan Katz, and two other roommates. It was a kinetic experi-ence from the minute Syd picked me up at the motel. On the way to his place, Syd made a stop at a convenience store. He pumped some gas, went in to pay, and came back to the car with a jar of peanut butter in one hand and a can of whipped cream in the other. He turned to me and with a wonderfully wicked twinkle in his eye said, "Susan really likes peanut butter and I *really* like whipped cream." I'm sitting there, a Haverford nerd who'd never so much as held hands with a girl. Yet I definitely caught the drift of what my big brother was saying.

Syd, Susan, and their two housemates all had what President Nixon would have called long hippie hair, and their three-bedroom house was just about the grooviest pad I'd ever seen. There was a killer stereo system cranking Joplin and Hendrix. Paisley fabric hung over the threshold of an empty closet, where "squares" might have had a door. At night, four colored floodlights in the closet blinked to the rhythm of the music from the stereo. Syd nodded to the couch and said it was all mine.

On Saturday night, Syd and his merry pranksters hosted a potluck dinner in the backyard. Friends and family came over but eventually took off. Those of us who were left, meaning Syd and his friends and me, sat in a circle and someone fired up a joint and it got passed around and reached me. I took it and looked at my brother. He smiled in such a way that conveyed, *Whatever you want to do, it's cool.* I trusted my brother. I felt comfortable among his friends. So I took a hit. Then I took another. I didn't feel stoned, or at least I don't think I was stoned, but who knows. Regardless, the real high from that night came months later when school resumed back at Haverford.

That fall, I ended up talking to Brock Dethier. Brock was in my year at Haverford. He was one of the cool guys at school. He was a wrestler—and we had been state champions for a decade. He was also the editor of the student newspaper and plenty smart—a National Merit Finalist. Even his name was cool—Brock. So I was talking to Brock and he mentioned he has smoked weed. As casually as I could, I said, "Yeah, man, me, too." Brock did a bona fide double take and looked at me. "Really?" he said. "Yeah, man," I said. Then, just as nonchalantly, I told him about my wild summer weekend up at Wesleyan with my super groovy brother and his hot girlfriend and the whipped cream, smoking weed in the yard. Suddenly, I'd done things and I'd seen things. I'd *lived*. I was far out. Brock brought me into his circle of friends, all of them among my class's smartest students, top athletes, and, naturally, the absolute coolest.

That year, my junior year, I attempted to grow my own pot. I put the feeble planting in one of those little red clay flowerpots with some planting soil. I put the pot with the pot on the ledge outside my bedroom window. Mom noticed and was not pleased. She said she didn't care if weed was not as "bad" as alcohol, as I had said. Her point was that weed was illegal, and therefore I was breaking the law, and that as long as I was in her house she would not tolerate me breaking the law. It's hard to argue with that kind of logic, but that doesn't mean I didn't argue with her.

I can't begin to imagine what Mom would have said if she had lived to see the day when Colorado would become the first state in the nation to legalize retail marijuana, and her son's administration would have to create the first retail marijuana regulations in our nation's history.

I finished my senior year at Haverford on the best high ever: hanging with the smart, cool kids, who until recently hadn't noticed me, and having the greatest sports moment of my life. My position on the Haverford baseball team was pitcher. Despite all those years practicing with Henry and playing with the Warriors, I wasn't exactly the star on the mound that I had hoped I would become. My junior year I didn't get in a game to pitch a single inning in spring training and was sent down to the junior varsity. But in my senior year I earned a spot as the number-two starting pitcher on the varsity, and we ended up in a three-way scramble for the league championship.

Near the end of the season, I pitched the game of my life. The day of the game was unseasonably chilly and wet. We were the away team on a foreign field, and I got sent to the mound against Germantown Academy. If we won, we would move into first place. During warm-ups, the opposing team lingered between their bench and home plate, watching me pitch. I could hear them laugh. I heard them talk about how they were absolutely going to knock the crap out of the ball. Just like the Wynnewood Cadet League days.

For me, the drama came in the first inning. One of the best players in the league stepped to the plate. Geezus, this guy was big. I felt like David with a slingshot looking at Goliath with a club. I had it in my head that if I could take this guy down now, I would have the confidence to handle any and all who came after him, including the next time I saw him at the plate. I got him with the curve. Strike one. He fouled off the next one. I threw another Hickenlooper curve and he popped out to our shortstop. I wish I had a picture of the look on that kid's face when he threw his bat down in disgust.

I pitched seven innings that day, giving up only two hits. With two outs in the fifth, Goliath returned to the plate and I walked him on four pitches. But other than that I never threw more than two balls to another batter. It was the only shutout I pitched in my short-lived career. I also laid down a pretty sweet suicide squeeze bunt. That year, 1970, the Haverford School baseball team finished first in the league; one of my fellow pitchers, Larry Ryan, was named the team's MVP, and yours truly was selected as MIP, the most improved player. I wrapped up my high school career feeling like I was one of the cool kids and a champion.

Persistence.

Five

THAT DECADE
I SPENT IN COLLEGE
(PART 1: THE BREAKDOWN)

Wesleyan.

After that far-out visit to Wesleyan University for my brother's graduation, how could I have chosen to go anywhere else? Just between us: at first, Wesleyan put me on the wait list; so, too, did Princeton. Wait list. Not quite good enough. I was beginning to think this was the story of my life. But the acceptance letter from Wesleyan arrived, and—*and!*—the very next day I received the acceptance letter from Princeton. Since "Wesu" was the first to take me, I figured, hey, Princeton, if you snooze you lose. No—joking aside, I chose Wesleyan over Princeton for a couple of reasons.

One: The fact that Syd had gone to Wesu made me feel as if I already had a connection to the school. During the previous four years I'd so often heard him go on and on about how great Wesleyan was; his stories made me feel as if I knew the place.

Two: Wesleyan was a place where diversity, creativity, and spontaneity mattered, where faculty spoke openly about how half of our education took place outside the classroom. While Wesleyan had all of the traditional academic programs, in 1970 it also had an amazing film program and the best world-music program in the country. Culturally, it felt like an alternative universe.

In truth, that visit to campus for Syd's graduation did influence my decision. Hanging out with Syd and his friends, sitting in that circle in his backyard with those groovy seniors, I kind of felt like I'd already been accepted by the community there. It was like, if I fit in with them, I fit in with Wesleyan. Besides, I had a feeling that Princeton would be a bit too conservative, too buzz-cut and buttoned-down for me, and that Wesu's long-haired liberal arts types would be more my crowd. Boy, I was about to learn just how correct my self-assessment was.

Speaking of self-assessments: Not long after I arrived on campus my freshman class took one of those tests that tells you which professions are best for you. The point of the test was to provide us with results that might help inform which classes we chose, what subject each of us selected for a major, and ultimately what sort of careers we should consider. It was called the "Strong Vocational Interest Profile," or SVIP. I still have it. "Properly interpreted," so goes the introductory page, "your scores may represent some of the most important information for vocational planning you will ever receive." Pretty heavy stuff, right? The kinds of results that an unmoored freshman such as myself ought to carefully consider.

According to the results, based on a blend of factors including standardized test scores, aptitude, and interest, I had the makings of a physician, librarian, artist, or music teacher. Just behind those was author-journalist. The professional classification that was closest to elected official was public administrator, which according to the SVIP rating was not the life for me. The results indicated I would have made a better farmer or physicist than public administrator. Then again, at the time, there's no way I would have considered a life in politics. Nixon was the president, presiding, as it were, over the war in Vietnam, which I thought was colossally misguided. As far as me and the draft, I had a college deferment. My draft number ended up being well above 300.

So looking down the list: Doctor, nope. I wasn't crazy about the idea of blood and guts, or for that matter, asking an old guy to turn and cough. Librarian? There was no way I had the patience or the discipline to catalogue and organize. More to the point, I couldn't see myself being happy cooped up in a building all day. Artist? Now that was interesting. I fancied myself a creative type. Maybe. But what sort of art? Sculptor, painter, photographer? I figured I would explore that at Wesu (and indeed I would). But art didn't strike me as the most viable career choice for me. Music teacher? Music and concerts were a huge part of my life— remember, as a kid I'd stuffed 45s down my pants. I played a mean air guitar in my room, but I had no musical training whatsoever. It seemed a bit late for me to learn all of what I would need to learn in order to teach music.

Author-journalist. *Now* we're talking. I liked the idea of being a journalist quite a bit, at least my fairy-tale idea of being a journalist. Here, I thought, was a profession that would not only give me license to explore different worlds but require and pay me to do so. How could you beat that? What most appealed to me about a career as a journalist is that it would enable me to meet some of the most interesting people in the world, to hang out and talk with them, to see how their minds worked.

Me and some of the most fascinating people in the world could become pals, hang out in the kitchen drinking beers.

Although one of my Little League baseball coaches who lived around the corner from me, Gil Spencer, was a hard-charging editor for *The Trentonian* and was on his way to winning the Pulitzer Prize, my more idyllic perception of journalism was based on my childhood interactions with my aunt Zef—Jozefa Stuart. Aunt Zef had been one of my mother's closest friends at Vassar and became one of the first female editors of *Life* magazine. On a couple of occasions my mom took us kids up to New York to see musicals. Mom loved musicals. The only records she played in the house were Broadway musicals. *Guys and Dolls, Oklahoma!,* and *The Music Man* were among her favorites. She knew the words to every song and would often shock us kids with some of the racy lyrics she sang. I daresay that I used to know most of the lyrics to all of the classics. I have fond memories of Mom taking us to see an Off-Broadway revival of *Anything Goes* sometime in the early 1960s. Aunt Zef was the entertainment editor at *Life,* which helped us snag some prime seats. We were third row, center.

Every time we'd go to New York we'd visit with Aunt Zef. She and her husband, Walker, had a grand apartment on the Upper West Side with a spectacular view of Central Park. I took a high school friend to New York to see the Beach Boys play with the Grateful Dead at the Fillmore East, and we spent the night at Aunt Zef's. When we got back to Aunt Zef's apartment after midnight, Aunt Zef and Uncle "Stu" were playing poker with friends. It was like a mini Algonquin Round Table. Aunt Zef matter-of-factly made introductions: "Say hello, Edward Albee. And this is Tennessee Williams, and James Agee." Over the years, I'd see these literary luminaries and others sitting there at her kitchen table along with her husband. Walker was no slouch himself. He was a successful movie producer. In 1963, his short film *That's Me* was nominated for an Oscar. The movie harnessed the best of the 1960s, music and community and social activism. The film was a comedy-drama about a young Puerto Rican guitar player and the conscientious social worker who tries to help the immigrant adjust to life in New York City.

As if Aunt Zef wasn't cool enough, her father was Bronislaw Malinowski, who wrote *The Sexual Lives of Savages*, the seminal anthropological work that posited the theory that sexuality drives virtually every aspect of culture. (The book was *not*, as some of my college pals thought, a book about sexual activity in primitive cultures.)

Yes, I liked the idea of author-journalist. After a few years reporting I figured I just might tap some of the fascinating people I would meet and adventures I would have and write a novel. So English it was, for my major. I had ambition. I wanted to do something with my life. Author-journalists had a shot at being famous. Why, Mom's favorite musical, *Guys and Dolls*, was based on the life and work of Damon Runyon, the early-twentieth-century author-journalist who indeed had led a wildly fantastic life. Also, it seemed to me that girls always went for writers. Lord knows, I needed all the help I could get in that department.

You haven't heard much about me and dating up to this point because there's not been much to tell. In high school, I was very aware of girls; and they were very unaware of me. While at Haverford I had gone on a total of three dates. I took Mary Nixon, daughter of Agnes Nixon, to a concert. I had just gotten my driver's license and picked up Mary in a new white Valiant station wagon of Mom's. Eight-years-old new. When I said Mom was frugal, I wasn't kidding.

I took Mary into South Philadelphia to see Jimi Hendrix at the Spectrum. I was nervous driving into the city. Doubly nervous because there was a live pretty girl actually sitting next to me, *and*—my Lord—we were alone. Such was the sort of thing on my mind and before I knew it I was in an exit lane of Interstate 76, which deposited us in a section of West Philly that made the urban wasteland in *Bonfire of the Vanities* look like Candy Land. We eventually got to the concert. Jimi was amazing on-stage. He did all of his hits: "Purple Haze," "Hey Joe," "Foxy Lady," "Are You Experienced?" Offstage, I was not so amazing. Definitely not experienced. This was my only date with Mary Nixon. The Nixon family was kind and charitable, but they had their limits.

My second date, I took Sherri LeFevre, another daughter of one of Mom's friends, into Philly to see Big Brother and the Holding Company. My big brother, Syd, essentially bullied me into asking Sherri. He had four tickets to the show at the Electric Factory and he wanted us to double-date. This was a rare example of Syd providing "fatherly" support. But Sherri was awfully cool. And what an incentive—Big Brother and the Holding Company. Are you kidding me?

Along with Jefferson Airplane and the Grateful Dead, this was one of *the* counterculture San Francisco bands. We're talking lead singer Janis Joplin. Their 1967 performances at San Fran's Avalon Ballroom and at the Monterey Pop Festival were already legendary. The most memorable thing about my date with Sherri that night was that Janis Joplin practically stepped over me on her way to the stage and I touched the hem of her dress. Let's just say I got much closer to Janis that night than I did to Sherri. But sensing the date hadn't been a total disaster, I decided to ask Sherri on a second date.

I was terrified. I didn't want to call her and seem uncool. Because I was nervous, afraid I would fumble for things to say, I prepared a list of six topics to discuss. I called her and rambled through my entire script in less than four minutes. Yes, as a matter of fact, I timed it. With nothing but dead space on the line between us, I asked her out and she said yes.

We went to a movie. Halfway through the film I tried to put my arm around Sherri, which she promptly returned to me as if it were a giant earthworm. That was my last date with Sherri.

At Wesleyan, I hoped for better luck. After all, I was a college man now and these were college women, and college women took time to read books beyond the cover. Surely, a romance was out there for me somewhere on campus. I was open to the idea that I might just find The One. At the very least, I fully planned on finally losing my virginity.

Enter Angela.

IT DOESN'T EXIST ANYMORE, but the main dining facility on the Wesleyan campus during my years there was McConaughey Hall, a massive, round, midcentury-modern building with huge windows that resembled the futuristic Colorado house featured in the Woody Allen sci-fi comedy *Sleeper*. I guess because the architect must have been really trying to show off, McConaughey was built into a hillside. Think 1950s flying saucer lodged into a mountain. Fittingly enough, it was inside this spaceship of a dining hall, in December 1970, that I had the outwardly banal yet ultimately cosmically altering encounter with Angela.

It was a gathering of the freshman class before the first-term break for the winter holidays. I knew a lot of people. I saw a girl I'd had a thing with. The only girl I'd had a thing with thus far at Wesleyan. We'd hung out and clumsily made out, but it wasn't right. We both knew it. Our dating, as it were, was mercifully short-lived. Spotting each other in the crowded spaceship, we waved and smiled.

I was hanging out after the main feeding frenzy. I guess you could say I mingled with a bunch of girls I had not yet met; one of them was Angela. I noticed her immediately. While she wasn't what you would call model-gorgeous, she was subtly yet unmistakably lovely, and naturally so. Long,

house . . . across the top of the page she wrote: "Drawings for John Hick-enlooper for his birthday."

Angela had thought enough of me to remember my birthday. She had thought enough of me to remember my birthday *and* get me a gift. Even more than that, she had sat at her desk in her dorm room and spent at least an hour putting a bit of herself onto the page, *making* something for me. That's not the kind of thing you do for just anybody, right?

We began to hang out a bit. I admired her. She emanated a grace, a centeredness. There was a goodness about her. It seemed to me that Angela saw the world the way I wished I saw the world. I have the distinct memory of thinking that she was someone I could trust, the way I trusted my mom. I know, I know. Paging Dr. Freud. But it's true, I had this sense that, like my mom, Angela might be one of those rare people who would refuse to enable the worst parts of me while empowering the best parts of me, that she would inspire me to become my best self. I loved her.

One day, not long after my birthday, Angela and I were walking on campus and I told her so. I blurted out that I loved her. Even now, I can't believe I said it, but there you have it. My first love. For what seemed like an eternity Angela didn't say anything. Finally, she spoke. As tenderly as could be said, she told me she liked me quite a bit, and then came the three words every fool in love dreads to hear—"as a friend."

Oh, the humanity.

Devastation set in.

For guys like my cool Haverford pals, this sort of thing was probably no big deal. Some guys do have all the luck. Then there's the rest of us. Angela told me she really cared for me, that she was touched and that she was sorry. "No big deal," I said. "No big deal." Meanwhile, it was a very big deal. It felt as if someone had taken my heart, jammed it in a blender in the spaceship cafeteria kitchen, and put the mess back in my chest.

I became the lame cliché of every unrequited love song ever written. Couldn't eat. Couldn't sleep. Couldn't think. Yes, I was that guy. None of my friends understood. Or maybe they understood better than I did. They kept telling me to get over Angela already, and really, that there was nothing to get over in the first place. I couldn't blame them. Intellectually, I knew my melancholy, which was slipping precipitously into a depression, was an overreaction. How can you feel you lost something that you never had?

But if you've been there, you know.

Because all I thought about was Angela and because they didn't want to hear it, and because it got to the point where I didn't want to hear myself talk about Angela, I stopped talking to my friends. I became more isolated in my . . . depression, for now that's what it was, depression, for sure.

After one of many sleepless nights, I was so desperate I went to the student health center. You know it's bad when you go to a college campus health center in the middle of the day. The health center was a room with an examination table and a nurse seated at a desk, doing a crossword puzzle. She took my temperature. Normal. She could see I wasn't normal, but she didn't know what to do with me. I couldn't bring myself to explain to her what I thought was wrong with me, that I had Angela-itis. The nurse told me to come back in the afternoon and talk with the doctor. I did; he gave me a half dozen capsules of lithium.

Heading into my freshman year finals on the lithium, I felt steady and energetic enough to turn my attention to another pressing matter: not flunking out of school. All of the classes I took that second semester were pass-fail. I had been so distraught over Angela, and such a slow reader, I was on the verge of failing every one of them. I took my exams and somehow managed to pass them all.

After finals, I returned home. I'd stopped taking the lithium. I was still a wreck. It took everything I had just to get out of bed and walk. I was a morose zombie. Mom saw it immediately. She rightly grew concerned about what would become of me over the summer. Once again she took action.

She called an old friend at the American Friends Service Committee, the Quaker version of Volunteers for America. At the very last minute, I got a spot with an AFSC work camp; there was a project up in Washington County, Maine. Next thing I knew, I was on my way to the town of Perry, where I would help convert a vacant sardine factory into a "free school," the earliest incarnation of a charter school, and where, unbeknownst to me, I would also learn to brew beer.

THE ORGANIZERS OF the sardine-factory-to-charter-school project were Tom and Susan Tureen. Tom was an attorney who did legal aid work for poor and indigent American Indians, frequently representing members of the Passamaquoddy tribe. Susan was a teacher. She had been teaching at the local public school, but the administrators of the school forced her out because they claimed she had hung pictures of Ho Chi Minh and a Communist flag in her classroom. I'm not kidding.

Susan was beloved by enough of the parents that they had banded together to start their own school, which with some degree of counterculture defiance they were calling "Our School." Tom and Susan had secured a grant and a portion of the old Sea Line sardine factory to begin the program. With the Quakers being big on schools, the American Friends Service Committee signed on to help with the effort.

I was one of thirteen college freshmen on the AFSC team who would work on the project, converting a portion of the abandoned factory into three multigrade classrooms and winterizing the place. Our quarters were a big, old, run-down farmhouse owned by a Mrs. Virginia Pottle. As

I learned that summer, Mrs. Pottle was an elderly widow who fermented elderberry wine in her living room, in her glass-topped coffee table. If you were lucky enough to be invited into her home and she took a shine to you she would serve you a glass. The widow Pottle owned quite a bit of property in the area and she'd donated the farmhouse to the cause for the summer.

The town of Perry is near the Bay of Fundy, and on our crew's first night together, before we set about our summer of work, there was a welcome party for us down on the beach. Technically, the first thing my team built together was a huge bonfire. Locals heaped wet seaweed on the bonfire, thus producing the perfect natural steam cooker for pounds and pounds of clams. The clams had been harvested earlier in the day from the flats of the bay. There was a giant pot of baked beans and a salad made of greens picked fresh that day.

As the sun set and we waited for the food to cook, a guy named Bob arranged a baseball game. Bob and his wife, Lisa, had four kids who would be enrolled in Our School. Bob's idea of baseball wasn't like any kind of baseball I'd ever played, but I did like it. In Bob's version, at every one of the makeshift bases in the sand there was a glass jug of his home-brewed beer. According to the rules, every time you stopped at a base you chugged from the jug.

My first couple of trips around the diamond I didn't care for the flavor of the Bob beer. It was thick, bready, yeasty. But the more I ran the bases, the more I enjoyed the beer—also, surprise, surprise, the more recklessly I ran. At the end of the game, Bob said he'd soon be brewing another batch of his Bob beer and he extended an invitation to any and all of us to come lend him a hand and see how it's done. I told him I wanted in.

Once the work on Our School got under way, however, there wasn't time for beer brewing. The long-abandoned Sea Line sardine factory was a massive building; Tom and Susan's school occupied about 10 percent of the space. Come September, about fifty elementary-school students would scamper in. We spent the summer fashioning sheets of plastic into storm windows, cleaning and painting, and building tables, blackboards, and sandboxes. Exactly the sort of manageable busy work and culture I needed in my life. My team members were all true believers, volunteers committed to doing whatever they could to help the community and help one another. We were united in a common goal and a common purpose that made it easy for me to forget about Angela for long hours at a time.

Put thirteen college freshmen like this together in an old farmhouse for a summer and it's bound to be a good time. The bonfire party on the beach was the start of many fun times we had together. At night, we'd gather and sing and drink beer and whoop it up. We had a stereo, and it seemed it was always playing that Carole King record with that song, "I feel the earth move under my feet. . . ." The girls all loved that song, and we guys liked watching them like it. Sometimes we'd find ourselves in thoughtful, wide-ranging conversations. We'd talk about all of the ways the older generation had messed things up, and how we were going to fix it. We were all in that phase of life between childhood and who we would become as adults; we were discovering who we were and what we believed. There was great trust and respect among us and we felt comfortable challenging one another's thinking. Romances blossomed.

I spent a good bit of time with a girl from Minnesota, Blair. Her dad was a college professor. She said he taught classes rooted in the connection between science and religion. From what Blair said, the gist of that connection as her dad saw it was that science and religion were not at odds with each other, but rather existed in harmony; that in and of themselves, neither science nor religion provided all of the answers for the universe, but when studied together, the package deal goes a long way to offer explanations for how and why we were all here. Where science leaves off, religion begins. Or, depending on your view, vice versa. Astrophysics explains the Big Bang, but what about the "nothing" that existed before the Bang? The nothing left room for everything of religion and other existential possibilities.

Religion and God had been part of my life growing up. Every Sunday, my family attended All Saints Episcopal Church, where my parents were married and my father's funeral service was held. After church, my siblings and I attended Sunday school in the church basement. For a while, Hick even taught at the Sunday school. Around the house, my mom would quote only Shakespeare and the Bible. But that summer in Maine, I wasn't sure what I believed. Some of my uncertainty had to do with a conversation I had with Mom when I was around fourteen.

It wasn't *all* bad between Mom and me as I grew up. During my junior and senior years of high school—with Tad at Stanford, Syd at Wesleyan, and Betsy out of college and off teaching at the Putney School in Vermont—Mom and I were alone in the house together. When I wasn't being a disrespectful ass, we had many quiet and perfectly lovely moments together. Frequently, our time together was dinner, not just eating together, but while she was preparing the meal. I'd sit on the countertop next to the stove while she cooked and we would talk.

One time, I can't remember why, I asked Mom whom she loved more, Bow or Hick. She was at the stove, stirring something. She stopping stirring and stood still for a while, as if this was either a question she had considered and wanted to carefully phrase her answer, or a question she had never before considered and was trying to first answer for herself.

After a few seconds she resumed stirring and said: "Bow was handsome and charming, but I was hardly with him. I was with him only a year when he went off to war. Then he died. I was with your father for twelve years. I knew everything about your father. I loved everything about your father. I had much more time to love him and for him to love me."

It was the first time I considered different depths of love.

During another stove talk—again, I can't remember why—I asked Mom whether she believed in God. This time she answered without hesitation. She looked over to me and said, "I have my entire life, but if there was really a God, he would never have caused so much intense pain to someone who was as wonderful as your father."

Mom's words stunned me. I had always had doubts about the logic of some of the Bible stories, but I never imagined that my mother might question her faith.

Hearing Blair describe her father's philosophy, this idea that science and the spiritual swirl together rang true to me. Certainly, it seemed to me that science had its limitations. Far as I could tell, science couldn't adequately address many of life's most important mysteries. Biology could explain why my heart raced when I got excited, and which part of my brain was responsible for my ability to hammer a nail over at the sardine factory—or, to be more accurate in my case, which part of my brain was responsible for the daydreaming that caused me to lose focus and hammer my thumb. But what was the explanation for why Angela was the one who made my heart beat faster? Why was she the one I daydreamed about?

Angela. I still very much thought about her. I never told Blair about Angela, although I trusted Blair and loved being with her. The one time Blair and I found ourselves in bed together, Angela was all I could think about and, well, I guess you could say I reversed direction, and that was that—or rather, there was none of that.

I had Angela on the mind, too, one afternoon when a parent of one of the Our School students sat down at a piano that had just been rolled into the school and started to play. She saw me watching her fingers on the keys. I was mesmerized. She asked me if I knew how to play. I didn't. She said it was easy. Sit down, she said. I did and she taught me the basics of "Für Elise." For the rest of the summer, whenever I got the chance, I stopped at that piano and played "Für Elise" over and over. Angela liked musicians.

Throughout that summer I'd been writing Angela. Brusque letters with no indication of affection. I told her all about Tom and Susan Tureen and Our School, and the work my team was doing to help make it all happen for the kids and that I was staying on at the school through Christmas as a teaching assistant. Knowing her last boyfriend had traveled into New York as a volunteer tutor for underprivileged kids, I'm not going to lie, I thought she might be impressed by my efforts. I told her, too, that I'd taken up the piano. I let Angela know I planned on returning to Wesleyan in October for a visit around Halloween. What I did not write is that after she said she didn't love me, I'd flipped my lid and went off to Maine to screw it back on.

Anyhow, at the end of the summer, while most of my AFSC crew members packed up and headed off to their respective colleges, I stayed behind as a teaching assistant at Our School.

And there was still that invitation from Bob to brew beer.

Six

THAT DECADE
I SPENT IN COLLEGE
(PART 2: STRANGE BREW)

One morning early that fall I headed over to Bob's place. You'd be hard-pressed to find a more homey home in which to learn how to home-brew. Bob and Lisa Szatkowski rented a small, weather-beaten three-bedroom house about fifteen feet off Route 1, the main thoroughfare. There was no real driveway to their place, and just a worn and rutted path up to the front door. The door opened into the living room, which was small and crowded with well-aged furniture. Bob led me through the living room into the kitchen, telling me to watch my step. Toys and books belonging to their four kids were strewn all over the place.

The kids had just finished breakfast. Bowls of granola and fruit were still on the kitchen table. It seemed every inch of countertop was covered with jars and food supplies and cooking utensils. Washington County, Maine, was then among the poorest counties in the nation. Folks did many things to cut costs and make ends meet. Lisa canned and jarred various fruits for their own use and to sell at local farmer's markets, which is what she was doing when we invaded her kitchen. She was also baking a pie, which filled the house with warm, delicious scents. Bob worked as a plumber, rough carpenter, ditch digger, really, whatever he could find, and, as was the case with many Washington County residents, he made his own beer. Bob would no sooner buy a case of Budweiser than he would a case of Champagne. Lisa said she'd take a break from her work and leave the kitchen to us. Probably because she had a good idea of what was coming and thought it wise to run for cover.

Bob's crash course in brewing beer commenced. First, he had me wash and rinse a five-gallon glass jug with a narrow neck called a carboy. We plugged the carboy with a black rubber stopper. A short bit of quarter-inch glass tube went into the center of the stopper, sticking out about a half inch. Bob said we'd need that carboy in a bit.

While we worked, Bob told me he'd moved to Maine years ago from Chicago, where he'd been a social worker. As he led me through the process of brewing beer I got the impression he must have been good at the social work. He had an easy way about him. He was patient. He made a point of explaining every step in the process. He was teaching me without seeming like he was teaching me.

Bob opened a three-pound can of Blue Ribbon Malt Extract. We emptied the malt extract into a three-gallon aluminum pot, filled it with water, and brought it to a boil on their dilapidated electric stove. Bob had me fetch the carboy. Using a dented aluminum funnel, we transferred the boiled solution of diluted malt extract into the five-gallon glass jug. We then boiled up another kettle of water and added it, leaving only a few inches of air atop the jug. Bob said this was our "wort" and we now needed to let the concoction cool down.

Bob opened the kitchen door and we stepped onto the back porch.

The yard was littered with all manner of broken household machinery and backyard equipment that I suspect had been waiting and would wait a long, long time for repair. Bob offered me a cigarette. I told him it might just be the first one I had smoked since I had been ratted out by little Chris Hansen for selling cigarettes after Sunday school at All Saints Church when I was barely six years old.

I explained to Bob how my dad had purchased each of us kids one share of stock in a public company. My share happened to be in the American Tobacco Company, which distributed a gift pack of their products every Christmas to their shareholders. I took my allocation to Sunday school and sold them, one cigarette for a nickel. That is, until Chris Hansen, just three years old, squealed on me.

Bob laughed and made some remark about how you gotta do what you gotta do. He said he had been a rough guitar player back in Chicago. He once jammed with "Spider" John Koerner's trio—Koerner, Dave Ray, and Tony Glover, and other blues greats like Sonny Terry and Brownie McGhee. Bob loved the music scene in Chicago and he enjoyed his social work in the community, but it didn't make him and Lisa much money. They were poor, he said, and they figured it would be easier to be poor in Maine than in Chicago.

We returned to the kitchen, where our "wort" had cooled but was still warm. We mixed up some wort with sugar and a package of Fleischmann's yeast, intended for baking bread. Again, don't try this at home with the Fleischmann's. Bob explained that when bread rises, it is actually the fermentation by the yeast cells that gives off CO_2, causing the rising of the dough. It also creates a low concentration of alcohol that, in bread, evaporates during the baking. Our yeast mixture immediately started to bubble. After a few minutes we added it to our jug. We stoppered the jug and manhandled it into their impossibly crowded hall closet.

We fitted one end of a long piece of clear plastic tubing over the nub of the glass tube sticking out of the stopper in the carboy. We placed the other end firmly at the bottom of a Mason jar filled with water, beside the glass jug. Almost immediately, the hose end in the Mason jar started bubbling. This, Bob announced as if he were revealing the meaning of life, is the miracle of fermentation. The yeast propagating, feasting on the simple sugars from the malt extract, reproducing, and giving off CO_2 and alcohol as by-products. Bob said it was like an orgy.

Decades later, I would find myself giving a group of old ladies a behind-the-scenes tour of the brewpub in Denver. I'd explain in formal terms the fermentation process, pointing out the importance of keeping the brewery clean and sanitized in order to prevent bacteria and contamination. Remembering Bob, I'd tell the ladies, "The fermentation process is like an orgy, and like any well-run orgy, you only want invited guests." Awkward silence. I had badly misread my audience and my joke fell flat, as would often happen in my political life.

Anyhow, Bob and I shut the closet door to try to keep the raging yeast party at a cool, consistent temperature. The closet was not perfect, but it was better than the living room, where the wood stove might be called into action on a cool autumn night. For the moment, our work was complete.

About a week or so later Bob called me back to his house for the bottling extravaganza. Like many home brewers of that time, he had been saving returnable beer bottles. The preferred brand up there was Narragansett: long-neck bottles, inexpensive for commercial beer, and the Narragansett Porter was quite tasty. Although the bottles had been washed when first emptied, we used a funnel and hot water to rinse them again. We would have used boiled water, but, what can I tell you, it wasn't that kind of high-class operation.

We removed the now barely bubbling glass jug from the closet and shimmied it back into the kitchen, removing the stopper from the carboy. The hose and decidedly funky Mason jar of water went into one of the sink's two basins. We hoisted the jug onto the kitchen table and placed the first case of rinsed empty bottles on a chair, a foot or so lower than the level of the table. Bob set a roasting pan on a nearby chair.

"What's the pan for?" I asked.

"You'll see," he said and smiled.

As I was about to learn, the other basin in the kitchen sink would have been a better filling station, but it was draining the last bit of blood from one of the Szatkowskis' chickens, which Bob had butchered that morning.

Into each bottle we sprinkled a pinch of sugar to trigger a final phase of fermentation. After we capped the bottles, this last brief fermentation action would generate CO_2, which under self-created pressure would carbonate each bottle. The amount of sugar was critical if somewhat imprecise. Too much, and the bottle was likely to explode its cap during the three weeks of bottle aging back in the closet; too little, and the beer would pour as flat as my joke to the old ladies.

Bob took a new length of clear hose, put one end deep in the jug, and put the other end in the side of his mouth and mumbled something.

"What?" I said.

With the hose still in his mouth, he mumbled the mumble again, only louder.

"Don't understand."

He took the hose from his mouth. Exasperated, he announced that what he was about to do next was the "suck-and-spit siphon starter" technique.

"Oh, why didn't you say so?"

Bob took a couple of breaths and sucked the hose until the raw beer entered his mouth. He pinched the hose, smiled like a Cheshire Cat, placed the hose in the first bottle, unpinched it, and the beer flowed into the bottle. Bob spat out his swill into the roasting pan. Well, mostly into the roasting pan.

"That," he said, "is what the pan is for."

Moving the hose from filled bottle to empty bottle was tricky. Bob would lose track of which ones were filled and which were empty. In fairness to Bob, the bottles were made of dark brown glass (dark to keep out sunlight, the natural enemy of good beer). By the time bottling was completed, there was beer everywhere. Lisa walked in, rolled her eyes, and walked out. She was a patient, patient woman, that Lisa. Did I forget to mention that throughout the bottling phase we were also drinking bottles of Bob's last batch? To ensure consistent quality, of course, like any good craftsman.

Although I didn't know enough to notice at the time, Bob omitted what most brewers would say is a critical ingredient: he didn't use hops. An honest citizen couldn't buy hops back then. That's why when I first chugged from the jug out on the beach it tasted so strange and bready. Very few commercial ales are made without hops. In addition to adding a distinct flavor, hops helps preserve beer. But Bob being Bob, it's not like his beer sat around very long, so that was not a concern. Bob was always more about the adventure than the engineering.

As imperfect as his methodology may have been, all in all, Bob covered the basics. He provided me with my very first course in the fundamentals of brewing beer—and also, for that matter, in the fundamentals of brewing politics, as I have since come to appreciate.

Brewing begins with natural ingredients: barley, malt, good clean water; in most cases, unless you're my friend Bob, hops. So does politics: ideas, people, passion, and in most cases, a just cause. The real brewing action, the fermentation, starts when you add the yeast. In politics, that's the activist, the engaged civic leader, coupled with the people's voice, which drives the democratic process, and often does so much to catalyze change. But for better and for worse, in our democracy, it takes a political leader with the will to take up the cause, to own it, as they say, to keep it clean, to take the slings and arrows, justified or not, to balance everyone and all of the energy and ideas together, in order to bottle a policy that usually isn't fancy or flashy, but is palatable, of value and lasting. That's the brewer.

Ultimately, too, it takes a politician to sell the seasonal yet hopefully timeless brew to the public at large. Abraham Lincoln put it best: "With public sentiment, nothing can fail; without it, nothing can succeed."

Thus the importance of the cult of political personality. Or, as political consultants like to call it, "the brand." It's a little like those last pinches of sugar Bob and I added to beer in the bottles before we capped them. That step, unique to home brewing, creates the effervescence in the beer. Without the smidge of sugar, or with too little of it, you just have varying degrees of flat malty beer. Too much, and your beer is so bubbly that you want to spit it out, or it explodes in the closet before you ever have a chance to taste it. Same could be said for political leaders. Those who lack effervescence, regardless of pedigree and intelligence, are not especially effective. Those with too much bubbling inside, well, they can be counterproductively explosive—off-putting, to say the least.

Naturally, I wrote to Angela and informed her of my newly acquired master home brewer skills. I received a letter from Angela's friend, Pat, the girl who also lived near me. She conveyed that Angela was *really* looking forward to seeing me. Pat and Angela were now living together. Pat said Angela wanted to have me over for dinner when I returned.

I couldn't wait to visit her at Wesleyan. But I was without a car.

Just before my sophomore year at Haverford, my big sister Tad and I had chipped in and bought a used Volkswagen Squareback. She drove the car more often than I did that year. After all, it wasn't like I had the sort of social life where I had friends to visit or places to go. The following year, Tad left home to attend Stanford University and the old beater of a VW more or less became mine. It's how I traveled to and from

Wesleyan my freshman year, and the Squareback is what I drove "down east" to the town of Perry, Maine, to link up with the American Friends Service volunteers.

The car was in fine shape when Tad and I first bought the thing. My brother, Syd, who was a gearhead, would give it a once-over when he was home on breaks. Tad and I also did our best to ensure that the car got to a mechanic for routine maintenance. Yet one day while I was driving from Perry up to Calais (pronounced *Callous*, which is fitting considering what happened next), the Squareback's engine started to knock and bang and then conked out. The road before me was downhill, and I knew I was not far from a farmhouse service station, so I figured what the hell—I shifted into neutral, opened the door, gave the Squareback a push, jumped back behind the wheel, and hoped momentum would get me there. I rolled down the hill and right into the Amoco.

A sign hanging in front of the service station read LAST AMERICAN GAS STATION. The station, as I had learned during my time there, was owned and operated by Eddie Brooks, at sixty-something years old, easily the oldest of the Our School parents. Eddie's Amoco was the last Amoco station, twenty miles south of the Canadian border, thus the sign.

Eddie appeared and asked what the problem seemed to be, with that particular down east drawl I had come to love, and I told him. He was a good listener, punctuating his nods with the occasional "ay-ah, ay-ah" that is pretty much the standard response to any story in that part of the country. He said, "Sounds like your Squareback might have thrown a rod." I gratefully accepted his offer to look at it. Eddie's working garage was out back. We rolled the Squareback over to his barn, where he did his work. Inside, Eddie had excavated a big hole in the barn's dirt floor, about eight feet by eight feet and at least six feet deep, with two thick wooden beams laid across the top of the hole. This was Eddie's mechanic's pit. A car in need of repairs went on the beams and Eddie went down under to do his thing.

While Eddie examined my car, his assistant, a kid in his late teens, arrived. He and I got to talking about engines and Eddie. Eddie was a legend in those parts. Where my brother was a mechanical whiz, Eddie was the Jedi Master. By way of example the kid told me a little story.

Eddie drove a flatbed truck that he bought cheap from "military surplus." For a while the thing had a bad engine. Eddie knew that any day the engine was going to die on him. So he traveled with a spare engine strapped in the back of the flatbed. Every Christmas season, Eddie loaded his flatbed truck with fir trees he'd cut down from the woods around his gas station and hauled the trees into Manhattan, where he sold them to tree dealers. Sure enough, one year, while Eddie was delivering his trees in Manhattan, the engine crapped out, right around Forty-second Street and Fifth Avenue—during evening rush hour.

Cars are honking. People are flipping the bird at Eddie. A cop pulls up and starts barking at him. Eddie doesn't get flustered. He listens, nodding his head and saying "ay-ah." He tells the cop he'll handle it, he'll get it fixed. He says he just needs some time. Right there on Forty-second and Fifth, in the middle of a cold, pissed-off New York, amid the holiday "cheer" of shouts and horns, Eddie yanks down three of the trees and some chains. He makes a tipilike engine lift out of the Christmas trees and chains. He hoists out the bad engine, installs the spare, and goes on his way. A complete engine swap, just like that.

"Pretty incredible, right?" the kid says.

I agree. Pretty incredible.

That story has stuck with me all these years later. There's something to it. Sometimes you just end up with a broken engine or a broken heart, or as was my case at that moment, both. And that's if you're lucky. If fate is *especially* cruel, you end up burying two husbands.

After Hick died, I remember Mom saying, "We can't always control what happens to us, but we can control how we respond." When she got word that Bow died in that plane crash, Mom kept scrubbing the bathroom floor. She went to work at the magazine. When Hick died, she turned her complete attention to raising her four kids. Thanks to the mess I had been, she spent a great deal of time on me. By the way, it wasn't like Sydney was an angel, or that my sisters didn't cause her worry. She dealt with each challenge as it came.

Angela had said she didn't love me. The engine in my chest threw a rod. But that summer I went to work. Took some time. Got myself fixed. Fixed enough that I was ready to return to school.

The Squareback with its thrown rod was another story.

The engine was toast. The car wasn't worth repairing. The VW ended up in the small junkyard behind Eddie's house. Eddie removed the car's front hood and his wife planted flowers inside. Maybe there's something to that, too: planting a garden where a busted engine used to be.

So in the fall of 1971, I hitchhiked from Maine to Connecticut, to Wesleyan, to Angela. Just as Pat had said, she had me over for dinner. As we ate the meal she had kindly prepared and drank a bottle or two of wine, I told her all about my time away in Maine—building, brewing, helping the kids. I left out the part about Blair. After dinner, Angela suggested that we go for a walk. It was a beautiful autumn night. We strolled down Middletown's Main Street, out over the Arrigoni Bridge, which spans the Connecticut River and connects Middletown to Portland. At the center of the bridge, we stopped to look out over the water and the lights from the two small cities. It was close to midnight.

We'd been having a lovely conversation. Everything was kind of great. Then there was this quiet moment. Just like in the movies. Seemed like the world stopped. Not even a single car crossed the bridge. Just us. We were standing there looking at each other. I got the feeling that Angela wanted me to kiss her. She kept looking at me. I kept looking at her and kept feeling like she wanted me to kiss her, and . . .

I did nothing.

I did nothing for a few seconds more.

Then it just got awkward.

Then she said, "Well, we should get back."

What happened? I froze. Simply froze. I had waited so long and thought so much about kissing Angela that when the opportunity was there, I couldn't believe it was there. Always doubting myself, I thought it wasn't possible that she would actually want me to kiss her. For all I know maybe she really didn't want me to kiss her. It could be just cruel wishful thinking I heaped on myself. Regardless, I was mortified. We walked back to her dorm, where our night owl friends swarmed me for stories of my adventures, and Angela slipped away. I spent Sunday morning on campus and then headed back to Maine to finish out the year working my teaching assistant job.

That Christmas of 1971, I returned home to Wynnewood. My Christmas gift to myself was a 1949 half-ton Ford pickup. I drove the Ford back to Wesleyan in January 1972 to resume my undergraduate studies and promptly set off on a road trip. In February, I drove my old Haverford pal Jed Rulon-Miller to visit a friend of his at Harvard. One day, I'm walking around the campus, seeing what all the Harvard fuss is about, and I spot the author Kurt Vonnegut, familiar from his photo on the book jacket of *Slaughterhouse-Five*. The best seller was published in 1969, my senior year at Haverford. It was the book that made Vonnegut a household name.

I took a special interest in the novel. Mom had told me she thought Vonnegut had been a friend of my father's while Hick was at Cornell. She wasn't entirely sure. That uncertain shred she had shared was enough for me to imagine they *were* friends and that they'd had great times

THE OPPOSITE OF WOE

together, and that the famous author knew and loved my father and probably had great stories to tell about Hick. Why, I would bet that Vonnegut even modeled some of his characters on Hick.

Actually, I wasn't the one who spotted the author. I was with Jed's friend and we were walking across the quad at Harvard, a big open lawn in the middle of ivy-covered, old stone academic buildings. It was drizzling, chilly. There was a mist. It was Jed's friend who pointed out Vonnegut, a tall, slender man with wild hair and a wilder mustache walking a few steps ahead of us. If Jed's pal hadn't been with me, there's no way I would have recognized Vonnegut. Seems a good time to mention, but I have always had a devil of a time recognizing faces, even movie stars or celebrities. This is not as rare as you might think, and in the extreme, it is a cognitive disorder called "prosopagnosia." More commonly it's known as "face blindness." I'm not at the extreme end, but it's presented challenges throughout my life. Try being in the social worlds I have been in and having a hard time recognizing people you should recognize. Makes for some awkward situations.

As I was saying.

Vonnegut's head was down. He had books under his arm. He was walking purposefully. He looked like he had somewhere to go and didn't want to be bothered. I imagined he was bothered now quite a bit, what with being famous and all.

I didn't often think of Hick. Almost never, actually. Funny thing, to have been alive when your father was alive, yet you hardly know him and almost never think of him. People didn't seem to understand what that was like. I would often pretend I remembered more about Hick than I actually did. Other people's stories became my stories. But I knew the truth. I hardly knew my father. I remembered very little. For just about everyone else in my life, his name triggered warm stories, but to me, my dad was little more than a character named Hick. A dead stranger. And that made me feel stupid, and robbed, and angry. So when I didn't have to pretend for someone that I knew my father better than they did, or as well as they did, I just didn't think about him. I didn't have enough of him to think about.

Seeing Vonnegut, though, took my breath away. It was like I looked over and saw Hick himself. I was overwhelmed by how unexpectedly overwhelmed I was. Here was a chance to maybe know Hick better. I decided I was going to approach Vonnegut. I was going to ask him: *Did you know my dad? What was he like? Did he have a girlfriend?* Certainly, if he really did know my father, if they really were friends, Kurt Vonnegut, being the brilliant writer he was, would be able to describe Hick in such a vivid way that he could bring him back to life for me, make me remember what Hick was like, make me feel him again, just for a few minutes. That's all I wanted. Well, that's not all I wanted. Meeting Vonnegut would give me a ripe plum story to tell Angela.

And so with Jed's pal I walked a few steps behind the author, planning what I was going to say and how I was going to say it. "Excuse me, Mr. Vonnegut. My name is John Hickenlooper. My mom . . ." Vonnegut looked like he didn't want to be disturbed. I was afraid to disturb him. I was afraid he might not have known my dad. That Mom was mistaken. Or worse, that he *did* know Hick and he remembered him vividly, but had nothing good to say. What if Kurt Vonnegut didn't like my father? But still, I wanted to know. Knowing was better than wondering, right? I stopped and watched Vonnegut walk off, disappearing in the mist.

BACK ON THE Wesleyan campus, Angela seemed uninterested in me, at least not interested in me the way I wanted her to be interested in me. I looked for reasons to get off campus. I put some miles on the Ford, let me tell you. Not long after the Harvard trip, over what I recall might have been a spring break, I traveled to another New England campus to visit a girl.

She was pretty. Originally from San Antonio, she had the greatest Texas twang. One night, in that spring of 1972, a few months after failing to kiss Angela, or at least I think after failing to kiss Angela, the girl from Texas and I got together. I needed a friend. We got especially friendly. I was smitten, and fate (and maybe pity) intervened, and I ended up losing my virginity to the San Antonio Rose. It was a magical moment, but it wasn't with the person I had hoped it would be with. We tried to make a relationship of it for a few months, but she wasn't Angela.

Playing "Für Elise" at Our School got me hooked on the piano. At Wesleyan, I started taking lessons. One of my favorite family stories was of my great-aunt, Lucy Hickenlooper. A piano prodigy en route from her hometown of St. Louis to study at one of the prestigious institutions in Paris, she had stopped for a couple of days with her favorite cousin, my grandfather Smith Hickenlooper. According to family legend, although you won't find it in her biography, Smith persuaded her to choose a new name from old Hickenlooper family names, something more befitting a classically trained pianist. And so the great Olga Samaroff was born that night in Cincinnati. Some years later, after moving to Philadelphia, marrying Leopold Stokowski, and then losing him to "that bitch" Greta Garbo, as Olga referred to the actress ever after, she became a prominent teacher. One of her students was Helen Doughten, my mother's mother. But I digress.

My formal piano instructor at Wesleyan was Leo Renwinski, a master with a strong Eastern European accent. My friend Athan Billias, who was a pretty good jazz pianist, gave me informal lessons. He taught me how to play boogie-woogie (a gift that I embraced for the rest of my life). Imagine if I could play jazz for Angela! Athan had both the rhythm and the disposition of a jazzman. Once we were walking down High Street in Middletown, I was defending a classmate as a "nice guy," and Athan countered that "nice guys are a dime a dozen."

In June 1972, after classes ended, I stuck around campus. I ended up crashing in an off-campus house with other students who, like me, were in no hurry to leave. One of them was Pete. Pete was cool. He played pedal steel guitar in a band. In the house we shared for a few days that summer, our bedrooms were directly across the hall from each other. (This detail becomes relevant in a second.)

At the end of the year, during the week of graduation, when it seems everyone who sticks around and not graduating is there just to party or work reunion events, I awoke early in my bed after a long night. As I wiped the sleep from my eyes, I looked across the hall and saw Angela coming out of Pete's bedroom. Angela saw me see her. With her hand on the doorknob, our eyes locked for a moment, and then she disappeared down the stairs.

The next morning, without saying much to Pete, I left as planned. I packed up my stuff and got in the Ford pickup. Once again, I was bound for Maine. Once again, heart-twisted over Angela. This time, I was off to learn ceramics. At the last minute, I enrolled in a workshop at the Haystack Mountain School of Crafts in Deer Isle. Pete or no Pete, I was designing my summer around what I imagined Angela would find intriguing. I know, I know—what a sap.

Within days of starting the class, I got crosswise with my ceramics teacher. Only I could get crosswise with a Haystack Mountain craft school ceramics teacher. I switched to a workshop in stained glass.

For my project, I chose to make a stained glass window of Saint George and the dragon. Like just about every kid growing up, I had heard the story of George's heroics many times. Riding his trusted mount, George stumbles upon a princess waiting to be devoured by a dragon—she's a sacrifice offered in order to spare her town from the dragon's wrath. The princess encourages George to continue along and save himself. George being the saint he is will hear none of it. He sticks around, slays the beast, and thus saves the princess and the town.

Would Pete have laid his guitar-playing, nice-guy butt on the line like that for Princess Angela? I don't think so. . . . Ah, who was I kidding? Yes, he would have done that for Angela. Fact was, Pete was cool, quietly self-assured; he probably would have taken on a dragon for anyone. Me? I wasn't even brave enough to kiss the princess on a peaceful, dragonless bridge. I'll say this, though: I made one heck of a stained glass window. I came up with the rather ingenious artistic choice to have the dragon's tail serve as the border and . . . oh, never mind.

I spent the rest of the summer traveling the country. Vermont, to see my sister Betsy. I hitchhiked to Montreal to catch the Canadian Northern rail line to Vancouver; from there I hitched to Eugene, Oregon, to pick up my truck, which I had loaned to a friend. Then down to Berkeley to hang with my brother, Syd. From there I headed back east.

This is how bad my Angela-itis was: I tried to collect adventures on the road and to learn unique artistic skills because I specifically wanted to be able to return to Wesleyan and describe my summer to Angela in fantastically true ways that made me uniquely worldly, that would make her want me. Long before there was that Dos Equis beer pitchman, The Most Interesting Man in the World, I wanted to be the most interesting man in the world for Angela. My awesomeness would be the dragon's head I would lay at Angela's feet.

What woman can resist a guy who can make a stained glass window?

ALAS, WHEN I returned for my junior year, Pete and Angela were on their way to becoming a couple. I could not be angry with them for being happy together, at least not openly. Though now I was lost on top of lost. I didn't have Angela and I still didn't have a clue what I was going to do when I grew up. I was starting to come to terms with the fact that I was not cut out to be a writer. I was living a life that may very well have been enough material to make for some interesting writing, but I had not actually done much writing. The most I had to show, as far as an attempt at anything literary, meaning the only thing I'd written at all, was the beginnings of a novel based on the life of Damon Runyon. All those years of Mom playing that *Guys and Dolls* record over and over in the house had made an impression on me.

Writing required that I sit down, be still, be alone. I was extroverted. I didn't like being alone. I wanted to be out and about. That SVIP test I took freshman year indicated that "artist" might be the life for me. Photography is an art. Photography is a way of storytelling. After all, a picture is worth a thousand words. Photojournalism is a way of meeting interesting people. I weaseled my way into an advanced photography class. One of the ongoing assignment themes was "light on skin."

One afternoon in the bathroom of my off-campus house, I rigged a camera high on a ladder above our old claw-foot bathtub. I filled the tub with warm water, jumped in the tub, and snapped a picture of myself, eyes just above the waterline, my shoulder-length hair floating around me, legs akimbo, knees high and dry. The Hickenlooper full monty. True artists put themselves out there. I was definitely out there.

Anything for art.

Despite the subject, it made for a compelling photograph, and that's not just me saying so. The photo won a local photography contest. I like to imagine the judges talking among themselves, discussing what each of them thought the photo says. *Who is this young man and what exactly is on his mind?* These would have been fair questions. I didn't know the answers myself. Truth was, the story of the photo was the guy got a little high and thought a naked self-portrait in a tub would be cool.

In the spirit of "light on skin," I shot some nudes of a classmate, Margie. Beautiful, free-spirited Margie. She was a friend of a friend whom I had met while taking a modern dance class. Margie lived in a house with women who were all focused on feminist studies. Margie could not have been a more stunning subject or a better sport, especially when the cop showed up.

At the time, my photography class was exploring the power of darkness and light. I suggested to Margie that I photograph her naked, standing in the center of Middletown's Main Street on a drizzling night, under a streetlight. Artists are daring. Might as well go big. Margie was game.

In the middle of the night, I staged Margie on one end of Main Street, and I ran down to the other end and cued her to walk toward me under a streetlight. From this distance she walked toward the lens, her fair white skin catching the light of the streetlamp, otherwise enveloped in the black of night. When I first developed the photo, I was struck by the fact that the most powerful light in that darkness appeared to be emanating from within her, Margie's natural glow. No, there was nothing going on between Margie and me. It was totally on the up-and-up. We were friends, and she was a lovely subject who agreed to put up with my aspiring artiness.

While we were at it, I noticed a nearby front loader. I floated the idea to Margie. How about "Beauty in the Bucket"? Wasn't I clever? Again Margie agreed. If any of the staged scenes tested Margie's patience it was this one. Climbing into the cold, wet, metal bucket of a front loader, nude, and then sitting there isn't exactly pleasant.

But it was when Margie posed in a telephone booth on Main Street that things got interesting. The Middletown police showed up. At night, a telephone booth is essentially a box of light. Margie got inside and as I was shooting, a cop car arrived. The officer rightly wanted to know just what was going on. I explained. His eyes rolled. I could practically hear his thoughts: *Damn college hippies.* He said he'd let us continue on one condition: that I send him one of the pictures of Margie in the phone booth. I told him that I couldn't do that. Margie, who had emerged from the phone booth, wrapped in a blanket, walked over and said that it was fine to send the cop a picture. She was flattered that he had asked.

The officer gave me an address. Later, after several calls from the officer to remind me, I mailed the photo.

A few months go by, and I'm in a diner in Middletown and run into the cop. He asks me if I would send him another picture of Margie in the phone booth. I say, "Oh, I don't know if I can do that. Why?" He tells me that his wife had been putting his clean laundry away, found the picture of Margie in his underwear drawer, and it just about started World War III in his house.

The officer managed to talk his way out of the doghouse. How the cop explained why he wanted the photo in the first place, I'll never know. But the officer's wife, he said, had torn up the picture and thrown it away. "So, if the photo caused all this trouble," I asked him, "why do you want another one?" He smiled and said, "I *really* liked the picture." I chose to take that as a compliment. Margie got a good laugh out of the whole thing when I told her and said, sure, send the poor guy another photo. Margie advised that I send along a note reminding the officer to hide the photo in a new spot.

It was also during my junior year that I met a lifelong friend in Mark Masselli and made my first real estate investment. My brother Sydney's dog had had a litter of puppies. I kept one, named her Hilda. As cute as Hilda was, the landlord of the off-campus house where I'd been living didn't allow pets. Looking for a new place to live, I turned to the classified ads in the local papers for "roommate wanted." I knocked on one door and Mark answered. He and another guy, Jim Ferrari, were renting a three-bedroom apartment in a dilapidated Victorian. Both Mark and Jim were my age; neither was a Wesleyan student.

Mark had lasted only three months at a small college in Ohio. College, he said, just wasn't his thing. He believed he could learn more, be more, by helping people. Jim was a social worker, a kindred spirit of Mark's. The rent was reasonable, Mark and Jim seemed cool. I moved in. We all got along. Jim had a terrific jazz album collection he graciously shared. As I had recently taken up the piano, Jim's collection provided me with endless inspiration. About the only drawback to the apartment was that there was an Indian rug merchant on the first floor who always seemed to be cooking something; our place smelled of incense and curry.

At the time, Mark had recently started a nonprofit Community Health Center. He rented some space on the first floor of a three-story building in downtown Middletown and recruited a local dentist to come to the center two afternoons a week and provide free dental care for the poor. Mark's CHC had grown dramatically. The clinic was now providing dental *and* medical care, treating hundreds of local people for free or close to free. Mark had expanded to the second floor, but the owner would not contribute to renovations that would allow Mark to improve his health care facility. The owner, however, would gladly sell the building for $40,000. Mark asked me if I wanted to buy the building with him. I invested $3,300, one third of the down payment, along with Mark and another friend of ours. It seemed a solid property investment, but even more, it struck me as the right thing to do. I felt I was investing in the community. We named our partnership Hilda's Associates, after you-know-who.

At the end of my junior year, I had a rather rated-X experience with my mom. Actually, it wasn't a "rather rated-X experience," it *was* rated X. I told you that Mom often quoted the Bible and Shakespeare; well, one of her favorite phrases to apply to me was the "Prodigal Son." When I walked in the door of our home my very first night back in Wynnewood for that summer after junior year, she said, "Ah, the Prodigal Son has returned. I have prepared the fatted calf."

From all of my Sunday school classes, I knew the Gospel story of the Prodigal Son well: A father has two sons. His younger boy asks his dad for his inheritance before the dad dies. The dad says sure, the kid takes the money and parties away his fortune. The definition of "prodigal" is "extravagantly wasteful." The kid ends up so broke that he eats pig slop with swine. He returns home, planning to beg for his father's forgiveness, thinking his father will shun him.

On the contrary, the dad embraces the younger son, even throws a party for the kid, kills their finest fatted calf, and serves it for the meal. The older son gets pissed. He skips the party and asks his dad why they were celebrating his selfish, dumb-ass brother when he had been there doing the right thing all along. The father tells the older son not to worry, that all that the father has will one day go to him, but for now they should celebrate his brother, for he was lost and now is found.

I knew Mom thought I was lost. And I was. But I was young. I felt like I was supposed to have some time to get lost. Getting lost was how you found yourself. Anyhow, I tried not to read too much into Mom's calling me the Prodigal Son. She hadn't killed the finest fatted calf for me that night, but she was in the midst of making me a fine dinner.

Being the insensitive lout I so often was to her, I asked her to hurry up because I'd made plans to go see a movie that night with Jed Rulon-Miller. Jed and I had remained close, and we have remained close to this day. When I first moved to Denver, Jed came out and worked with me on a screenplay about Damon Runyon, and later, when I opened the brewpub, he moved to Denver to help open it and eventually became our bookkeeper.

Anyhow, I tell Mom to hurry up with the dinner because I'm going to see a movie with Jed. The minute I said it, Mom's face fell, but she didn't say anything. She just kept preparing to serve the Prodigal Son his dinner.

I felt like such a heel. It then occurred to me—really, I'd say, for the first time since I'd gone off to Wesleyan—that Mom spent every day alone in our empty house. Hick dead, kids all gone. She had been looking forward to seeing me and spending time with me that evening. I asked her if she wanted to join Jed and me for the movie. She looked up, a huge smile on her face. Her eyes were so happy. "Yes," she said, "I'd love to join you."

The thing was, Jed and I were going to see *Deep Throat*, one of the first and most famous or, depending on the perspective, infamous X-rated films of all time.

In my defense, I'd never before been to one and wasn't entirely sure what an X-rated film was. They were a pretty new thing. Don't get me wrong: I had some idea it was going to be racy, but this was the 1970s, and free love was in the air. And I was now into photography and had gained a broader appreciation for the aesthetic value of nudity. I had completely missed the big obscenity lawsuit over the film in New York. In the spring of that year, a judge had found that the film was indeed obscene and described it as a "feast of carrion and squalor," "a nadir of decadence," and "a Sodom and Gomorrah gone wild before the fire."

After dinner, Mom and I get in her car and we pick up Jed and head into Bala Cynwyd to the Band Box theater to see *Deep Throat*. Now, I'm six foot two, Jed is six foot three, and Mom is barely five feet tall, and there the three of us are at the ticket window: two tall college guys in their early twenties and this little, proper fifty-year-old woman from Wynnewood, and I say, "Three for *Deep Throat*, please." The woman inside the ticket booth gives us a long look-over and says, "Are you sure?"

"Yes, we're sure." At least, I think we're sure.

We got there late. The only seats unoccupied were among the very front rows. Mom sits between me and Jed.

The first scene is the film's star, Linda Lovelace, driving through her suburban neighborhood. Typical, normal. Seems okay to me.

She parks her car in the driveway. As she rolls down her window, the credits begin to roll down, too. I'm thinking, *Hey, that's hip. Arty. This should be fine.*

Linda walks in the kitchen door and there's a woman sitting on the kitchen countertop, her legs open, and a guy has his head between them. There's movement—not too much, but enough.

Uh, boy.

I just about slid down out of my seat. I could not bring myself to look over at Mom. But I did. Very, very, very slowly, I turned to her. She was looking straight at the screen.

"Mom," I whispered. "Should we leave?"

Mom kept looking at the screen.

"No," she said, softly, matter-of-factly, "it'll be okay."

And so Mom, Jed, and I watched *Deep Throat.*

The whole thing.

My mother, who rarely swore, was nothing if not flinty. Back in the car, after what you can imagine was a rather awkward silence, she told Jed and me she'd been wondering what an X-rated movie was like. Jed and I were stone quiet. *Was she serious?* She looked over, after another moment of even more uncomfortable silence, and said, "It certainly was sharply in focus." I swear that in the faint light from that familiar dashboard, I saw her smile.

Seven

THAT DECADE
I SPENT IN COLLEGE
(PART 3: ROCKY FOUNDATION)

Senior year, 1973–74. Four years coming to an end. I'd fallen in love, had my heart broken, dodged a nervous breakdown, worked on a community school, learned to brew beer, taken up the piano, at last lost my virginity, made a stained glass window, gotten high and taken some (very artistic) naked photos, watched a porno with my mom, *and* managed to pass all my classes. Not bad.

Not good was that it had become pretty clear to me that I wasn't going to become a writer. There was no getting around the fact that writers have to write. I didn't see a future as a photographer, either. I just didn't feel that was the path for me. I was an okay amateur, but that was about it.

So, what now?

So I didn't know.

I didn't know until the second semester of my senior year. Then I knew. I knew about ten minutes into a class I wasn't even required to attend.

For no reason other than that I had time to kill and my friend Tracy Killam invited me to join her, I went to Tracy's geology class. It just so happened that the class I audited that particular day was taught by a guest instructor, Skip Pessl, a glacial geology expert with the U.S. Geological Survey. He was teaching this course on land use planning. The theme of his presentation that night, as Skip said right off, was to show how practical and useful geology is in our everyday lives. At that moment, I was looking for practical and useful in my life. Skip had my attention.

To make his point, Skip focused on a topic that was about as far from sexy and about as practical as you can get: leach fields, or, more specifically, how unscrupulous developers use geology to misrepresent leach fields in order to lower their costs and ultimately screw home buyers. Wastewater from city homes flows into municipal sewage systems, whereas most rural and many suburban single family homes have leach fields.

Leach fields, as I learned that day in Skip's class, work like this: Wastewater runs from a home to a septic tank that captures most of the sewage. (I told you it wasn't sexy.) The wastewater then flows from the tank into a leach, or drainage, field, typically a subterranean trench work of perforated pipes and porous materials such as gravel. A properly functioning leach field catches and neutralizes the remaining pathogens, then releases the water, or effluent, into the surrounding subsoil. A good leach field ensures that the ecosystem is not unduly disturbed. If, say, contaminants were to percolate to the surface soil of a farm, it could harm livestock.

A basic component of a home inspection is a percolation, or "perc," test, which evaluates the integrity of the leach field. Not surprisingly, most local health departments require a perc test. And as Skip pointed out, during wet months, like spring thaws, leach fields are pushed to their limits as water saturates the ground.

If you're a home owner, you want to make sure your perc test occurs then, because that's when the moisture and the local geology will reveal the competency, or incompetency, of the leach field. If crap is ever going to bubble up, that's the time. If you're a shady developer or seller who knows you have a weak leach field and you don't want to pay to fix it, you'd want the perc test to occur in a dry month, like July. A leach field that passes in August, but then fails in rainy April, can cost a small fortune to replace, but if you've already purchased the home, that's now literally your shit to deal with.

I loved it, right from start. Going into the class with Tracy, my plan had been that if it was boring, I was going to bail. I stayed for the whole thing. I had taken but a few notes in all my English and writing classes. In this class of Skip's, I scribbled furiously, not to pass a test, not because I had to, but because I was interested. I remember walking out of that class with at least six pages of notes.

I know, I know. Leach fields. What can I tell you? All I know is that listening to Skip Pessl talk, I felt as if I'd been introduced to a world where concrete problems could be solved, where mysteries could be unearthed and demystified. I know that's part of what appealed to me.

My life already had been filled with so much that was unexpected and could not be explained; I was immediately drawn to the certainty of geology. In geology, if you know the science, if you do the research and you add up the facts, there you have it. Outcomes are predictable. Unexpected shit won't bubble up in your yard. You won't get screwed. Or if it does and you do, you can determine the reason and understand why, and set about fixing it. In geology, most things are solid as rock.

Wesleyan had and still has a special master's program for nonscience majors called Earth and Environmental Sciences. I went to the chair of the department and asked if I could apply to the master's program. The response I got was a "maybe." First, I was told, I would have to meet certain requirements, meaning I would have to pass the math and science classes I'd so masterfully avoided during my first four years. That spring of 1974, I graduated with my bachelor's degree in English literature and rolled right into becoming a "special student."

In the summer of 1974, as President Nixon resigned, I successfully completed a chemistry course at Harvard. During the academic year of 1974–75, at Wesleyan, I took physics, calculus, and some other coursework to qualify for the Earth and Environmental Sciences master's. My former Wesleyan profs would see me on campus and ask what the heck I was still doing there—"John Hickenlooper, didn't you just graduate?" A couple of my geology professors called me into an office one day and with good-natured pomp and circumstance presented me with a piece of parchment paper, which I still have. On it they wrote:

Wesleyan University and the faculty and students thereof hereby award to *Mr. John W. Hickenlooper* tenure at this institution for his unflagging pursuit of excellence as a STUDENT.

Thus, to my knowledge, I became the first and only student in Wesleyan history to be granted tenure.

ON FEBRUARY 7, 1975, I got a phone call from Mom. I figured she was calling to wish me a happy birthday. That day, I turned twenty-three. Mom said she was phoning to tell me she and Bill were soon to be married. It wasn't a complete surprise. By then, she had been seeing Bill MacDonald for quite some time. The whole family had met Bill and liked him. He was a splendid man. He'd gone to Harvard, was retired from a successful business career, played the violin. Just a kind, elegant man. He adored Mom. And he was a younger man! Bill was five years Mom's junior.

I had figured things were going well between the two of them. My brothers and sisters had joked with Bill that if he and Mom married, he'd better enjoy life, because he probably wouldn't have long to live. We informed him that our mother is very hard on husbands. Mom and Bill would marry three months later in a small ceremony. We were all there. On that February phone call I congratulated Mom and wished her the best. She was so excited she forgot to wish me happy birthday, the only time in my life Mom ever forgot my birthday. Later, on a visit home, I noticed that Mom was reading *The Joy of Sex*. Good for her, I thought.

I passed the required special student science and math requirements and was accepted into the master's program. At the end of that special student year, I was fried. I wanted to take a year off before three more years of working on the master's degree. My geology professor Jelle de Boer thought that was a good idea and proposed an opportunity. He had a grant to fund research in Costa Rica and offered me the chance to work on it. The mission, if I chose to accept it, would be spending the better part of eight months charting gold deposits in areas of hydrothermal activity— in other words, dormant volcanoes. Sounded like a fine adventure to me.

I was mostly by myself in Costa Rica. I didn't speak much Spanish, so even among people I felt alone. Evidently, when I opened my mouth in Spanish I made even more of an ass of myself than when I shot off my mouth in English. I walked into a pharmacy and asked a teenage girl behind the counter for a comb. Or I thought I was asking for a comb.

"*¿Tienes un pene?*" I said.

The girl behind the counter's eyes opened wide; she gasped and covered her mouth. "*¿Pene?*" she said.

"Sí. Un pene."

"¿Pene?!"

"¡Sí! ¡Pene!"

An older Swiss gentleman in heavily accented English said, "Sir, you are asking for a penis." With a compassionate smile, he informed me that the word for comb was *peine*.

In the fall of 1976, with my new Costa Rican *peine* (just so we're clear, that's *comb*), I returned to Wesleyan to begin my master's coursework. I moved into a little red house—or as it had been known for years around Wesleyan, "the Little Red House on Long Lane." I rented it with a fellow geology grad student, Tom Metcalf. Tom had come to the master's program from Swarthmore College, where he'd majored in history. A non-science major like me, he had also done the special student requirements at Wesleyan, which is how we met.

Tom was the ideal housemate for me. He was smart and disciplined, a serious student. I knew he would be a good influence, help keep me focused. If I needed assistance—and who was I kidding, there was no if about it—I had the smartest grad student at my side. All the professors favored Tom. So did all the girls, which was the other reason I felt fortunate to live with him. Tom was tall, slender, with broad shoulders. Handsome, with a confident, easygoing manner. Having been half raised (all his summers) in his mother's homeland, the beautiful Annapolis Valley in Nova Scotia, he emanated a rugged independence. Women buzzed to him like bees to a flower. I figured Tom couldn't possibly date all the girls around him. Once in a while, one would have to settle for me.

Plus, I loved Tom's dog, Aslan, a beautiful Samoyed-like breed that was probably smarter than me. Aslan accompanied Tom everywhere. Aslan was so sharp and well trained that when Tom would bring him to class on the fourth floor, if Aslan had to take care of business, the dog would leave the class, walk down the hall to the elevator, wait till someone came along, hitch a ride down to the first floor, go out, pee, then make the return trip to class. The girls also loved Aslan.

Alas, despite Tom's fine example, other pursuits often distracted me from my studies—namely, real estate and, color me a glutton for punishment, love.

I had begun to think I just might stick around Middletown after school. I loved the town, the culture, the people. It already felt like it was my home. It *was* my home. I felt secure there. I could see a future where I'd find work as a geologist and just stay put. Even if I did leave after school, I envisioned returning one day. After all, I did have tenure.

In 1977, the Little Red House went up for sale. It was owned by the college, and the asking price was $26,500. I bought it, putting $3,000 down. I tried to get Tom to go in on it with me, but he passed. The deal seemed low risk. (That's how I started to talk, saying things like "the deal seemed low risk.") The mortgage and tax payments were less than the rent we'd paid the previous year. If I ended up living in Middletown, I had property, a place to live. If I left, I could sell it and would likely make a profit. Property values around the college were only appreciating.

Around this time, Mark Masselli's real estate attorney, Bill Howard, told me about a real estate injustice: The city was going to demolish the Mather-Douglas House, a large, stunning, but run-down historic mansion. It had been abandoned for years. City officials said traffic in the area around the old house was a problem, but Bill and anyone else who paid attention knew that this was a thinly veiled plan for the city to attract tens of millions of federal transportation dollars. I had been by Mather-Douglas a thousand times. It was an incredible building, and, it seemed to me, in a prime location. It was historic, a fixture in Middletown for 165 years. I arranged to go down and tour the inside of the building. Yes, it was a bit run-down, but boy, did I see possibilities. My two real estate investments had armed me with just enough confidence to be dangerous. I was now seeing things not merely for what they were but also for what they could be. I was convinced that the "problem" was merely a ruse to cut patronage deals on road construction. I was pissed.

Walking around inside the Mather-Douglas House, I saw a fine dining restaurant. Throughout the ten rooms, I saw seating for 175 people. I wasn't sure I could pull it off, but I figured if it all came together, I'd be preserving a treasure that was built when James Madison was president. I asked Tom to come down and do a walk-through with me. On top of being the super-man he was, Tom was also one hell of a carpenter. His father and genera-tions of Metcalfs before him all had been carpenters. Tom had been working as a contractor on breaks from school from the time he was a kid. Tom saw what I saw. He thought I was a little bananas, but like me, he didn't buy the city officials' rationale. Neither of us liked the idea of tear-ing down something that had intrinsic value for the sake of politics.

Tom and I formed a real estate development company, Aslan Associ-ates, named after Tom's remarkable dog. The "company" comprised Tom, the dog, and me. A friend's family ran a successful restaurant in New Haven and were eager to help. He drew up some plans and we hired an architect to draft a rendering of what was possible. We set a budget of $200,000, with $63,000 going to the purchase of the 42,000 square feet of Mather land. Tom and I put all this into a proposal and went before the Middle-town city council. We petitioned to buy the property and dared to ask the local officials for help to apply for a restoration grant from the federal government.

The Middletown Press reported our presentation like this: "For the moment, the plans of Aslan have collided with those of the official plan of the city, which calls for the demolition and relocation of the house to en-able a highway change. . . . It is clear from the proposal that the two part-ners have done their homework." Ultimately, we lost out, but we stopped the demolition. The building was converted into a medical center. While

Tom and I were disappointed, I had learned a great deal about a lot: design, consultants, zoning, how to navigate the real-world politics of local government.

Perhaps most importantly, I discovered that I loved that sense of creating something that didn't exist for a purpose that others didn't recognize. And I discovered an emotional attachment to historic buildings.

Ah, well. Tom and I were off to a geology conference in San Diego and, because we'd gotten a screaming deal on Eastern Airlines, we tacked on a midterm escape to St. Croix. In the airport on St. Croix we got to talking with two women our age from Sweden, Annica and Ellinor, who went by the name of Nålen. We might have gotten to talking to them because they were attractive and actually responded to us when we spoke to them, small talk that Tom and I tried to drag into a longer conversation. They had wonderfully thick Swedish accents. Soon enough they went their way and we went ours.

Until we checked into our hotel room.

Tom and I were opening the door to our room, still discussing the Swedish sisters, when, what do you know, they came walking down the hall and opened the door directly across the hall from ours. Tom and I could hardly believe our eyes. "Hey, didn't we see you at the airport?" I said. "Yes, hello," Nålen said, friendly enough, as they went into their room and closed the door.

The next morning, Tom and I woke at dawn and rented the cheapest car we could find. We hustled back to the hotel, left our door ajar, and lingered around a good three hours until Annica and Nålen emerged from their room. We invited them to tour the island with us. We had an offer we hoped they couldn't refuse: we had a car, they didn't. They said yes and off we went. We explored the small island that is St. Croix. We found that the "other end" of the island, anchored by the town of Frederiksted, had been ravaged by a hurricane the previous year. Debris was still everywhere.

Within walking distance of the town we came upon a string of two-story fourplexes on the beach. They were largely empty. Each one had two spacious bedrooms with two double beds, a kitchen–dining room, and a living room that opened onto a balcony overlooking the beach. The kicker: the rent for the whole place was the same price as five days of only one hotel room. Tom and I hatched our plan on the spot. We would, all four of us, split the week's rent. With the rental car, we'd pick up a week's worth of groceries, drop them off at our new pad, and still have time to see *Heaven's Gate* at the island's only movie theater. The girls agreed. To everything. Well, *not everything*.

Tom and I had crushes on them both, although we both fancied Nålen, partly because Annica had a boyfriend back in Sweden. For those seven days we did everything within our feeble powers to impress them. We cooked every meal, washed every dish. I mean, we were besotted. We bought two bottles of rum, which Tom and I put to good use but the girls hardly touched. We told hilarious anecdotes—or at least we thought they were hilarious—and submitted oh-so-keenly-insightful observations of human nature. We took long walks along the moonlit beach. But it was always the four of us. The sisters never separated. Well, almost never.

There was one day when Nålen and I spent a good bit of our time in the water together, swimming around each other. The sun was bright, no wind, the water calm. I asked Nålen to make a muscle. She smiled and flexed her biceps. Impressive, I said. Flirting clumsily, I asked if her legs were as strong. She frowned and playfully shook her clenched fist at me. There was a chemistry between us.

When Annica and Nålen left, Tom and I still had a couple of days to go in St. Croix. The girls were bound for Guatemala. They were on a six-month North American tour together, with stops in the United States. As we said good-bye, Tom and I gave them our address, the Little Red House, Long Lane, Middletown, Connecticut. "If you get anywhere near our neck of the woods," we told them, "please, stop by," never expecting we'd ever see them again.

Back on campus, in 1978, my thesis adviser, Jim Gutmann, a fine scientist who finally taught me how to write with clarity, informed me that he was taking a sabbatical and I would have to get my thesis to him six months early. I threw myself into the work and Tom did everything he could to help. I'd wake around 6:30 a.m. and eat a breakfast that he prepared. I'd drive to campus, work until noon, and come back for lunch that he had waiting. I'd return to campus until it was time for Tom's dinner. During that period, Tom not only cooked; he took care of *everything*. He did the dishes. He cleaned the house. Sometimes the guy even nudged me awake in the morning. Tom Metcalf mothered me through my thesis. As we ate together, I'd think out loud to him. He was genuinely curious about my thesis, and his feedback went a long way in helping improve my thinking.

There was, however, a brief period of three days when Tom was not on hand.

One night we heard a knock on the door. It was a Middletown cop—no, it wasn't that cop looking for another photo of Margie; this was a different cop. He said, "Do you know an Ellinor?" It couldn't be. I asked the cop, "Did you say Ellinor?" He said yes, and explained that there were two Swedish girls wandering around the bus station in town looking for a bus out to the Little Red House on Long Lane. "Well, where are they?" I asked. He said he'd offered to give them a ride. He pointed to his patrol car. "They're right there."

Annica and Nålen stayed with us for three days. Tom and I gave them our rooms. He and I took turns on the couch, with the other getting the floor. Because I was behind on my damn thesis, Tom was the one who took them out every day and showed them the town. Mystic Seaport, the Hartford museums. I'd work on my thesis from early in the morning and then spend time with them from late afternoon into the evening. I might have taken off with them one afternoon. I wanted every second I could get with Nålen, but the sisters stuck together and then they were gone. Back to Sweden. Just like that, Nålen and I were pen pals. In letters, we acknowledged that we had a connection, but she was in Sweden and I was in Middletown. With Tom's assistance and Gutmann's good grace, I did manage to turn in my thesis. I got my degree in February 1980.

I was in no hurry to leave Middletown. I hadn't even begun looking for a "real job." I was thinking about staying—doing the real estate entrepreneur thing, with a side of geologist work. I was already feeling like a real estate entrepreneur. I took out a loan on the Little Red House and invested in a three-story Victorian with my friend David Mauldin and his wife. We bought the house for $50,000, with David and me each putting in $10,000 for the down payment. The deal we struck was that David and his wife, Annie, would pay the mortgage, utilities, taxes, everything; and he would spend a year working on the house full time, doing improvements, carpentry, painting. Whenever we decided to sell, I'd take a third of the profit.

Meanwhile, I invested in another property with Mark Masselli: the Bank House, another historic fixer-upper. The place was teeny, and the proverbial money pit. The stone core of the house was believed to date back to 1700. We paid $20,500 for it, and then spent about $24,000 to renovate it, starting in the fall of 1979. I did virtually all the contracting work. Sixty hours a week for eleven months.

Well, that's not all I did.

I started dating Gwynthlyn Hoag Green. She was gorgeous, smart, five years older than I was—for whatever that matters—and very much part of a wonderfully brilliant and artistic family. Her father, Sam, chaired the Wesleyan art department. Her brother, Sam, orchestrated one of Andy Warhol's first shows and curated one of the first group shows of the American abstract expressionists.

Gwyn was the best of both her parents. She was an anthropology grad student, keenly interested in the witches of South America. She traveled just about everywhere with a small green and red parrot on her shoulder. The bird's name was Loro, Spanish for "parrot." There were times when I couldn't tell if it was Gwyn or the bird nibbling on my neck.

I found everything about Gwyn, her bird, and her family eccentrically charming. There was an aura of style and elegance around Gwyn and the Greens. Their home was a massive colonial on the top of a hill in the center of Middletown, with a forest-enclosed backyard garden that seemed like a page from a fairy tale. One warm evening, I joined her family for dinner in the yard. Gwyn's brother Sam was in town, and he brought his artist friend Yoko Ono. That Yoko was the wife of John Lennon often overshadowed the fact that she was an artist in her own right, a prominent figure in the New York art scene, which is how she came to know the Green family.

After the meal, Sam and Gwyn took Yoko and me up to the bathroom on the second floor to see the Green family portraits that covered virtually every inch of the walls. As we looked at the photos, we heard the stories behind each one; we laughed and talked.

After we'd been dating for, oh, maybe six months, I presented Gwyn with the very same engagement ring Hick had given to Shrimpy and asked her to marry me. She said yes. If it sounds like a rash decision that possibly was made in a surreal haze, it was. Within months, the more time we spent together, the more we realized we didn't fit. Much of it had to do with the fact, I think, that she was dealing with her own demons, and/or smoking a lot of marijuana to avoid them. I would frequently return after a long day to our small apartment at the back of her parents' home, which I noted to myself at the time was originally the "slave quarters," and find her reeking of pot with nothing to show for the day.

I'm sure it didn't help that in doing that renovation of the Bank House,

I made a couple of colossal, almost ludicrous mistakes. I was a stubborn screw-it-up-myself type who had to learn everything the hardest way. Every day I'd come home to Gwyn, frustrated with myself, and I'd find her on the couch, clearly stoned, sitting with the parrot on her shoulder. Gwyn and I went from bad to worse, to worse still. I regretted that I had allowed myself to be so quickly swept into the moment and had proposed. I wanted out of the relationship almost as much as I wanted to be free of the Bank House.

Both happened in short order.

In 1980, just about a year after we'd purchased it, Mark and I sold the Bank House. For all the blood, sweat, and tears I'd put into the project, I cleared a whopping $460. I once heard a friend say of his first renovation, "If we had known at the beginning what we know now, we would never have done the project, and what a shame that would have been." I felt the same way. Well, in truth, my perspective might not have been quite so Zen in the moment.

The Bank House was the first renovation I took on myself. Although it didn't bring a windfall profit and arguably was only marginally more successful than my failed efforts to secure the Mather-Douglas House, both of those experiences were invaluable. The way I see it, the only true failures are in not learning from mistakes, and in failing to take on the dreams we dare to dream.

If I had not done the Bank House renovation or made a run at the Mather-Douglas deal, what a shame that would have been, for the real payoff came a few short years later. They'd given me the baseline knowledge and confidence to take on the renovations for the Denver brewpub.

Eight

DENVER

In the summer of 1981, I landed a geologist job with an oil and gas company based in Denver. One hundred and twenty-two years after the Fifty-Niners struck serious gold in what would become the great state of Colorado, I was a young man of twenty-nine heading west to stake my claim.

That January, Ronald Reagan had succeeded Jimmy Carter as the fortieth president of the United States, and Iran had released the fifty-two Americans who had been held hostage for 444 days. Two months later, in March, President Reagan and his press secretary, James Brady, along with two police officers, had been shot outside a Washington, D.C., hotel by John Hinckley Jr. And in August, as I arrived in Denver, Mark David Chapman was sentenced to twenty years to life in prison for the murder of John Lennon.

The next time I saw Yoko Ono after that late summer night at the Greens' house in 1980 was the following December: December 8, to be exact. I saw her on television, during the breaking news coverage of the assassination of John Lennon. Lennon had been killed outside the Dakota apartment building in New York City, where he and Yoko had shared a home. An evidently deranged Chapman had shot Lennon five times, putting four bullets into his back. Chapman was arrested at the scene, reading J. D. Salinger's novel *The Catcher in the Rye*.

That summer night at Gwyn's, the Yoko I met was happy, blissful. There was light and laughter in her eyes. The Yoko I saw in those television reports the night of the murder was a shell of that woman: a fresh widow with a blank face, her eyes utterly empty. Her sadness, her lost happiness, seemed an expression of the grief and disbelief that millions of people around the world felt as they mourned her husband's death.

John Lennon had come to personify a movement of love and peace. As the nation entered the 1980s and exited the tumultuous decade of the 1970s, trying to make sense of the costly Vietnam War and the price of free love, Lennon's voice had been a powerful, healing whisper that encouraged the next generation to imagine—imagine living life in peace, with nothing to kill or die for. He called himself a dreamer, but he believed he wasn't the only one. When Lennon was killed, it seemed the world he imagined for us died along with him.

Eight months after his murder, as I arrived in Denver with Chapman's sentencing in the news, a song by Lennon was posthumously making its way to the top of the charts: "(Just Like) Starting Over." The song managed to capture what beginning again feels like. The song was a mixture of melancholy and optimism; it seemed a fitting theme of the moment for the nation, and for me.

My new employer was Buckhorn Petroleum, formerly owned by Frederick Mayer. I had a tangential connection to Fred. His son Tony had attended a New England boarding school where my sister Betsy and her husband, Dan, were both on the faculty. Dan had been a mentor and something of a counselor for the kid. As a student, Tony had been a character, mischievous, but in the way that the teachers who knew him found charming. Well, not all the teachers.

Tony might have gotten himself into a disciplinary jam with the administration. I'm not saying he did, just that it *could* have happened, and if that were to have occurred, my brother-in-law, Dan, would have advocated for Tony. Fred knew that Dan had taken an interest in Tony, counseled him and believed in him. Even after Tony graduated, Dan and Betsy remained friendly with Fred.

During the homestretch of my master's degree work, my brother-in-law told me about Fred. He suggested I send Fred a letter and inquire about possible openings. Dan said he'd ask Fred to keep an eye out for my résumé. It turned out the company was hiring. I was one of a small handful of geologists Buckhorn hired that year.

When I left Connecticut bound for Denver, Gwyn and I had been talking—sometimes rather loudly, and over the parrot squawking—about ending our engagement. We had agreed Gwyn would stay in Middletown while I got settled in Denver. The time apart, we said, would be a good time for us to take a break. Fact was, we both knew our relationship was perhaps irrevocably stressed.

Buckhorn hired me for the position of exploration geologist. It was a great first job. My starting salary was $26,500. They gave me a company car, a brand-new 1981 Buick Skylark, all expenses paid. The first couple of weeks, Buckhorn put me up at Denver's Brown Palace Hotel, one of the grandest hotels west of the Mississippi. The Brown Palace was drenched in five-star western hospitality and history. Denver's "Unsinkable" Molly Brown had stayed at the hotel only two weeks after surviving the *Titanic* disaster. When presidents came to town, when the Beatles came to town, they stayed at the Brown Palace.

A bellhop told me that the hotel was the site of one of the city's most infamous murders. In 1911, in the hotel's Marble Bar, a fellow by the name of Frank Henwood fatally shot a Sylvester Louis "Tony" von Phul, accidentally killing an innocent bystander as well. Henwood targeted von Phul because they both evidently had a hot and heavy thing going with a Denver socialite, Isabel Springer, who happened to be the wife of a wealthy local businessman and political candidate, John W. Springer. The high-profile murders played out in a series of high-profile trials. The West, it seemed, was indeed wild and lusty.

I was excited to be an exploration geologist. Like those Fifty-Niners who came to strike gold, I envisioned I would be setting out into the hinterlands of the rugged West, a scientist-speculator testing the geology, looking for evidence of oil and gas deposits. When I'd find the promise of black gold, I'd give a whistle and say, "Over here, boys!" The boys would rush out and set up a rig. As the drill twisted into the spot I had marked, I would watch as they struck it rich. With oil raining from the sky, dripping down their happy faces, the boys would hoot and holler, then turn and cheer, "Let's hear it for the geologist!"

I moved into one half of a duplex in central Denver, on the 500 block of East Center Avenue, just west of Denver's beautiful Washington Park. To the west was a breathtaking view of the city's skyline and, beyond that, the Rocky Mountains under a vast and stunning sky. Indeed, it seemed the sky was the limit.

In early fall, Buckhorn sent me to Durango, in southern Colorado, for an annual conference of the Rocky Mountain Association of Geologists. There are few places more Colorado-spectacular than Durango. The old mining town is on the Animas River, surrounded by the rugged San Juan Mountains. When I reached Durango that September, the air was still warm. The leaves were changing color. People were in the streams fly-fishing and kayaking. Hunters were parking pickups on the roadsides and heading into the mountains. Hikers were packing up and heading off.

The conference supplied us all with tickets for the Durango & Silverton Narrow Gauge Railroad. The steam-powered tourist train travels round-trip through the mountains, from Durango up almost three thousand feet in elevation to the historic mining town of Silverton, above nine thousand feet, a route it's followed since the 1920s. I had thought I would never see a fall as vibrant and as stunning as the ones I'd witnessed in New England; now I realized how wrong I had been. If Mom could have taken in the view from this train—seen that sea of gold, red, and orange fluttering on mountainsides dense with aspen, the clear streams bubbling over the stones—she might have felt the divinity in the place.

One Saturday not long after the conference, I was in my duplex unboxing my stuff, moving around my three pieces of furniture, as a party raged in the other half of the duplex. It went all afternoon and late into the night. The next morning I was running errands, and through my neighbor's window I could see what looked like nearly a dozen people all dressed in blue and orange Denver Broncos gear. They were sleeping, sprawled all over the place, on the couch, on chairs; a bunch of folks were on the floor. Seemed to me this crowd was going to wake up and have a rough morning.

Nope. Sunday morning the party resumed. Kickoff for that day's Broncos game wasn't until the afternoon. My new neighbor knocked on my door to see if I had any tonic water. Colleen Feely explained that she was from a big family born and raised in Denver. She said her family and friends did this just about every weekend during the season: got together the night before, stayed over and had a brunch, and then either watched the game on TV or headed over to Mile High Stadium. She invited me over for brunch and to watch the game.

Durango and Denver in the fall had already convinced me that Colorado was indeed the most beautiful state in America, and after hanging with Colleen's clan, I couldn't imagine more passionate fans than those in Broncos Country. I was all in.

Colleen was a wonderful neighbor and we quickly became close friends, but outside of work, she was one of the very few friends I made early on. After nearly a decade in Middletown, where I had a vast network of friends, where I felt like I knew everyone, in Denver I once again felt like an outsider. For an extrovert like me, loneliness is a terrible thing.

In my isolation, I became an avid letter writer. I also got into the habit of photocopying my correspondence at Buckhorn before mailing it off. I figured if I kept an archive of the letters I sent, I would have them for reference when I received letters in response. This was long before e-mail; now, we take records of "sends" and "receives" for granted. If you ask me, I was ahead of my time. Anyhow, I wrote letters and photocopied them this way for my first decade in Denver.

All these years later, I still have them and I'm glad I do. At least I think I'm glad I do. They remind me of details and emotions I otherwise might have forgotten, like how insecure and self-centered I could be and what a dreadful writer I was. In any event, the letters are a time-capsule reminder of who I was and all that occurred during my transition from oil-busted geologist to beer-booming entrepreneur. All of that, plus the beginning and end of my second engagement.

MOST OF THE LETTERS I wrote during my first months in Denver were to the old gang from Middletown. I invited anyone and everyone to visit me in Denver. Begged them, was more like it. "I must admit that I'm a little lonely," I wrote to an old friend on September 6, 1981. "I feel a general shyness toward the world after so many years of the 'social security' in Middletown." I wondered to another buddy if he thought Gwyn might come to see me in Denver. "Her ways which irritated me most seem irrelevant to me now and I don't think it's just the distance." I even missed the parrot.

Man oh man, when I wrote that I had no idea what was really going on back in Middletown, but I soon learned all. Gwyn was *never* going to visit me. Three weeks after I left, she and Tom Metcalf, who was still at Wesleyan working on his thesis, had begun seeing each other. I was not pleased, mostly with Tom. I felt betrayed, and I told him so in a letter:

> *Dear Tom,*
>
> *First, you are an asshole. You don't date your best friend's ex-fiancée three weeks after he leaves town. . . .*

That must have gotten it out of my system, for with some degree of humor, I went on to suggest that Tom consider marrying Gwyn.

> *She is a rare beauty, inside and out. . . . She's independent, yet affectionate and wouldn't mind long absences for fieldwork. . . . As regards to her, how shall we say, eccentricities, which are admittedly many, they are, for the most part, cured with a little patience, which I unfortunately lack and you luckily have in abundance. Many of the eccentricities were, I think, incubated by my own particular variety of eccentricities. . . . She doesn't go with someone unless she's pretty sweet on them. And she's ready to settle down, despite what she says from time to time. . . .*

As if I had any right to suggest such a thing to Tom.

I closed the letter by wishing Tom well on his thesis and signed off, "Take care, your pal (still), John."

And so, moving on, I moved on.

My job, as fortunate as I was to have it, didn't turn out to be all that I had imagined. I did a bit a fieldwork and got some training on sites. I learned how to collect and read seismic and magnetic data. Then it was back to the office in a Denver skyscraper. I spent 90 percent of my time at a desk, poring over maps prepared by other geologists. I'd review rock strata that previous or existing drilling operations had encountered in the region. Using that data, I'd create new maps that attempted to predict what sort of rock formations and opportunities we might find deeper down. I felt a bit like a geologist Sherlock Holmes. I enjoyed taking the limited facts provided and speculating on an idea, a reality, we could not see. I studied the maps and then produced reports or gave presentations in which I'd make the case for the best spot to set up new drills.

In no time, it seemed that whenever I wasn't leaning over a map, I was writing a letter to Nålen, or reading a letter she had sent to me. Ever since her visit to the Little Red House, Nålen and I had kept up our correspondence. We transitioned from pen pals to something more rather rapidly. With each letter, we drew closer to each other. It's clear from our letters that we felt less inhibited to share what was on our minds and in our hearts. From a distance, we got to know each other more intimately, more quickly, than if we had been living in the same town. Or so it seemed to us at the time.

We began to fall in love.

I know, I know. I'd just broken up with Gwyn. I was feeling lonely. I should have known better. Should have been more cautious. But what happened, happened.

Nålen was afraid of the strong feelings we had developed and had expressed for each other. She didn't see how anything could come of it, for all the obvious reasons, and this made her sad. I convinced her that we could and should try. "There is too little of time to waste it with unhappy thoughts," I wrote in the late fall of 1981. Then I added this ridiculous gem: "Thinking really doesn't provide solutions very often." Sure, why bother with thinking?

The frequency of our correspondence intensified, and so did our emotions. Nålen's letters, as I wrote to her, were "furnace-like," arriving "like tissue paper to a flame." I was trying to be funny, but still, not the greatest phrase. You get the idea. Soon we were also mailing audiocassettes back and forth; we wanted to "speak" to each other, to hear each other's voice. International calls were still wildly expensive and we were both wildly frugal. While we talked periodically on the phone, the letters and cassettes were our primary connection. To avoid astronomically high phone bills, we devised a system where I'd ring her once and hang up just to let her know she was on my mind. She would then ring back and let it ring twice and hang up to let me know the same.

We decided I would visit her that December. "I will arrive in Sweden on December 24th," I wrote. "I must leave on January 3. That is only 9 days, 216 hours, more or less." Apparently, I wanted to make sure we made the most of our time together. That twenty-nine-year-old me also wrote, "This matter of love is such that we must trust our hearts." Reiterating the point, I suppose, that we ought not think too much.

My time with Nålen in Sweden was idyllic. I met her family. We took long walks through her town. We finally held hands and held each other. Once again, as happened with Gwyn, I became enveloped in the moment and I proposed. It was a roundabout proposal, but still, a proposal all the same. As we walked one evening in Sweden, I suggested we marry and Nålen answered with "I guess that means we are engaged."

Once I was back in Denver, as Nålen and I corresponded about how soon she would come for an extended visit, my honeymoon period with Buckhorn began to wane. One year into the job I was bored. I didn't like being cooped up in the office. I also thought we were exploring in the wrong places. In a letter to a friend, dated June 1982, I wrote, "I am working on my first big project in the oil biz. Our division chief requested $6.3 million for me to buy seismic data and drill two wells to test some rather silly ideas. It's a lot of dead weight responsibility, especially for someone like me, like being a basketball star or a politician, but maybe not quite." If there was any doubt that I didn't think much of politics, there you have it. Reading this letter all these years later, I cringe at how my younger self, with only a year's experience, thought he knew better than geologists with three decades' experience.

Two months after my trip to Sweden, Nålen came to Denver for a visit. By then I had moved out of the duplex and bought a house on the 2200 block of West Center Avenue. Colleen Feely, my first neighbor in Denver, and our mutual friend Jody Chapel, an aspiring graphic artist, each took one of the upstairs bedrooms for $100 a month. A cheap deal for them, which made the mortgage cheaper for me. Nålen stayed with me for almost six months. I took her cross-country skiing in Aspen; we toured Denver. But mostly we hunkered down in my new house. We got a puppy (daughter of Tom Metcalf's Aslan) and named her Pie. We planted strawberries in the backyard. We visited with my rather small circle of friends. Near the end of her six-month visa, we went on a ten-day camping trip to Wyoming, where we met up with my thesis adviser, Jim Gutmann, and hiked the glorious Beartooth Mountains. Glorious days. Saying good-bye, we talked about how this would be the last time she would come and go; next time, she would come and stay.

Only that would never happen.

I loved Nålen. She was beautiful, to be sure, with dark hair, high cheekbones, wide eyes that seemed to see into people, into me. She was at once one of the most empathetic and independent souls I have ever known, generous to all around her, naturally so. I lit up and felt good whenever she entered the room.

Reflecting on her visit, however, I couldn't shake a feeling I had: I came to believe that we were not compatible. She was as introverted as I was extroverted. At parties, she stood off to the side by herself, content, happy, but still I worried for her. I was continually introducing her to people. She was happiest at home with me and Pie and the garden. I worried I wouldn't make her happy, that ultimately she would be disappointed in me. I would feel guilty if I stopped for a beer and to visit with friends after work rather than come directly home. She was happily independent, but still, that feeling of mine, I couldn't shake it. The more I thought about it, the more that feeling grew. She wanted to settle down. Her vision of our life together was akin to that Crosby, Stills, Nash & Young hit song of 1970, "Our House." You know, I'd light the fire. She'd put the flowers in the vase. Two cats in the yard . . . That wasn't me. I felt like my life was just getting started. I wasn't in the "settling" phase of my life. I wasn't ready to make the commitment she deserved. I broke it off.

On November 9, 1982, I wrote:

> *Perhaps this will be the letter [where] I can finally say some things that for too long have been unsaid. . . . What I think I fear most is how much I have been affected by my culture, growing up a man in the United States. We are raised to take our strength, our pride in ourselves, from women, by convincing them how good we are, by winning their love. When successful we reflect their love as our own self-respect.*
>
> *Almost all men I know have little real confidence or self-respect, and they cover or disguise this with macho, or by making a lot of money, or owning expensive cars, etc. And those of us who are too smart to be macho, or too poor to buy expensive cars, I think what we do is fall in love. Again and again.*

There are of course some few men who actually grow up,
mature and become adults or almost anyway. They can love
for only love itself, not for newness or excitement, not for
some abstract feeling that they are a new man each time they
fall in love. I hope and I think that I am like that, that I can
love someone just because [of] who they are and not because
I need to prove something to myself. . . .

Here I am with the opportunity to settle down with
perhaps the one girl I will meet who I am compatible with,
and instead of delight, I feel terror. Instead of looking
forward into the doors that could be opening, I am frozen
in place, looking around at all of the doors that will be
closed. . . . There really are no reasons for my fear. But
sometimes emotions carry more weight than reasons.

I daresay that I was *thinking*. And I guess I was beginning to stumble
into moments of introspection. Incredibly, or perhaps not, Nålen understood. Being as intuitive and practical as Nålen was, I suspect all along
she had thought that such an ending was possible, if not inevitable. She
had resisted. I had convinced her that it was possible. Nålen and I
remained friends and we have remained friends ever since. Years later,
when she married a handsome Alaskan, Nålen gave me the honor of
being godfather to her two children.

I understand that some people may find this an odd turn of events. I
understand the desire to want to make sense of such things. The best I
can offer is—*karass*, a term coined by Kurt Vonnegut in his 1963 novel
Cat's Cradle.

In the book, the character-narrator, John, is a writer who finds himself on odd and mostly wonderful adventures in odd and mostly wonderful places, where he meets odd and mostly wonderful people—people

who are all connected and not always for the reasons it at first seems they are connected. John encounters a religion, Bokononism—a religion Vonnegut made up. One of the fundamental concepts of Bokononism is *karass*, which is a group of people linked in cosmically significant ways that aren't immediately clear.

Call me a Bokononist, but I believe the people who have entered and most influenced my life—some of the biggies up to that point being the Baird boys, Angela, Bob Szatkowski, Tom, Gwyn, Nålen—are part of my *karass*, just as I am a part of theirs. At first, Nålen and I thought we had entered each other's lives to be a couple. That turned out not to be the case. Nevertheless, our love and affection for each other was meant to be, only in a different form, and it has endured. And I'm grateful, grateful that she has been in my *karass*.

For that matter, I'm grateful that Kurt Vonnegut and I became part of each other's *karass*, or rather discovered we had been part of each other's *karass* for quite some time and didn't know it until we did finally meet. Although I chickened out of approaching Vonnegut that day on the campus of Harvard, I did eventually. We talked about Hick and about beer. I even made a special Kurt Vonnegut brew based on a recipe that had been in his family for generations.

But here again, I'm getting ahead of myself.

IN 1983, two years into my time with Buckhorn, the company began to feel the effects of an economic crisis that had hit the oil industry—an aftershock caused by the geopolitics of the previous decade.

In the 1970s, the United States heavily relied on the Middle East for its oil supply, and for the first time Americans began to see why this was a terrible idea. In 1973, with President Nixon in office, the United States supported Israel as it defended itself in the Yom Kippur War against

Syria and other Arab nations. OPEC retaliated by raising the price of oil by 70 percent, then cut production, and then embargoed oil shipments to the United States.

The American Automobile Association estimated that 20 percent of the country's gas stations ran out of fuel at least one week during the crisis. There were reports of drivers waiting in line at the pumps for up to three hours. Left with no other choice, Americans learned to conserve and consume less. Fewer homes were built with gas heating systems. Congress legislated that 55 miles per hour would be the maximum speed limit on highways. Temporarily, daylight savings time went into effect year-round in the hopes of reducing electrical use. These and many other changes reduced oil consumption in the United States by as much as 20 percent.

The year 1979 was a lot like 1973. In the wake of the Iranian Revolution and the Iran-Iraq War, virtually all oil production in Iran, then the world's second-largest oil exporter, came to a halt. The price of crude doubled. In the United States, there were long lines at service stations, and pumps ran empty—the whole paralyzing shebang all over again. I remember seeing the signs at stations that read SORRY. NO GAS. For the second time in six years, Americans did yet another round of belt-tightening. President Jimmy Carter and Congress implemented additional policy changes. Americans continued to find ways to adapt and consume less oil. From 1979 to 1981, oil consumption in the United States dropped by at least 13 percent.

So then along comes the early eighties. Middle Eastern oil flowed back into the United States. This oil surplus or "glut," as *The New York Times* called it, combined with the reduced consumption, forced a dramatic drop in oil prices. There's an argument to be made that the market merely returned to the "normalcy" that had preceded the one-two punch of the 1970s. Regardless, between 1981 and 1986, the barrel price of oil fell from a 1980 peak of $35 to around $10.

In the spring of 1983, Buckhorn laid off about 15 percent of its 160 or so employees: "Black Friday." Too many days, I found myself with colleagues in a conference room, gathered around a cake as we said good-bye to another laid-off coworker. Offices were emptied. Desks were moved. "Consolidation." Tensions and anxieties escalated. What was happening at Buckhorn was happening industrywide. All of us with the company felt we were on the brink of a bust and more downsizing. Of course, at that point, we didn't know just how right our worst suspicions were.

I began to think about my next act. I wrote to the local newspaper and tried to cajole an editor into hiring me as a freelance entertainment reporter. I pitched myself as someone who often finds himself at unusual events, such as a recent performance of the Marimba Orchestra of Zimbabwe, which had the virtue of being true. No dice.

I bought a dog.

I bought a parrot, named it Lucy. Lucy was a South American breed, identical to Gwyn's Loro. Why did I buy a parrot? I have no idea. I can't believe I did. Damn bird was vicious.

I began contributing as an associate editor and then coeditor— *la-di-da*—to *The Mountain Geologist*, a quarterly technical journal published by the Rocky Mountain Association of Geologists.

Updating a friend on my recent flurry of activity, I wrote, "I guess some are doomed eternally to such vagaries of direction."

In November 1983, as the industry continued to struggle, there were more layoffs. One of my close friends got canned. I took it personally. As I wrote to a friend, it seemed to me that this particular guy was one of the ones laid off due to "FTSA (failure to suck ass)." I was all the more determined to master my own fate, though still unsure of what that might look like.

I sold my house on West Center Ave. for a modest profit. I'd paid

$70,000 for it, and during the ten months I was in it, I'd made enough improvements to sell the place for $74,500, my first real estate success in Denver. I purchased and moved into a house on the 4500 block of Moncrief Street. It was on a hill, one of the highest points in Denver, with a stunning view of the mountains. The place was pretty run-down. I thought this might be the beginning of the development company I had envisioned starting in Middletown. I reached out to an architect friend in Philadelphia, and he made noises that he was in. I saw us buying three houses a year, renovating and selling them. Alas, my friend was offered a plum job in Philadelphia and stayed put.

I wrote to Tom Metcalf. Tom and Gwyn's romance was short-lived, and so, too, was my anger over the whole affair. That letter I'd sent him was my catharsis. Tom being the relentlessly mellow fellow he was, he took my dopey rant in stride. Meaning, he'd read the letter, he understood why I was pissed, and disregarded the rest, chalking it up to the fact that I was a hothead. Knowing Tom had recently completed his thesis at Wesleyan and hadn't yet found a job, I asked if he was interested in coming out and for a good hourly rate working on my new place. So Tom came out, stayed a few months with me in the new house, and did much of the rehab work.

I got the idea that I'd start my own oil consulting business. There was opportunity in all this volatility. Upon hearing this idea, Mom wrote to me that she worried I was not "hard-hearted" enough to run my own business. Well, one thing I knew for sure, I'd learned in my corporate world the type of boss I didn't want to be, and I felt confident I could pull off running a business, even though Mom had her doubts.

I had met a fascinating young Kenyan geologist, Bill Okoth, at a two-week continuing-ed symposium. To save the Kenyan government some cash, he spent the second week in my spare bedroom. We stayed friendly when he returned to Kenya. Bill had the idea of me setting up a consulting company to provide exploration services for Amoco, Chevron, and other companies that had committed to spending more than $200 million in the next five years in Kenya. Oil companies were aggressively looking for oil outside the Middle East. In June 1983, I traveled to Kenya to talk with Bill. We made the rounds and plotted out a strategy that never did come to fruition.

Throughout 1984 and 1985, the oil industry was in a full-on crisis and the climate within Buckhorn's offices was full-on toxic. In the summer of 1984, I got into a major blowup with my bosses. A letter I wrote to Mom captures all the intrigue:

> *I got my annual evaluation and for the first time received some very disappointing comments. These were not with regards to my technical skills. Rather I was told that a) I did not get along well with people b) I lacked communication skills c) I had a bad attitude. As it turns out, my nemesis, Art Anderson, the Vice President of Exploration had refused to accept my boss's original eval until these certain negative changes were made. I was furious and spent the weekend drafting a scathing letter to the VP with copies to the president and my immediate albeit ineffective boss, which was tantamount to a resignation. Monday saw cooler heads prevail. Wednesday, the president called the whole exploration group into a meeting and announced that Art had been fired.*

I suppose upon receiving this letter, Mom might have been tempted to send out the old behavior modification chart.

It felt like management was trying to drive employees to quit. One of my good friends did. Jack Ebel, an attorney with Buckhorn, got so fed up with his relentlessly unreasonable supervisor and the corporate bullshit that he just walked out. Losing Jack was a morale blow. He was one of the kindest men I have ever met. Throughout the tumultuous period of layoffs, Jack would circulate around the offices, checking on people, doing his best to assuage their fears. If Jack heard that a colleague needed money, he'd lend it, never expecting to be repaid. When a woman we worked with died of cancer, it was Jack who took it upon himself to organize a collection for the education fund for the woman's children; I have little doubt that Jack contributed the most. When Jack quit, he had nothing lined up, and he and his wife had a nine-month-old son. With Jack gone, the culture felt all the more heartless. Shortly thereafter, the company laid off ten geologists. The only reason I think I continued to survive was because my salary was so low, no one noticed it. But it was just a matter of time.

That time came in early 1986. Buckhorn was taken over by Occidental Petroleum. The American oil industry was in free fall. The consolidation happening throughout the oil business was not unlike the roll-ups Hick's grandfather Andrew Hickenlooper had pioneered. All of us who had survived the waves of layoffs thus far knew this was it for us. That March, we were told we would be laid off in July. Occidental's acquisition of Buckhorn was a "friendly" takeover, and while being laid off is no fun, Occidental did make it about as friendly as they could. We were all promised we would receive a fair severance package, and in the months leading up to our last day in July, the company would provide us with training and support they hoped would help us find our next jobs.

One of the seminars Occidental arranged was about how to start your own oil consulting company. During one of the sessions, I wrote a letter to Nålen:

Presently sitting in a large meeting room with probably some 200 other geologists. It is a beautiful, sunny Monday morning, but we are probably 10 meters underground below the Radisson Hotel. We are all in this seminar called "A Consultant's Workshop." The progression of lawyers, accountants and other geologists are teaching us the essentials of starting your own company.

Of course if all of these people start companies there will be lots more companies than work. The reason these experts are free is because there was not enough work to be done to justify their previous company that continues their employment. It is sort of depressing. Not to me, of course, except I feel sorry for all of my poor friends. I am excited more each day by the prospect of my freedom. I have so many dreams, so many plans.

Over the course of a few weeks, I met with a small handful of current and former colleagues, like Jack Ebel, and we indeed talked of launching our own oil company. I described what we had in mind in a letter to a friend:

Our plan would be to go East and to Texas and California to ferret out investors then buy proven oil reserves. Already discovered but still in the ground, at a price of, say, $12 a barrel. There are scads of small operators with looming bank debt. And they are almost giving away reserves. It would be a sound though modest investment. But these reserves take years, say 20 years, to produce when prices rise and everyone's in clover. A little like being a vulture, but without the guilt.

This scheme, however, also was short-lived, because the would-be founding partners had families and mortgages; as they found good-paying jobs elsewhere, they did the pragmatic thing and took the paychecks.

I didn't have those obligations. By then, I was convinced I wanted to do my own thing. I did want to start my own business. Whatever it was. At the time, "entrepreneur" wasn't the buzzword it would become. Entrepreneurs weren't seen as cool. If anything, entrepreneurs were fools. Unless they were successful—then they were geniuses. But even then, they weren't referred to as "entrepreneurs." If you had luck starting a business or doing your own thing, people would say you launched a business or you did your own thing. I was disappointed that my attempts to launch my own oil-related business hadn't worked out. Truth was, my heart wasn't in it. "I must confess," I wrote to a friend, "that I'm still enamored with John Hickenlooper—Big Writer."

I was still a wannabe Damon Runyon.

Runyon! It occurs to me that thus far I have neglected to mention that he was from Colorado—Pueblo, Colorado. And lo and behold, I was in Colorado. I dusted off that lame novelized version of Runyon's life that I'd begun and never finished while at Wesleyan. I thought I'd take a stab at writing a Runyon biography or maybe even a screenplay for a television miniseries about his life. I'd gotten the idea of writing a screenplay from a Hollywood producer, Nat Mauldin. Nat was the brother of David Mauldin, the guy who was my partner in the old Victorian in Middletown. Nat was then the producer of a hit television show called *Night Court*. Nat and I got to talking; I told him I wanted to be a writer. He said that Hollywood was always looking for scripts. All it really takes is one, he said; sell one and you'd make a killing and you'd be in the game.

What did I know about screenwriting?

Nothing.

But I'd never let that stop me before. The way I figured it, everyone starts knowing nothing. Runyon started knowing nothing.

Over the course of a couple of months I took a local screenwriting seminar in the evenings after work. Recognizing I didn't have the discipline to count on myself to do the writing, I recruited a partner. My old friend Jed Rulon-Miller was home in Philadelphia with time on his hands. Jed also had aspirations of becoming a writer. Only difference was, he was actually writing. Though he was a poet and unpublished, I knew he was quite talented. If, together, we could craft a Runyon biography or screenplay, or heck, maybe both, that was as poetic as it was marketable, that was fine by me. Jed liked the "idea," as it were. He flew out and stayed with me while we researched Runyon's life and set about working on the biography-screenplay.

As if my *karass* wasn't filled with enough characters and activity, enter my next girlfriend. Eileen Kelly was a Wesleyan grad and a writer—a good writer. We had mutual friends. Somehow Jed and I ended up visiting her in Hoboken, New Jersey, driving up from Philly.

Eileen had graduated a few years behind me. She was acting with the Provincetown Players and working on a novel. Eileen was indeed impressive. She had graduated Phi Beta Kappa, and was the winner of the university's prizes for academic achievement in both English and psychology. I'm not entirely sure what she saw in me, but we hit it off. I went to Provincetown to see her in *The Night of the Iguana*. She was fabulous.

We started dating long distance and soon the two of us were collaborating on a script for a musical comedy for the stage. We roped in David Mauldin, who was a musician and painter. Our musical would be based on *The Prince* by Niccolò Machiavelli. I figured a sixteenth-century treatise on power and politics was the perfect material for a black-comedy musical.

All of this was in play when Occidental finally cut me loose in July 1986.

Truth was, I could not have been happier. After five years with the company, I left with a year's worth of severance. In several letters of that time, I mused on my future. "With a modicum of frugality," I wrote to a friend, "I should have two to three years' financial grace to pursue my personal chimeras. Or at least to find out what they are." In another letter, I acknowledged all that I had going on and how none of it immediately showed promise of a financial return, or for that matter, amounted to much of a bridge to a "real job." However, I wrote, "on the rockiest of foundations, great bridges have been built. I just made that up, but doesn't that sound like Churchill or someone?" I closed another letter with "I guess now the real fun begins."

I had no idea how right I was.

Nine

LIQUID GOLD

When I told everyone that I wasn't concerned about being laid off and that I was actually looking forward to it, I meant it. Even before the corporate changes and the toxicity, I knew I wasn't meant to be an oil and gas geologist, or for that matter, a company man. If I hadn't been laid off, there's no telling how long I might have done the sensible thing and stayed on, feeling unfulfilled, misplaced; my real life might never have begun.

I realized, too, how fortunate I was to feel excited about being pink-slipped or otherwise forced out of the company into the great unknown. I didn't have a family depending on me, as so many of my colleagues did, as my friend Jack Ebel did with his wife and baby boy. For me, twelve months' severance was quite a cushion. If it became necessary, I had those few properties I could unload: the two houses in Middletown—the Little Red House and the piece of the Victorian with David and Annie Mauldin—and the stake in Mark Masselli's health clinic building. Also, I could always sell my house in Denver.

Some of my optimistic talk was bravado cover for the real anxiety I felt. I wasn't wealthy; I would have to earn money. Being laid off takes an emotional toll. That job, even though I did not love it, even though I knew it was not my *calling*, was more than a paycheck. During the previous five years, "oil and gas geologist" had become part of my identity. It was part of what defined me. In fact, in lieu of knowing who I really was and what I really wanted to be when I grew up, it was just about the *only* thing that concretely defined me. If I had died while still at Buckhorn or Occidental, my obituary would have read, "John Wright Hickenlooper, an oil and gas geologist . . ." Now I was an unemployed thirty-four-year-old. I woke up every morning, looked in the mirror, and wondered just who that guy staring back at me was. I was a little scared.

Okay, maybe more than a little scared. One response to this anxiety was what I called my "frugal splurge." Buckhorn (which had become Harper, which had become Midcon and was about to become Occidental) gave us the news about who would go and who would stay on the Friday before the Fourth of July weekend. Ample warning. They even brought in "industrial psychologists" from Boston who spent an hour with each of us individually. I remember one of the psychologists saying, "All change involves loss, even change you desire, and all loss must be mourned." Yeah, I got it. Another one of the shrinks had said, "Find a small indulgence, to soften the loss."

That Monday morning after a pretty sad Fourth of July, I opened the paper to the classified ads, and as my eyes ran down the page they locked on a "1967 red Chevy Malibu convertible for $6,000 obo." I needed a car. I no longer had my five-year-old company vehicle. I got a lift down to Highlands Ranch, to the home of a petroleum engineer who had lost his job with Petro-Lewis eight months earlier. I offered him $4,200 and he took it. To this day, it's the best $4,200 I ever spent.

Within a few short weeks of my being laid off, Eileen came to visit. She was also between jobs. With time and togetherness on our hands, we embarked on a couple of adventures.

My brother Sydney was living in Berkeley. His wife, Thelma, had just given birth to their son, Sydney Jr., born two months premature. On top of that, the bakery they owned and operated, with the exquisitely Berkeleyesque name of "Leaven and Earth," was in the midst of a crisis; several employees had quit. As if that wasn't enough, when the infant was born, my brother was midway through reroofing their house; the job was still half done. Considering I was out of work, I offered to come out and lend him a hand. Eileen was game to join me. And my '67 Chevy Malibu demanded a road trip.

One night, after a long day of shingling Syd's place, he took me out for a beer. He said I had to see this new thing, a brewpub in Berkeley. Really, what he said was I had to taste the beer. We went to the Triple Rock Brewery and Alehouse on Shattuck Avenue. There was a line out the door and halfway down the block. On a weeknight! I thought, *you've got to be kidding me.* I was excited to taste what all the fuss was about.

I ordered a beer and couldn't believe the flavor. Compared with the usual beers I drank, this one was richer and less carbonated, smoother and softer on the palate, and with a real bouquet. I thought to myself, *I would have driven twenty minutes out of my way without thinking twice about it to have a beer or two like this.* Brewpubs were just becoming a thing. There were a few in the Bay Area; nothing like it existed in Denver. But I didn't think much more about it.

I was on my way to Hollywood.

I visited Nat Mauldin in Los Angeles. His older brother, Dave, my partner in the Victorian, was out visiting Nat, building a redwood deck on his brother's home. On my way back to Denver with Eileen, we stopped in for a few days. Heaven knows I had the perfect wheels for a cruise down Sunset Boulevard, which we did, twice. I helped Dave with the deck, and Eileen and I picked Nat's brain on writing for Hollywood. Eileen spent more time with Nat. While I worked on the deck, she went with him to work on the lot at 20th Century Fox.

I told Nat I'd taken a screenwriting course in Denver. Eileen talked with him about her novel-in-progress and her acting. It wasn't just the Provincetown troupe; she had been acting on the stage since Oddfellows Playhouse in Middletown. We talked with Nat about our ideas for the black-comedy musical of *The Prince*. I shared my vision, as unclear as it was, for the Runyon biography-miniseries. We must have sounded wildly naive, certainly I did, but Nat never rolled his eyes. He was patient and remarkably encouraging.

He gave us what seemed a practical yet lofty goal. Nat said two of his former protégés were producers of the hit television show *Moonlighting*. It was a comedic drama with Bruce Willis and Cybill Shepherd costarring as private detectives in perpetual romantic tension. To hear Nat tell it, the producers were always looking for good story ideas, and all the better in script form. "They'll look at anything," he said. Nat offered to help. If Eileen and I wanted to work on a script "on spec"—Hollywood lingo for writing an unsolicited masterpiece for free—he would get on the phone with us and coach us along; when it was done, if it was in shape, he'd submit it for us.

In the Malibu on the way back to Denver, Eileen and I got to work. Most people who visit the Grand Canyon are enthralled with the peace and splendor. As Eileen and I hiked the canyon, we got lost in discussing Cybill Shepherd's shifting hemline. Inspiration struck Eileen over dinner at a nearby Best Western. As we talked out most of Act 1 we became so boisterous a woman at a neighboring table shushed us. Eileen and I had the outline for the entire script done before we crossed the Painted Desert and the first draft completed within a week.

Eileen and I found ourselves having typical arguments over wording. I thought Eileen was going to lambaste me for demanding inclusion of the word "starched," which by the way never made it into the script. The good news was, after working with Nat over a couple of months we had a script he was willing to take to the show's producers. He told us they liked it and I believed him.

That fall, Eileen and I volunteered for a political campaign—technically, my first foray into politics. In 1986, Tim Wirth, a six-term United States congressman representing Boulder and the Denver suburbs, was running for the U.S. Senate. Wirth was hoping to fill the seat vacated by Senator Gary Hart, who was campaigning for president. Wirth's longtime aide David Skaggs, another Wesleyan alum, was a candidate to fill Wirth's congressional slot and retain it for the Democrats. It was the midterm election of Ronald Reagan's second term—a referendum on Reaganomics. The D.C. balance of power was at stake.

Wirth struck Eileen and me as one of the white hats. He was a reformer, but a probusiness reformer. Other than voting, I had never before participated in a campaign. I was curious and, let's be honest, bored. Eileen and I spent three evenings working a phone bank, encouraging Coloradans in the district to get out and vote. The day of the election, we walked a crucial precinct for Wirth. It was a long day. We didn't get to bed until around one a.m. But it was worth the effort. We woke to the news that both Wirth and Skaggs had won. Nationally, Democrats took eight seats and regained control of the Senate for the first time since the Republicans assumed the majority in the slipstream of Reagan's victory in 1980.

Our screenwriting campaign was not as successful. The show's ratings declined; script development was on hold. According to news reports, both actors wanted to move on. Bruce was coming off his *Die Hard* success and wanted to be a movie star; Cybill had given birth to twins and wanted to focus on her real-life role as a new mother. Sure enough, the show was canceled.

Eileen and I also decided to cancel our romance. Incredibly amicable. Once again, I wasn't ready for a long-term relationship. Maybe, I was starting to think, I would never be ready. We remained good friends, even to this day, although our collaboration on the black-comedy musical evaporated. So, too, did my Runyon project. Throughout all our writing endeavors, I kept telling anyone who would listen about how great this brewpub in Berkeley was.

I MENTIONED THE Triple Rock to one of my best friends from the Buckhorn days, Jerry Williams. Jerry was a geophysicist who had dabbled in home brewing. During our five years at Buckhorn he and I had spent many a night after work at our neighborhood Lakeview Lounge, playing table shuffleboard, drinking beer, and discussing how the world ought to work. We lived a block apart. His wife, Martha, and their three children welcomed me as if I were family. Jerry had often waxed rhapsodic about the magnificence of British pubs. He, too, had been laid off. I suggested he consider trying to open a brewpub in Denver. Jerry asked why I didn't give it a go. We thought about it for all of about four seconds and agreed that *we* would give it a go. That was the fall of 1986. Within two years, we moved from the conversation to a grand opening with astonishing speed and utter cluelessness. Ignorance sometimes is indeed a blissful advantage. When you don't know what you don't know, anything seems possible.

We needed start-up capital. Which meant we needed a business plan to entice investors. Neither of us had ever seen a business plan. We didn't have MBAs. We were a couple of rock-head geologists who wanted to launch a brewpub—something few, if any, venture capitalists or bankers, or for that matter, *anyone* in Denver, had ever heard of.

Jerry took out library books on how to write a business plan. In the beginning, it was like reading Latin. We didn't even know what "pro forma" meant. The more I looked at how to craft one of these things, the more I realized it wasn't all that different from the methodology that went into our stratigraphic maps: gather data from the field—in this case, market analysis—summarize the facts, and present it to show the sweet spot to drill for the gusher.

The facts, in short: In 1988, there were only a handful of brewpubs in the country. We couldn't find a brewpub anywhere between New York and California. Of course, there was not a single brewpub in Denver. It was still Coors country. In the lexicon of the oil and gas world, we were looking for speculators to stake us as we set out to strike liquid gold, only the beauty of this operation was, all we had to do was brew the liquid gold ourselves. At least, that's what we told ourselves.

Our pitch was straightforward. We would brew and sell beer as the beer gods intended: made of all natural ingredients, without adjuncts or preservatives, sold and served fresh on the premises. As customers drank the beer, they could look through the windows into the brewery and see where all the magic happened. Along with our fresh, all-natural micro-brews, we would serve international pub fare with everything made from scratch. No cans. No mixes. We figured since we would be selling better-tasting, higher-quality beer we would hold ourselves to the same standard for our menu. In business school jargon, this allowed us to "expand our target market." Another way of looking at it might be that man does not live by beer alone.

Of course, we had to do market research on both our competition and the beer market. One night in the revered Wazee Supper Club, a couple blocks from our eventual home, Jerry and I spent a full evening sketching floor plans on cocktail napkins. As the evening went deeper, we extended our wisdom, arms waving, to what the Wazee owners should have done to make this thriving establishment really successful. After about an hour an older, heavyset man with thick, furrowed brows stepped over and asked what we were discussing. We gave a sweeping description of what should be here and there. And after listening patiently to our blarney, he gently but firmly introduced himself as Angelo Karagas, who had built the Wazee in 1974. Luckily, he didn't hold our youthful exuberance (and inebriation) against us. We became friends. Later, we worked together with other pioneers to promote this district of Lower Downtown, but more about that in a bit.

Other times our research would be at other taverns, where we would befriend the afternoon or evening bar manager to see how much beer and especially imported beer (at the higher price points) they sold. Sometimes we learned more than we asked. Late one night at the West End Tavern in Boulder, after befriending the barkeep at the upstairs bar, I couldn't help but notice how well he helped his wait staff, especially Suzy, a remarkably attractive young woman. As she gave him her stack of cash for her evening checkout he asked if she wanted to wait around to grab a late drink. She gave him a spectacularly devastating smile, a sly wink, and said, "Oh, Tommy, you know I don't like you like that." As she walked out the door, long hair swinging, he looked over at me and with a rueful smile said, "God, it's hard to go slow in a car that goes fast." As Jerry and I moved forward with our brewpub plans, we would think of that line a million times, though not the way Tommy meant it.

As all the management books we'd never read pointed out, a key ingredient was talent. The business proposal books advised us to highlight the expertise of the team. But we had no talent. We lacked plenty of expertise—most noticeably, a brewer. All I could whip up was "Bob beer," and I homebrewed less than a dozen times since my training all those years ago with Bob Szatkowski. I suspect that Bob likely would have been available and game, but no disrespect to Bob, I didn't think his Bob beer would sell very well. And as his wife, Lisa, could attest, he was awfully messy.

My partner Jerry had much more brewing experience. He home-brewed during college, so we figured that qualified him for brewmaster-in-chief. Like I said, rock-heads. As we got under way getting under way, Jerry began brewing up a storm in his basement. At one point, he produced twenty gallons in three weeks. Jerry was more than willing to handle the minutiae of brewing, and I was more than happy to do the necessary taste-testing. We thought it was critical to have a signature Colorado beer. We wanted something that had the flavor, or at least the *bouquet,* of the Colorado prairie. So we came up with idea of a "Sagebrush Stout." Jerry himself hiked off into the wild, handpicked some sage, and tried adding it as an ingredient at several different stages of the brewing process.

Jerry's beers weren't half bad. But nothing like I'd tasted at Triple Rock. We both knew that to be a successful brewpub we needed something that was much better than half good. We served one of his beers to a potential investor who, after a sip, instantly made clear that he was not a potential investor. And so Jerry and I did a road-trip tour of brewpubs and microbreweries around the country to get wise. In late 1986, he and I drove to Commonwealth Brewing in Boston and then down to the Manhattan Brewing Company in New York City.

Inside Manhattan Brewing, we had a beer and checked out the place, the big gleaming tanks, the cavernous space, the giant TVs. There was a good crowd for a dank, cold Sunday afternoon. As it turned out, the Broncos were playing the Cleveland Browns for the AFC Championship, with most of the New York crowd barely watching. After Cleveland took the lead, 20–13, with five and a half minutes left, and the Broncos misplayed the kickoff and had to fall on the ball on their own two-yard line, the bartender switched to the Giants-Redskins game. Jerry and I howled. I mean, we howled. But alas, to no avail. This was New York.

I ended up giving the bartender $20 to put the Broncos game back on, on one of the TVs off to the side. Jerry and I watched one of the greatest clutch drives in football history. John Elway drove ninety-eight yards to tie the game, and the Broncos won in overtime. According to what *Sports Illustrated*'s Rick Reilly would tell me years later, after we met and became pals, while the Broncos were in the huddle on that two-yard line, Denver guard Keith Bishop said, "We've got them right where we want them."

We made arrangements for Jerry to head off to Albany, New York, right after Christmas 1986, for an apprenticeship at a microbrewery there. As Jerry packed his bags, we read about a local guy who had won the 1985 home brewer of the year award from the Association of Brewers. Russell Schehrer was only twenty-eight years old. Charlie Papazian, who founded the Brewers Association, wrote *The Complete Joy of Home Brewing*, and helped create the craft beer revolution, told us there was no better.

We figured what the hell, why not try to taste what this Russell's got, and if his beer was *that* good and he was interested, we would try to rope him in. We'd have a great, unique product, and what's more, if we could market that we had the home brewer of the year in our lineup it might help persuade investors, not to mention eventually draw customers. We called Russell and he invited us to his home for dinner to talk.

Home brewing was then a macho world. A brewers' convention was filled with bearded guys in flannel shirts. Most of these Paul Bunyans brewed beer in their workshop laboratories using cobbled-together systems that looked like the board game Mouse Trap. Russell was none of that. He was a craft-brew hipster before there was such a thing as a craft-brew hipster. Tall, handsome, with rockabilly hair and thick-framed black eyeglasses, Russell had an Elvis Costello vibe. Not only did he have style; he was eccentric, a home-brewing folk hero with a reputation. Legend had it that Russell arrived to pick up his home brewer of the year award riding an elephant. He showed up to another brewers' event dressed as a woman and ended up in the pool, naked or near naked. Why? Because he was Russell.

I liked Russell *immediately*. He said he had been considering doing a brewpub independently of us.

When he took us into his basement brewery, we could hardly believe what we saw: a masher, a fermentation kettle, the works. Some pieces of his equipment, like the heat exchanger, were actually his inventions. Everything was immaculate and industrial quality, or so it seemed to Jerry and me. No other home brewer had this kind of setup, because it was impossible. Russell poured us a few beers. While we drank, we looked at the abstract paintings on the wall. Russell, home brewer of the year, was a computer programmer by day and still found time to paint. Jerry wasn't a big fan of the paintings, but we both agreed Russell's beers were works of art. By night's end Russell said he wanted in—in fact, he and his wife, Barbara, both wanted in. While Russell worked with us, he would keep working his day job, at least for a while.

We still needed a chef. We'd find one. Meanwhile, my cousin Peter Lind, who was the flavor designer for Ben & Jerry's ice cream, and formerly a chef instructor at the New England Culinary Institute, agreed to create a menu for the business plan. If we found ourselves in a pinch when we opened, my old friend David Mauldin's stepbrother from Portland, Oregon, would fill in. I mean, we were doing the best we could. Hard to go slow in a car that goes fast. We were moving.

For investors, we started with us. Russell and Barbara had saved $20,000 they were willing to invest. Barbara's father, a Vermont lumber baron of sorts, provided $25,000 more. I put up $50,000 out of my severance. Jerry and Martha could do $10,000. Another good friend, Judy Goebel, and her father invested $10,000. We started asking everyone we knew. One of my Little League coaches invested $10,000, telling me, "You couldn't do much with a bat but bunt, but still you never quit."

Then there was my mom.

"I don't understand," she said. "Why would anyone want to eat in a brewery?"

"But Mom, you don't understand, it's not a brewery. It's more like a bakery. The beer is fresh. Fresh! Beer is not like wine; it gets worse, not better, as it ages. . . . It's a brewpub restaurant. And beer is food!"

I was wasting my breath.

My mom confided in me that her real hesitation was that if she invested in my project, she would, in fairness, have to invest in my brother's ventures, and she wasn't as confident of his business savvy. I'm sure she said the same thing to him about me. She just hated risk.

I knew in my heart it would kill my mother to invest in something like a brewpub. She had lost so much throughout her life, and growing up in the Depression, money was something never to be risked. I didn't bug her. Most guys at their core are momma's boys. But I've never met a guy who owes more to his mother than I do. Mom's younger sister, my aunt Jane, who was widowed and lived comfortably in the Highlands of Scotland, invested $10,000. I think part of her motivation was that she knew my mother could not.

LOCATION, LOCATION, LOCATION. It ain't everything, but it's a lot. We wanted to be in the city of Denver. But because we knew we would have to invest significant money in the renovation—interior design, contractors, and the like—not to mention the cost of everything else involved in establishing a brewery *and* a restaurant, not to mention the fact that we weren't exactly flush, prime real estate wasn't an option. The challenge, then, became to find a "B" or a "C" location that had the potential to become an "A" location. It's like the hockey great Wayne Gretzky said: the secret is not staying with the puck but, rather, going to where the puck will be. A natural place, or so I thought, to look for just such a location was the Lower Downtown section of Denver. Outside of the Wazee Supper Club, the beautifully restored (but at that time bankrupt) Oxford Hotel, and a few other businesses, there was little retail activity in the twenty-six-block district. There were a number of art galleries, and there was some urban-planning wisdom that art galleries hinted at development, a sign that a lifeless neighborhood was on the cusp of a rebirth. *Denver Post* columnist Dick Kreck had recently dubbed Lower Downtown "LoDo." It had been Denver's commercial center at the turn of the century. People had been predicting its resurgence for a couple of decades. But in that deep recession that marked most of the 1980s in Denver, there was not much going on. Tumbleweeds literally blew through the streets. There were plenty of old abandoned buildings and warehouses. As I told my new partners, these buildings had fine bones. I was five years into renovating my third old house, and I had developed an abiding affection for old and especially historic buildings. We were going back to the historic way of making beer; what a fine excuse to breathe life into an abandoned jewel of a building, a frog prince waiting to be kissed.

I found what I thought was a striking building at a sketchy location near Twenty-fourth and Blake streets, on the far fringe of an area the city was just beginning to consider "historic"—and across the street from a homeless shelter. But I thought the building was just grand—the Pony Express building, which dated to the 1880s and was one of the oldest structures in Denver. As the name implies, the building had served as a Pony Express station and stables. It was all brick, seven thousand square feet on each of three floors. The main floor, where the wagons had been loaded, had a completely open floor plan. Perfect for filling with a brewery and a restaurant. It was owned by a Louise Vigoda, who introduced herself as "the Dragon Lady."

After much negotiation, we agreed to a low rent of four dollars per square foot per year, with the rent increasing in four years to eight dollars per square foot, and then three years later to twelve dollars per square foot. Louise agreed that she would provide $100,000 toward the renovation of the building. This was $100,000 I wouldn't have to raise, and the fund-raising was going very slowly. We were still stuck at about $200,000 in commitments.

My former housemate Jody Chapel, a student graphic artist, sketched a killer logo based on the original Pony Express logo. You know, with the galloping horse and rider. Jody's soon-to-be husband Mark Stevens, a journalist I'd met at the YMCA, had been the first person to commit to invest in our fandango. We slapped Jody's logo on the cover of our ever evolving business plan and waited for potential investors to come to their senses.

We waited a lot. Having a building helped. We asked everyone we knew. We resorted to asking people who else they knew who we could ask. It was a hard slog. We were still well short of what we thought we needed. Finally, I went to the owner of the building, the Dragon Lady, who wasn't such a Dragon Lady. She was a well-known investor who provided me with savvy advice then, and for years to come. I told her we were giving up. We just couldn't swing it.

When I left Middletown six years before, I had walked away from a small development project I'd been pursuing. Mark Masselli kept me up-to-date on how another young developer with a little more experience and a little more patience had done the same development and had walked away a year later with half a million dollars. My instinct then had been correct. Now I was convinced a brewpub would work. Would really work. This was my shot and I was not going to throw it away.

The next day, I went to look at a building with a young broker named Charlie Woolley. Charlie was just starting his career after spending his first five years out of college as the manager/caretaker of the historic

Denver site and museum the Four Mile House. He loved historic build-ings as much as I did. I have always been partial to people with double *o*'s in their names. And this building was on Wynkoop Street.

The J.S. Brown Mercantile Building, erected in 1899, was simply mag-nificent. Five stories with a full basement, 11,600 square feet per floor, more than double the size of the Pony Express building. Old western regal, constructed of red brick and rhyolite, with spectacular seven-foot-high arched windows along the two sides of the building that faced the intersecting streets of Eighteenth and Wynkoop. Reminded me a bit of the old Mather-Douglas House in Middletown. Not architecturally speaking, just that it was big and historic and emanated history and pos-sibility. The kind of building you look at and think, *That would make one hell of a something.* The Eighteenth and Wynkoop location was infinitely better than that of the Pony Express.

The J.S. Brown Building was closer to the center of downtown, at the far western end of the relatively new 16th Street Mall retail district, and directly across the street from the long-neglected Union Station and the rail lines that carried tourists and lifted skiers to and from the resorts. There were still tumbleweeds blowing down the streets and there was a potential red flag only one block away, in the form of the historic Oxford Hotel. Pioneer preservationist Dana Crawford had renovated the hotel in the early eighties, but it was now in bankruptcy. There were very few signs of life in the neighborhood. One warehouse just a block away had been converted to a design center; another around the corner had been redeveloped for office space and residential lofts.

Inside, the J.S. Brown was inspiring. The fourteen-foot-high ceilings were still clad in the original turn-of-the-century pressed metal. I walked across an area of the floor; a large piece of the surface was chipped away and I could see that the original floor was maple, scuffed but clearly with the potential to regain its polished shine. There was finish trim around the doors and windows. Throughout the building were columns, all painted a grotesque orange. But when Charlie and I scraped a column with my pocket knife, we saw the most beautiful golden oak. Looking up at the twelve massive wooden arches . . . there was no way we could afford this place.

It was like Charlie read my mind. "If Mr. Barton likes you, he'll make a fair deal."

Most recently the J.S. Brown Building had been used as a furniture warehouse by the nearby Kacey Furniture store. Jack Barton owned Kacey and the J.S. Brown. He had moved his inventory to a single-story warehouse; evidently placing and retrieving furniture spread out among five stories had become too much of an inefficient hassle. Charlie said he thought Jack was ready to cut a deal.

"How ready?" I asked.

"A dollar a square foot."

That was the rent for the first three years and then, similar to the Pony Express, the rent would increase to four dollars per square foot, or 5 percent of our gross sales, whichever was higher. In the negotiations over the next month, Jack agreed that if we spent more than $190,000 on renovating the building, we would receive a 12½ percent equity interest in the building; we would own one eighth of the place. After Jack agreed to this, I almost couldn't sleep for a week.

We were still short investors. I took the business proposal around and pitched banks and lenders. Ten pitch meetings, fifteen pitch meetings, twenty pitch meetings.

Nothing.

After being turned down by banks and other lenders *thirty-two times,* we at last secured two loans: $50,000 from the Women's Bank and a $125,000 economic development loan from the City of Denver. The latter loan came with 9 percent interest and a balloon payment due in five years.

Women's Bank required an additional $150,000 collateral on top of the new $175,000 brewery and all our kitchen and restaurant equipment. I put up my interest in the three buildings in Connecticut and all the partners put up our homes. In answer to my whining about the unfairness of it all, the bank representative pointed out that banks don't like risk; that was our department. In total, we ended up with thirty-five private investors.

We decided we could proceed despite being some $60,000 shy of our bare-bones budget of $400,000.

Our designer, Vilis Berzins (that's Bill Birch in Latvian, he told us), charged us one tenth his usual rate. He was brilliant. At one point explaining why the large island bar was so close to tables along the windows, he shouted out, "Friendly friction!" He said when people have to gently brush against people seated at the bar, they are more likely to talk to them, to talk to strangers. This is advice that would end up serving me in politics as well. Opening a restaurant is a uniquely risky proposition. Most new restaurants fail. Near as we could figure, one of the reasons they failed was because they took on too much unnecessary debt. Much of that is due to lavish spending on design, furniture, plateware, and silverware. I was determined we wouldn't do that. We would buy new only as a last resort. As with the oil business, there was opportunity in volatility. With so many restaurants closing, that meant a good bit of what we needed was likely available at auctions.

It felt like we hit every auction on the Front Range of the Rocky Mountains. We picked up the Cadillac of stoves, hardly used, for half the $5,000 it would have cost off the showroom floor. Cash registers, same deal. The Brown Palace was unloading its plateware to upgrade. I scooped up their gold-trimmed hand-me-downs, formerly fit for a Palace, for a pittance. I scored an entire stereo system for a song. Our chairs didn't match, but came at a very good price. Though it never occurred to me at the time, Hick would have loved such fruitful treasure hunting.

By now, we're in early 1988 and we planned a July opening. We even took out an ad in the program for the Association of Brewers conference that would be in Denver. We had hired a great young contractor who believed in us. And even better, his was $50,000 below the other two bids. Turned out he could do this because his workers, a salty crew, seemed as likely to take a day off for every day they worked. In reality, with the cheap rent we had time, but little money. Saving money was more important than the schedule.

Which reminds me of the toilets. A friend of mine was rehabbing a 1920s mansion in the swanky Cheesman Park part of town. My old pal told me that if I removed six toilets I could have them for $25 each. We're talking about gorgeous old porcelain thrones, a perfect art-deco period match to the building. So I go over with two newly hired hands to remove toilets. These suckers were bolted into the floor. Upon closer inspection, I realized the toilets were still full—as in, full of years-old, maybe decades-old, dried feces. Apparently homeless people had squatted in the house, literally.

At $25 a pop for these six beauties, I was undeterred. There, among the flies and maggots, I saw opportunity. The two guys and I spent most of the day unscrewing the rusted bolts and carrying the toilets to a pickup truck. On the way back to the pub, we stopped at an outdoor car wash and set about cleaning the bowls. We put on rubber gloves and with hammers began whacking away at the crust on the waste-caked bowls, breaking it up and then scooping it out. Again, just to be clear, that's by hand. (In a few years, as governor, I would learn that legislative politics on a statewide level can be very similar: whacking away at layers of crap to get to something useful.)

Investors remained elusive. Everything that could go wrong with the building did go wrong. The last straw was when Brent, our general contractor, called me down to the basement to meet with the plumber.

There at the base of the stone wall was a pipe six inches in diameter, but it was so clogged with the rust and gook of ages that I couldn't have fit my pinky into it, not that I tried. This, they explained, was the only waste pipe out of the building. That's when things really got crappy.

It was going to cost $18,000 to dig up the street and put in new sewer connections and all the rest. I went to my desk and had a panic attack. We simply didn't have the money. We were tapped out. I sat there knowing that unless I figured out how we were going to pay for the repair we'd be out of business before we had a chance to start. All the investors—friends, family, Little League coach—would lose their money. And the banks, geezus—we would all lose our homes. It appeared as if that was indeed about to happen. I couldn't squeeze the money from anywhere. I was *this* close to telling all my investors that we were done.

I got a call from Jack Barton. He said, "Johnny, how's it going over there?" Truth was, Jack was understandably concerned we were going to fail and he would get screwed. I said, "Jack, I'm not going to leave you with a half-finished restaurant in the building, but the sewer main is clogged, we've got to rip up the street. It's gonna cost us eighteen thousand dollars." We were already behind on what we owed him; he could have kicked us out. Not only did this wonderful Jack Barton not kick us out, he said, "Johnny, life's too short to worry like that. What if I put in twenty thousand and buy a couple of shares?" Old Jack Barton saved my hide. And it wouldn't be the last time.

That spring, we found a stellar chef, Mark Schiffler, and we finally settled on a name.

OH, THE NAME of the brewpub.

As just about any Coloradan could tell you, we called it the Wynkoop Brewing Company. Of all those names we had put on the list of contenders that we shopped around to the bar patrons in Lower Downtown, Wynkoop was the one that tested the best. Meaning, just about every person who ranked our list put that one smack-dab in the middle. All the locals had heard of Wynkoop. Nobody loved it. More important, nobody hated it. And few people really knew why the name mattered. We put that name on the list for a few reasons: the J.S. Brown Building was on the corner of Eighteenth and Wynkoop streets; it was the least polarizing name; and we wanted a cool-sounding Colorado-ish name that everyone already knew but didn't really *know*, so that we could more or less create the brand.

But when we settled on the name, I researched it and that sealed the deal. Wynkoop was a true western hero.

At dawn, on the morning of November 29, 1864, well over 600 heavily armed United States cavalry approached a bend in a dry riverbed on the western plains, at Sand Creek near Eads, Colorado. Most of the troops were members of the Third Colorado Cavalry, with a contingent of about 125 troops from the veteran First Cavalry. Their commanding officer was Methodist preacher Colonel John Chivington.

In the riverbed below the U.S. forces was an encampment of 200 Cheyenne and Arapahoe. Weeks earlier, the Cheyenne chief Black Kettle had met with Governor John Evans in Denver. That meeting was brokered by our guy, Major Edward Wynkoop. Wynkoop had put himself at great risk in arranging the meeting, but he was a man in pursuit of peace. He had encouraged the native people to trust him and his leaders. Black Kettle agreed to a truce and was assured—or so he thought—that his people would have safe refuge at Sand Creek.

A month later, when Chivington and his men arrived at Sand Creek, most of the tribes' young warriors were off hunting the buffalo they would need to survive the winter. The majority of the Indians left in the camp were asleep in their tipis, wrapped in blankets, rightly thinking they had been promised no harm. Looking on the sleeping tribes, Colonel Chivington rallied his troops by reminding them that Native American warriors had killed white settler families. Then he gave the order to charge.

When the attack began and the shots rang out, Black Kettle exited his tent. He raised a pole with an American flag. The flag had been presented to him by the commissioner of Indian affairs. So there could be no misunderstanding, Chief Black Kettle also raised a white flag. But the bullets kept coming and Black Kettle retreated.

Another chief, White Antelope, ran toward the commanders. A member of the U.S. forces later testified that White Antelope "[held up] his hands and shouted, 'Stop! Stop!,'" speaking in plain, clear English. As the firing intensified, White Antelope folded his arms and calmly began to chant what would be his death song: "Nothing lives long, except the Earth and the mountains." Riddled with bullets, Chief White Antelope crumpled in the creek bed.

The first Denver newspaper reports of Sand Creek told a story of cavalry heroes fighting off brutal savages. The men of the Third Cavalry returned to Denver parading their souvenirs. "Cheyenne scalps are getting as thick here now as toads in Egypt," the *Rocky Mountain News* reported.

Major Wynkoop knew the truth of what happened. From friends who had been on the scene he learned the massacre lasted for nine hours, well into the afternoon. At one point, after several cavalrymen were killed, the U.S. forces turned howitzers on the Indians and cut them down at close range. Captain Silas Soule, who refused to allow the men in his command to participate in the slaughter, wrote to Major Wynkoop:

I tell you Ned it was hard to see little children on their knees have their brains beat out by men professing to be civilized.

One squaw was wounded and a fellow took a hatchet to finish her, she held her arms up to defend her, and he cut one arm off, and held the other with one hand and dashed the hatchet through her brain.

Wynkoop was devastated. He felt betrayed by his commanders and by his governor. Congress appointed Wynkoop to lead an investigation that proved the U.S. forces had slaughtered Indians to whom he had promised peace. Once again putting himself at great peril, Wynkoop revealed Chivington to be the mass murderer he was, and the investigation led to his condemnation. Still, it was Wynkoop who became hated as an Indian lover, while Chivington was never punished.

That summarized history of the Sand Creek Massacre and Wynkoop's role was part of a speech I gave as governor to recognize the 150th anniversary of the atrocity. On behalf of the people of Colorado and with the full support of all four of the state's living former governors, I apologized to descendants of these tribes who were gathered with me on the steps of the state capitol. It was one of the rare apologies ever offered to American Indians by an elected government official in American history. Indeed, it seemed very little, very late, but our hope was that it would continue to improve relations with the tribes and help ensure that this terrible chapter in American history would never be forgotten.

Suffice it to say, we incorporated stories of Ned Wynkoop into our menus and marketing whenever we could.

In September 1988, we felt we were close to being ready to open. The kitchen and the brewery were in place, and my brother Sydney had arrived to put his carpentry skills to use building back bars and furniture, and helping us pour our forty-eight-foot concrete island bar top. Our chef, Mark, was busily cooking up the menu. Russell was holed up in the basement fermenting a portfolio of tasty ales and stouts. We were all working ninety hours a week. At the end of the month, we gathered in a circle on the as yet unsanded floor and tasted Russell's maiden batch of beer, a classic English bitter. It was everything we could have imagined. "Here we go!" Jerry shouted.

Opening day was October 18, 1988. I had thrown in the last $40,000 from my severance to reach the $400,000 in total investor funds we had promised the bank. We still owed the contractor, Brent, about $40,000. Needless to say we didn't have the $75,000 our business plan had dedicated for marketing. We decided our opening would be the only marketing we'd get for a while.

We had a couple of soft openings for friends and family and investors. Mom and my stepdad, Bill, came out. Mom smiled and had a beer. She was pleased as punch we had managed not to fail, thus far. I think it was Russell's wife, Barb, who had the idea that since we were brewing beer with pre-Prohibition techniques and ingredients, for our opening night we should sell our beer for pre-Prohibition prices, twenty-five cents per glass. Of course, we invited all the media. I had already decided that journalists would always get their first beer free.

The Denver Post's Dick Kreck had a widely read man-about-town gossip column. He had been stopping in every few weeks. His vanity license plate was "Mr. Beer." He liked Russell's beer. That Tuesday we opened, he ended his column with "for the best twenty-five-cent beer in town check out the grand opening tonight of Colorado's first brewpub."

Naturally, us being us, we had no idea what to expect. When we opened our doors that afternoon there was a line around the block. The place was packed from open to close. We had six beers on tap, among them a light Timberline Pale Ale, St. Charles Extra Special Bitter, a spectacularly pungent wilderness Wynkoop Wheat Beer, and, of course, Sagebrush Stout (or as one customer dubbed it, "cup o' mud"). The menu offered diet-plate classics such as shepherd's pie, fish and chips, Gorgonzola ale soup, and various bockwurst platters. That day at lunch, Mayor Federico Peña, whom none of us had ever met, came early for a brewery tour before cutting our red ribbon. All the TV stations came. We were after all the first restaurant of any kind to open downtown in five years. Luckily, the TV cameras all left before our auction-scavenged point-of-sale system melted down and people waited up to an hour for their order to be served. I gave away forty-five free lunches that day. Many of the clients were charmed by how hard we were trying and became devoted customers.

All night long the crowd around the bar was five to six people deep. In the kitchen, Mark never stopped. He ran low on supplies several times, and Jerry made a few runs to the local King Soopers to restock. Like all of us, he was frazzled. When you've been working eighty- and ninety-hour weeks for months on end, your wits tend not to be at their sharpest. Jerry likes to tell the story of going to King Soopers on a cabbage run. He was checking out and his nerves were already on edge; then the clerk behind his register fell to the floor and went into epileptic spasms. Jerry caught her as she fell and thought, *This cannot be happening*. Jerry's unspoken but implied point is, just about everyone on staff that night started at least one sentence with "You're never gonna believe this. . . ."

At one point, I saw Mom and Bill standing like islands in a surging sea of young people. I rescued them and took them into a side room where you could hear yourself think. Bill looked dazed but happy. Mom's eyes were twinkling like, well, like the day she married Bill. As you all know, Mom didn't get excited often. She put both hands on my forearms, pulled me to her, and said, "You did it." Her voice was soft. She said it again: "You really did it." I was sure she was about to tell me how proud she was, but Jerry's wife, Martha, came in to find us and we were swept back into that wonderful maelstrom of energy.

Russell was adamant about serving his beer English style, which as he put it, as in literally put it on signs throughout the Wynkoop, was, WARM AND FLAT IS WHERE IT'S AT. And that's how he served it: almost room temperature, and almost no carbonation. Customers seemed to enjoy it. We sold six thousand cups of Russell's beer that night. As I happily fell asleep afterward, all I kept thinking was, why didn't we sell the beer for fifty cents per glass. That, and the fact that I'd actually made my mother happy, that she was proud of me.

By any and every measure, opening night was a smash. With the exception of our chef, Mark, none of us had ever before worked in a restaurant. Question was, what would happen the next day when we went from twenty-five cents a beer to $2.40, and the day after that, and the day after that?

Answer was: incredible. As one restaurant reviewer—in a rave, by the way—wrote, "the Wynkoop is always a full house." By our second month we were earning a profit; suddenly there was money in our account. Eighteen months after opening we had retired our bank debt and a third of the rest of our debt.

That's not to say it was all a smooth pour.

Our accountant was a sweet woman but inept. It took her five weeks from when she got numbers to when she gave us our profit and loss statement. The summer after we opened—July Fourth weekend, 1989, I remember—I was driving up to Boulder to go see this incredibly attractive lady from Oklahoma, and I was in the car thinking of May's P&L statement and that our sales were down 10 percent. I realized how much we had in the bank account and that we didn't have enough to make payroll on Monday. I remember pulling over to the side of the road and sitting there wanting to cry. My brother, Syd, loaned me $50,000 to get us over the hump.

But like any start-up that survives and thrives, we learned from our mistakes, we fixed, we tweaked, and we were constantly improving—

the business and the beer. I tried to work every Wednesday through Saturday night, and I tried to get to every table to get feedback and catch problems before they turned into bigger problems. People always seemed especially appreciative when they learned I was one of the owners. I learned to let them know in offhand ways. Like when they said "fine" when I asked how everything was, I would say, "Hey, fine isn't good enough. My house is up for collateral for all the loans for this place."

For months after the opening we tried to get Russell to give us a cold, carbonated lighter beer. When we opened, during the winter months, the warm and flat was particularly suited for the season. Come spring, we needed to offer a lighter brew with more fizz and served colder. Russell wouldn't listen to any of us. It was my old friend from Buckhorn Jack Ebel who persuaded him. Jack had launched his own consulting business and it quickly became a success, even in the oil and gas downturn. He was a regular at the Wynkoop, always holding court and cracking wise. Russell loved him. He made the carbonated light because Jack made the ask. Jack, who was a vegetarian, also persuaded Mark to add his favorite recipe for vegetarian green chili stew to the menu. Jack had found the recipe in a tiny café in Pojoaque, New Mexico.

Also in 1989, something great and not so great happened. First the not so great: On my way home from an employee's birthday party, I was arrested for drinking and driving. I didn't fight the charge of "driving while ability impaired." I did what I did and it was stupid and dangerous. I could have killed myself, or worse, someone else. I did my community service, but also changed the way the Wynkoop did business. We became the first restaurant in Colorado to offer a designated-driver program. Now the great thing: In March, five months after we opened, the Downtown Denver Partnership, one of the city's business organizations, recognized our founding team and presented us with its namesake award for business. In my speech, I quoted Mark Twain's *Roughing It*, which was about how to make it in the West: "The cheapest and easiest way to become an influential man and be looked up to by the community at large was to stand behind a bar, wear a cluster-diamond pin, and sell whisky." It's a quote that my ancestor Anthony Morris, brewery founder and mayor that he was, would have liked.

We were grateful for the recognition, and it also helped promote the business. I was obsessed with promoting the Wynkoop and the neighborhood. We had unilaterally put up fliers in our vestibule when we first started, promoting the Wazee Supper Club and what few other businesses were then in LoDo. I told our staff who thought I was crazy that maybe our real competition was the TV and that our goal was to get people off the couch, out the door, and enjoying life with family and friends—in LoDo. When one of us is a draw, we all benefit from the foot traffic and bustle. We are a community. If we were the draw and other businesses could benefit, that was good. Good for LoDo and good for the city. It was the old rising-tide-lifts-all-boats mentality. We started buying pint glasses with our neighbors and together got *The Denver Post* to sponsor the LoDo Brewers Festival. Our best events, however, were the ones we did ourselves.

Without a doubt the most talked-about PR stunt we pulled was our annual October "Running of the Pigs."

To celebrate the second anniversary of the Wynkoop, we threw a pig roast outside the brewpub. Who needed another Oktoberfest? Even with the pig twirling on the spit, we decided we needed a little more pork. The following year, we arranged to borrow about a half dozen swine and stage a "Running of the Pigs" down the alley behind the Wynkoop, à la the Running of the Bulls in Pamplona, made famous, of course, by Ernest Hemingway in *The Sun Also Rises*. You could convince the wannabe writer he was no writer, but . . .

It was a marketing success. Drew a sizable crowd. Everyone from families with kids to college kids dug it. The third year, animal rights activ-

TOP LEFT: My great-grandfather Andrew Hickenlooper was a Civil War hero and a pioneer with the gas and electricity industry. As the history buff that I am, I would love to have had the chance to hear his stories. And I am sure that we would have had much to discuss about the changes in the energy industry.

TOP RIGHT: My maternal grandparents, Boppa and Granny, loomed large in my life. As you can see here, even after Boppa's distillery went under, their joy and happiness endured. I suppose Boppa and Granny, by their example, taught my mother resilience and the importance of seeking out reasons for joy and happiness.

BOTTOM LEFT: My mother, Shrimpy, and her first husband, Bow, on their wedding day in October 1942, before Bow flew off into D-Day heroics.

BOTTOM RIGHT: Mom and Hick on their wedding day, September 25, 1948. I think it's pretty obvious that mom is holding Sydney in place and Betsy is being her typically angelic self.

TOP LEFT: This is my favorite photo of my father, Hick. That smile.

TOP RIGHT: Even as a child I was inquisitive. Not sure how long that frog stuck around.

MIDDLE: So here we are, my siblings and me in the family station wagon. From left to right, that's Betsy, yours truly, Tad, and Syddo.

BOTTOM RIGHT: My sister Tad and me on a small mountain, West Rattlesnake, overlooking Squam Lake in New Hampshire, where our extended family has long had a vacation home.

TOP: My siblings and me in one of the many poses stage-directed by Hick, who appeared in very few photos because he was almost always behind the camera.

BOTTOM: Mom in the kitchen. She read two to three hours every day. I love this photo of her. Amazing how she put up with us. This was taken in 1969, not long before I left for college.

TOP: The Wynnewood Warriors! That's me in the first row, third from left. At least I think that's me.

BOTTOM LEFT: Me in the seventh grade, looking quintessentially dorky during my first year at the Haverford School.

BOTTOM RIGHT: That's quite the sport jacket Mom made for me when I was in the eleventh grade at Haverford. I still have it. Keeping it for Teddy.

Haverford's soccer coach presenting me with the Michael G. Dowling award during my senior year. The trophy went to the kid who had made the most of his ability. In other words, I had more passion than athletic talent. The award meant a great deal coming from Coach Smith, as he had played on the 1928 Olympic soccer team.

Me as a senior at Wesleyan University, with one of my many dogs, Hilda.

Here I am during a break on a road trip in the early 1970s. I crossed the Sierras in my old Ford and picked up hitchhikers who could pay their fair share. The dogs are mine and rode for free.

LEFT: That's me with Mom in 1972. I'm home from Wesleyan for Thanksgiving. Between us is my new nephew, Bowman. His hair is considerably shorter than mine; for that matter, so is Mom's.

RIGHT: Me with my first fiancée, Gwynthlyn Green, during my farewell party just before I left Middletown, Connecticut, bound for Denver.

Look at me jamming. My dog, Pie, is not amused. Photo taken by my pal Patrick Dunne.

Here I am, the budding entrepreneur with plans to build the first craft-brewpub restaurant in Colorado. Photo taken by local journalist Bill Husted.

My siblings and me with Mom at the house in Squam in the summer of 1998. Counterclockwise from left to right is me, Betsy, Tad, Sydney, and Mom smiling away.

TOP LEFT: The J.S. Brown Mercantile Building before we converted it into the Wynkoop Brewing Company. Isn't she a beauty?

TOP RIGHT: The Wynkoop Warriors (left to right): me, Bill Pugh, Jerry Williams, Martha Williams, Mark Schiffler, Russell Schehrer, and Barbara Macfarlane. Darn right, we look tired, but happy.

BOTTOM LEFT: My brother, Syd, and me, arm-wrestling in the Wynkoop during our grand-opening weekend in October 1988. I let him win that one.

TOP RIGHT: Here I am with the famous, or perhaps infamous, Wynkoop toilets learning about politics, although I didn't realize it at the time. (Read the book.)

ABOVE: I'm seated with my late friend Kurt Vonnegut, who helped bring my father's ghost to life for me. This is at a luncheon fund-raiser for the Colorado Endowment for the Humanities in 1997. *Photo by B. J. Ruley*

RIGHT: Syddo by my side once again—this time at the grand opening of the Phantom Canyon Brewery in Colorado Springs. Another brewery that almost didn't happen.

ABOVE: My pal Tony Mayer and I got the brilliant idea of posing in our birthday suits for the invitation for our joint birthday party, which we held at the Wynkoop on February 11, 1992. He was turning thirty; I was the old man at forty. You missed a good one.

LEFT: Another shot by my journalist friend Bill Husted for *The Denver Post*. My first scooter, a lovely shade of brown. 1998.

A framed copy of the *Rocky Mountain News* from June 2003, marking my first political campaign win as mayor of Denver.
Photo of framed Rocky *by Evan Semón Photography*

A shot from a 2010 gubernatorial campaign ad. My pockets are turned-out empty because our campaign was fund-raising. That car is mine; it's a 1981 Checker Marathon Deluxe.
Photo by Evan Semón Photography

Another shot from one of our 2010 campaign commercials. This one we filmed in beautiful Evergreen, Colorado. As you can see, I'm focused on the task at hand.
Photo by Evan Semón Photography

Ah, the famous shower ad. This one was another from my 2010 run for governor. In the commercial's opening moments, I say that political attack ads make me feel like I need to take a shower. I think most Americans feel the same.

Photo by Evan Semón Photography

During my first term and into my second term, I was extraordinarily fortunate to have Joe Garcia, the best lieutenant governor in the United States, as my running mate and friend. This is a shot from our first campaign on the eastern plains of Colorado.

Photo by Evan Semón Photography

BOTTOM LEFT: This is our 2013 holiday card, which was taken at the Denver Center for the Performing Arts complex. Helen, Teddy, and I are with our dog, Skye. *Photo by Evan Semón Photography*

BOTTOM RIGHT: On January 11, 2011, Helen and I made the walk across Denver's Civic Center Park, from the City and County Building, where I had been mayor, to the State Capitol, where I was to be sworn in as governor. It was a rather short walk of exactly 663 steps, and yes, I counted.

Photo by Evan Semón Photography

Bill Ritter, the forty-first governor of Colorado, and I celebrate on election night, November 2, 2010. That's the incredible Roxane White to the left of Bill. Helen is looking on from the right.

Photo by Evan Semón Photography

Our 2013 cabinet during a goal-setting retreat.

I'm enjoying a stop in Colorado's Rocky Mountain National Park on the one hundredth birthday of the park in the summer of 2015. Getting Rocky Mountain National Park open in the wake of the flood was critical to the businesses of the surrounding communities, but we did it.

Photo by Evan Semón Photography

Thousands of people gather at the Aurora Municipal Center for a prayer vigil for the victims of Friday's movie theater mass shooting, July 22, 2012, in Aurora. *Photo by Evan Semón Photography*

The three daughters and one son of Gordon Cowden, fifty-one, gather at the memorial set up near the Century 16 movie theater just three days after the mass shooting. Their father was the oldest of the twelve victims who died from their gunshot wounds, according to the Arapahoe County coroner's office. *Photo by Evan Semón Photography*

Ketch Secor, the lead singer of the band Old Crow Medicine Show, is a friend. Here he is making me sing in front of a sold-out show at Red Rocks.
Photo courtesy of The Denver Post

Isaac Slade of The Fray has been a longtime friend. He and his band have done much to highlight just how amazing the music scene is in Colorado. He performed at one of my gubernatorial fund-raisers in October 2010. I can't remember what he's saying here, but probably pointing out how terribly I sing.
Photo by Evan Semón Photography

During the 2014 reelection campaign, Joe Garcia and I are appearing at a rally of Latino voters. *Photo by Evan Semón Photography*

The Salazar family has had a tremendous influence on Colorado for decades. Their mother, Emma Salazar, was the matriarch of the family, which resides in the San Luis Valley. It had become a tradition for me to visit their ranch during my gubernatorial campaigns and receive her blessing. When Emma died in January 2016, the Salazar family and Colorado grieved the loss of a remarkable woman. *Photo by Evan Semón Photography*

In 2014, I was the chair of the National Governors Association, and Utah governor Gary Herbert was the vice chair. Here we are meeting with President Obama in the Oval Office and I am presenting him with a gift: some nighttime reading. *The White House, photo by Pete Souza*

Morgan County farmer and entrepreneur Keith Bath is a lifetime Republican but became a strong supporter of mine in both gubernatorial races. What's more, he became a great friend. Here he's visiting me during a stressful time, election night 2014.

Photo by Evan Semón Photography

On Saturday, January 16, 2016, Robin Pringle made me the happiest man in the world by marrying me. The ceremony was at St. Andrew's Episcopal Church in Denver. My son, Teddy, was my best man. I guess you could say on this day, the rest of my life began. *Photo by Evan Semón Photography*

ists informed us that the running in the sun was hard on the pigs. We also learned that piglets don't run in straight lines. In the alley they were hard to corral. Actually, what we learned is that pigs aren't big on running. In the spirit of innovation, and to protect the squealing swine from the sun, for the next Running we put sun bonnets on the pigs. Bill Husted, a *Rocky Mountain News* columnist, dubbed the event "Pamplona on the Platte."

By the time we got to the fourth annual Running of the Pigs, in 1993, it was big news. J. R. Moehringer drew the short straw that day over at the *Rocky Mountain News*. No one could have captured the color of the event better. Like a matador getting out of the way of a bull, it is best if I step aside and let J.R.'s prose run wild. Harnessing the style of Hemingway, it began thus:

The pig stepped in something and went down hard.

The crowd watched him lie there, snorting and refusing to get up, like a man on a sofa when Saturday comes.

Everyone stared in horror at the pig's dangerous snout, which could not gore a man but sure could kill an appetite. Smeared with breakfast and its aftermath, the snout looked like death in the afternoon. . . .

Just then a father with a bizarre sense of humor put his 8-year-old son into the pigpen. The little matador happened to be wearing a Chicago Bulls T-shirt, and when he ran in fear from the pigs, it was something like a running of the bulls, and everyone gasped in mock terror. Except the boy, whose terror was real. Did the title *Old Man and the Lawsuit* occur to anyone?

"Every year we do this," said a man who works for Wynkoop owner John Hickenlooper, a man they call Matthew McAleer. "And every year I wonder why."

The man they call Hickenlooper walked over with an answer. In one hand he held a Bloody Mary. With his other hand, he gestured at the balconies above, promising that when his pig-running is world famous, people will hang from those balconies cheering the pigs on to greatness.

J.R. would go on to win the Pulitzer Prize and become a celebrated author. That he did not win a Pulitzer for this masterful bit of reportage was an outrage.

Due to continued concerns raised by animal rights activists, we switched from pigs to prairie dogs. "Prairie Preservation Day," we called it. So it goes.

WITH THE WYNKOOP an established success, we added a billiard hall on the second floor and put a jazz club in the basement. And we looked to expand.

Representing our founding partners, I began trying to replicate our success elsewhere. In 1989, we became partners with a talented young manager, Scott Smith, to start CooperSmith's Pub & Brewing in Fort Collins, about an hour north of Denver. That was a success, a big success. Still is. Next, we headed south of Denver.

In 1991, after getting a call from an acquaintance who owned a liquor store in El Paso County, I bought the only registered landmark in downtown Colorado Springs, an hour south of Denver. I made the offer four days before the bank that owned it had scheduled its demolition. Two years later we were trying to launch the Phantom Canyon Brewing Company and I learned one of the most valuable lessons of my life.

Even with our successes to the north, investors remained skittish. The bank had financed my purchase, but I'd fallen behind in the payments, and while the contractors were ready to set to work on the Phantom

Canyon and make it a reality, I couldn't seem to find the last $150,000. I didn't have the money to pay for the project. My general contractor was Chuck Murphy, a burly Irishman and as fine a man as I've ever worked with. Here's the kind of guy Chuck is: A few years ago, he was standing with his wife, Mary Lou, and some friends at their big bash celebrating their fiftieth wedding anniversary; he was asked the secret to their marital longevity. It was easy, he said, as they beamed at each other. Chuck explained that he and Mary Lou had decided from the get-go that he would make all the big important decisions and she would make all the little ones that didn't matter. For a moment, everyone looked shocked. Chuck and Mary Lou continued beaming at each other. Then Chuck went on: so far, he said, there's never been a big decision.

So I didn't have the money to pay the contractors for the work on the Phantom Canyon, and Chuck got an idea. He assembled all of his subcontractors who had bid the job and were waiting for it to start. He gave them the bad news first: I was still short. But then he said he was going to become an investor and they should, too. So I gave them the same pitch I had been using all along, describing the wonderful potential of the building and business, and the kinds of returns we were hoping for. They had all been up to eat at the Wynkoop and they knew the building. Pretty much every one of them after some discussion and a little hemming and hawing decided to invest.

We were all partners, and what a difference that made. A month in, Jay, our electrician, suggested using better ceiling fans, the same quality without the brand name, but ones that came with a lighting fixture attached and at the same price. He was worried that otherwise the bar area might not have enough light. Turned out he was right. Most electricians, if you were lucky enough to have one, who took that kind of initiative would have a narrow self-interest and would add an extra charge, a change order. Not Jay.

Now we all had an alignment of self-interests. We all had skin in the game. No one succeeded unless we all succeeded. The alignment of self-interests is that magic place where difficult projects, or in politics where initiatives or policies, suddenly take off.

Remember I said that Jack Barton's buying some shares in the Wynkoop wasn't the only time he helped us out? Well, in 1991, he agreed to sell us the whole J.S. Brown Building, and he suddenly had reason to dramatically increase his asking price, but he did not. Like me, Jack didn't care much for contracts and lawyers; he was a handshake-on-a-deal guy, which is what we did when we had agreed on the purchase price of the J.S. Brown. But just before we were to sign the necessary paperwork, news broke that Coors Field would be going into Lower Downtown, just a few short blocks from the Wynkoop. This news instantly increased the property values in the surrounding area, by a lot, including Jack's J.S. Brown. Jack, however, stuck with the price we had agreed to with that handshake. He said, "A deal's a deal, Johnny."

Now I obtained a loan from the Small Business Association and we converted the second floor of the building, just above the Wynkoop, into a vast pool hall, and we got a construction loan from a bank to build lofts into the top three stories.

Over the next seven or eight years, we expanded beyond Colorado. With local partners, we opened brewpub restaurants in Wyoming, Nebraska, Iowa, South Dakota, Wisconsin, Kansas, West Virginia, San Francisco, Kentucky, and more. Our idea was to take the template for the Wynkoop and partner with local business and industry expertise. Each brewpub had a different name and regional investors—in other words, a different local operating partner—but we all used the same backroom systems and designer.

We soon realized that our business plan was flawed. The profit from the well-managed brewpubs was negated by the brewpubs with poor management. We struggled to create a common culture, a unified training system. We lacked structure. We made one or two terrible choices in location. For all of the travel and the effort, we weren't making much money. So we divested and refocused on local and slower deals. We bought six area bar-restaurants. We learned the hard way how critical it is to have the right team and a strong structure. We learned to walk instead of run. We learned that when you make a mistake, you admit it. One of the places we bought was the Wazee Supper Club. Remember Angelo Karagas? Well, when he died in 1994, his wife insisted that we be the ones to buy their much-beloved landmark.

WITH ALL THE HOURS I was putting into being a big-shot brewpub entrepreneur, there wasn't a lot of time to date. Fact was, since I first signed the Wynkoop lease with Jack Barton before Christmas 1987, I had done nothing but work. I became better friends with that broker Charlie Woolley, and together we did a twenty-unit LoDo loft project just as the Wynkoop pool hall and lofts were finishing up. I also got to know Joyce Meskis, the founding owner behind the legendary Tattered Cover Bookstore, and one of the most inspiring individuals I have ever met, anywhere. She had reached maximum capacity in the 40,000-square-foot store in the Cherry Creek neighborhood and I approached her about doing her shipping and receiving in LoDo, with maybe a retail footprint as well. She, of course, had already considered this in detail, along with half a dozen other possibilities. While she was quiet and invariably polite, there was always a strong current moving in her thoughts. We formed a partnership, one in which I agreed she would always have the deciding vote. I trusted her that much. We spent months walking Lower Downtown, imagining what a project focused on community building would look like. I liked her so much, I introduced her to my old pal Jed, who had moved out permanently to be the bookkeeper of the brewpub. One of my first official acts when I was elected mayor was to preside over their wedding. Talk about a happy day.

Together, Joyce and I purchased the abandoned Morey Mercantile complex, which had once been the major competitor to the J.S. Brown Mercantile Company, where my brewpub was rocking and rolling. The Morey Mercantile was an assemblage of four glorious buildings, more than 200,000 square feet in all, which we bought for less than $10 per square foot. We brought in a financial partner that shared our values, Coughlin & Company, and in the end built ninety-one loft apartments that we designated as affordable housing. In addition to the Tattered Cover shipping and retail, there was a locally owned restaurant, and a little wine store in the alley that we leased to Jed, which cost me a good bookkeeper.

Joyce had every employee train for two weeks before they could begin work. She let me take the first day of that training, which she always taught herself. She made sure that every one of those employees understood and believed in their mission: the more books in more people's hands, the better the world is. She did her best to teach me patience and how to really listen. But in truth I still need remedial work there from time to time. Joyce was a great partner and a better friend.

So I was opening brewpubs and rejuvenating historic buildings at a breakneck pace, but talk about a lack of balance. I was beginning to think more and more about a wife, someone who could share my life and tolerate me and my frenetic ways. I started to think it was never going to happen, that I was too fragmented, that no such person existed. One night, late in the bar at the Wynkoop, a table of friends openly scoffed that I would never make the time to find the right woman. Laughing, I said that I would pay $5,000 to anyone who introduced me to the woman who would become my wife. A bride bounty. I was joking, but the next day, Bill Husted, the columnist at *The Denver Post*, called to see if I was serious. His cousin had a three-hour layover and he wanted to bring her over to meet me. I laughed again and said, sure. Naturally, this ended up in the local media. Fine by me. The more people looking out for me the better. Also, it was more publicity for the Wynkoop. What I didn't expect was that I'd end up on the most popular afternoon television talk show of the 1990s, *The Phil Donahue Show*.

"All right," Phil said as he started the show, pacing about the audience with his hand to his forehead like a confused professor, "our guests today believe it's very difficult to find the man or the woman of your dreams, especially in this day and age, so they're willing to offer big bucks to the person who introduces them to the person they subsequently marry."

Phil turned to me first and said, "Am I lying to these people, John Hickenlooper? You of all people. John, you're from Denver, you've never been married. But you've been engaged twice."

"I just say that to keep my mother happy." I was on the stage dressed in a sport jacket, plaid vest, and tie. I was never one to dress for success.

"Five G's to the person who introduces you to the person that you subsequently marry?"

"I own a restaurant. I own this place called the Wynkoop Brewery in Denver. It makes its own beer and I've had it for five years and it's busy, and I wasn't meeting anybody."

"You got that plug in pretty quickly, John."

Indeed I did. Pretty proud of myself for that one. As far as a promotional opportunity for the Wynkoop, *The Phil Donahue Show* made the Running of the Pigs look like, well, the Running of the Pigs.

Phil turned to a man in the audience, my friend Ken Gart, a plant. Phil revealed that Ken had introduced me to a woman whom I had now been dating for about a week. Phil then introduced that woman, onstage to my left, Devany McNeill. Devany was great and took it all in stride. She had a terrific sense of humor, one of the many things I liked about her.

Phil, God bless him, pointed out that Devany was twenty-nine years old and with great fanfare asked the audience to guess my age. Shouts from the audience were early to mid-thirties. Phil had the best audience. He announced that I was forty-two.

Gasps all around.

"Well preserved," I said. "It's all that beer." Another plug!

"Hickenlooper, first of all you've got a problem with the last name. Who wants to be Mrs. Hickenlooper for the rest of her life?"

Indeed, Phil's question was a good one.

In keeping with my pattern, I dated Devany for three years, and she understandably got tired of merely dating, so we split, though we remained friends.

And who wanted to be Mrs. Hickenlooper for the rest of her life?

THE CITY SUPPORTED US, and I tried to do my part to support the city. It was the right thing to do and good for business. I became engaged in many charitable and civic organizations. At the Wynkoop we hosted all kinds of groups for luncheon and dinner meetings. We'd deliver and donate beer for local charity events. Upon request, for some affairs, we'd print special labels to stick on the bottles or even brew a special beer. In 1995, we got such a request from Bill Havu, who asked if we would brew a specialty beer to celebrate the Havu Gallery's hosting of author Kurt Vonnegut and some of his silk screens.

Not only was he a celebrated novelist; Kurt, as his legion of devoted fans knows, was an accomplished artist. He did Picasso-esque drawings that were as wildly imaginative as his novels. Bill told me Kurt also wanted to meet me because his grandfather had been a brewer in Indianapolis and won a gold medal at the Paris Exposition in 1900. One week later, I'm in our big open office, I answer the phone, a deep voice asks me if I'm me. Then Kurt Vonnegut introduces himself. I was a big fan, had read all his books. Was completely starstruck. He then asked before we talked beer if I knew whatever happened to a guy he had gone to Cornell University with, a guy who had the same funny name as mine. I spoke in a monotone and said that was my father; he died of cancer in 1960. Long pause. "That's so very sad," he said. "He was a good friend of mine. He was a kind and funny young man."

Our meeting when Kurt came to town was the beginning of a friendship that lasted until Kurt died, on April 11, 2007. I told him about almost approaching him on the campus at Harvard all those many years ago. In return Kurt shared with me his memories of my father.

They were fraternity brothers. Kurt and my father shared a similar sense of humor and a penchant for nicknames. Kurt ended up calling me "Hop'n'hedger" or "Hedgehopper." Of course, when Kurt told me stories of my dad, they were wonderfully rendered, especially when he wrote them down and sent them to me, as he continued to do after our first meeting. We corresponded by fax and letters. One faxed memory that he sent captures Kurt better than I ever could:

To: HEDGEHOPPER FROM FUNNYGUTS

Delta Upsilon Fraternity at 6 South Avenue in Ithaca, New York, now a thuggish football player's animal house, was before World War Two, genteel, although incipiently alcoholic, traditionally the crew house. We had crossed oars on the walls of our dining hall and no varsity or basketball or track types. In my time, we had the stroke and the bow man and the coxswain of the varsity crew. The coxswain was a diminutive but scrappy John Hickenlooper, or is my memory playing tricks on me?

We also had big shots traditionally on publications, the Sun and so on. I myself was one of those, and had become a member because my father, Kurt, Sr., had been a DU at MIT. Reason enough!

Hickenlooper and Brother John Locke had a little snack and cigarette and soft drink concession in a big closet on the second floor of the fraternity house, which they called, "Hickenlooper's Lockenbar," but which came to be known as Lockenlooper's Hickenbar," or "Lickenbarker's Loopen Hock," und so weiter.

John Hickenlooper was an invariably kind and funny young man when I knew him. I think he was two years my senior. Two years was a whole generation back then.

To play varsity soccer or be a varsity swimmer was acceptable. To date a coed was strengst verboten!

Of course, we crafted a beer just for Kurt. His maternal grandfather, the noted American brewer, was Albert Lieber, who owned the original Indianapolis Brewing Company. Lieber's lager won a gold medal at the Paris World Exposition in 1900. By this time, Russell had left the Wynkoop and died tragically, falling down a flight of stairs while working at a brewpub in New York City in April 1996. But Russell had trained his protégé, Tom Dargen, well. Tom whipped up a batch of the Lieber dark lager that won the gold, or at least a close approximation. Although the recipe was never written down, according to Kurt, the secret ingredient was coffee, in a Duesseldorfer-style lager. We called it "Kurt's Mile-High Malt." The label image featured a silk-screened Kurt Vonnegut self-portrait.

Later, Kurt and I collaborated on another project. In 1995 and 1996, my pal Lew Cady, a Wynkoop customer and local public relations whiz, decided that the Wynkoop should brew a special beer to celebrate the dedication of the new $91 million Michael Graves–designed Denver

Public Library. We called the brew Denver Public Libation. Better yet, we got famous authors Clive Cussler and John Nichols to write very short stories that would fit on the beer labels for twenty-two-ounce bottles. The second year, Amy Tan said no. Dave Barry said yes. The man they call J. R. Moehringer, who reports on pigs, kindly obliged. So did FunnyGuts.

Kurt wrote "Merlin," a wee tale about a British science fiction writer named Kilgore Trout, who appears as a character in many of Kurt's novels. In this story, Kilgore is deprived of beer growing up, thanks to Prohibition, and so he escapes into science fiction books and grows up to write such stories himself. Kurt describes how Trout sets his first novel in the Court of King Arthur; Merlin the magician casts a spell that equips the knights with Thompson submachine guns. All in 160 words. After all, it had to fit on a label. Fun stuff.

Kurt's most recent novel had been published six years earlier. Since then, the literary legend had stayed relatively quiet. Sensing opportunity, I orchestrated an event at the library where some of the writers would read their stories to the public. Naturally, I issued a press release on Wynkoop letterhead featuring Kurt. "A reading of a beer bottle label by internationally acclaimed Kurt Vonnegut . . ." The Denver library event made big news. Even *The New York Observer* covered it. "Kurt Vonnegut is about to break his literary silence," so went the article. "The septuagenarian has contributed a 200-word short story to a beer label." I was quoted, and the Wynkoop got some nice ink and went big-time in the *Observer*. We sold the literary brews in collector cases of twenty-two-ounce bottles of Denver Public Libation, proceeds to the library.

Kurt told me that part of the reason he had not written in so long was that he had not felt inspired. He had lost his muse, he told me. He had been struggling with what would be his last novel, *Timequake*, and decided to slip in apparently random vignettes, mostly about his family and the loss of loved ones. Once again, he featured Kilgore Trout, and—and!—Kurt wrote me and my father into the book and mentioned the Wynkoop Brewing Company. In chapter 44, he described our first meeting and our discussions of my father. Pegged to the book's publication in 1997, I did an interview of Kurt for *The Bloomsbury Review*. At last, I was published in a respected literary publication.

THE WYNKOOP BREWING COMPANY'S success triggered a revival of the entire Lower Downtown area. As *The Denver Post* reported this Wynkoop effect, "Beer flowed out, money and people flowed in. Other businesses opened up, along with galleries and pioneering residents." The former ghost town of abandoned warehouses and tumbleweeds was now cool "LoDo." Restaurants (with valet parking!), retail, lofts, hotels. The fact that Coors Field was built in the neighborhood may also have accelerated the transformation. When Coors Field opened, in 1995, it was the first new National League ballpark since Dodger Stadium opened in 1962. Chiseled into the edge of the Platte Valley so it was lower and more in scale with LoDo, Coors Field had only 4,500 parking spaces, despite being expanded from 43,000 seats to 50,000 seats while under construction. This seemingly inconsequential fact was the result of a bunch of LoDo entrepreneur types lobbying the Stadium District. The Stadium District liked the idea because it saved them money. We liked it because it would force fans to park in the large multistory garages along Eighteenth Street and compel them to walk the three or floor blocks to experience LoDo firsthand. Almost like free marketing, and boy, did it work. When our pool hall opened, we jumped from $2 million to $4 million annually in sales. When Coors Field opened, we jumped another 50 percent in monthly revenues, with modest increased expenses. And it wasn't just all summer. While the sellout crowds marched to and from the stadium, the winter months were up 50 percent as well. Coors Field had marketed LoDo as no amount of paid advertising could have ever achieved.

LoDo became the hippest, most happening hood in Denver. The Lower Downtown story has often been cited as one of the most vibrant instances of urban redevelopment in the United States. LoDo indeed felt like a community. All for one, one for all. Celebrating one another's successes. Doing what we could to help one another avoid failure. As a Denver city councilman once put it, the West was won because in the Old West there were a lot more barn raisings than there were shootouts. That's consistent with the spirit of the West. If you ask me, that is at the heart of the Colorado brand and the secret to our success—collaboration.

And partly from all that collaboration, I was rich. Or at least, I felt rich. The Tattered Cover project was a success. Our other real estate projects had boomed as well, and we had learned our lessons from national brewpub expansion and were successfully concentrated in Colorado. Vonnegut once told me about a conversation he had with his friend Joseph Heller, who wrote *Catch-22*. They were sitting on the front porch of some gargantuan estate on Long Island, and Kurt asked him if he was bothered that this mogul whose guest they were would likely make more money just over the weekend than Heller would earn in forty years of royalties from *Catch-22*. Kurt told me that Joe turned to him and said, No, not at all. He had something the mogul would never have— enough. And that had left me thinking.

IN 1999, I found myself the unlikely leader of a community-based effort to protect what was arguably Colorado's most important brand, and one once thought to be untouchable: the Mile High part of Denver's Mile High Stadium. The Broncos were in the midst of erecting a new stadium, or rather, the region's taxpayers were. But the Stadium District didn't want to call it Mile High. The organization wanted to sell the naming rights to the highest bidder, ostensibly in order to help finance the construction.

My old pal Lew Cady—he of Denver Public Libation fame—got in my ear about it. Lew was a lover of beer and sports. And was as colorful a character as he was civic-minded. His point was that "Mile High" was synonymous not only with Denver, but with the entire state of Colorado. The way Lew saw it, selling away the name "Mile High" was like selling away the name of a beloved family member when you wanted to build a new house. (Maybe not the best analogy, but as I said, Lew liked his beer.) He didn't think it was right for the Broncos organization and the Stadium District to sell off something that was so meaningful to taxpayers, especially since their taxes were funding most of the construction costs; they were selling something that didn't belong to just them.

I appreciated the need to find creative ways to finance a construction project, but Lew was right. I imagined how my very first next-door neighbor in Denver and dear friend, Colleen Feely, and her family would react if the Broncos sold away our Mile High Stadium. There might be a shootout, after all. Seemed to me, there were millions of Broncos fans who felt the same as Lew and I did. He asked me if I would go public with my feelings, as a member of the business community with something of a profile. Lew thought it would matter. I said sure.

I talked to a reporter from *The Denver Post,* and the next day there was a big story about how business leader John Hickenlooper opposed selling off the naming rights. Everywhere I went for days, everyone was talking about that story. I thought, *Well, that's interesting.* I had said what I said because I thought it was the right thing to do, but there was also an ancillary marketing benefit for the Wynkoop. I got more involved.

I did some research. I got a blue-chip consulting company to estimate how much the name was worth. The appraisal showed that the brand value of "Mile High" to the metro Denver area was well over $100 million.

A bit more research showed that increasing annual city taxes for individuals by $4.24 per person would cover all of the proposed revenue from selling the name; then all Coloradans could keep their beloved Mile High Stadium name. I asked a local pollster and Wynkoop regular, Floyd Ciruli, if he would add a couple of questions to one of his polls to find out how willing taxpayers might be to pay for that. Almost 70 percent of locals surveyed said they would gladly pay. Floyd told me that was unheard of—that many people willing to pay a tax for *anything*. Again, as Lincoln put it, with public sentiment nothing can fail; without it, nothing can succeed.

We called a "press conference"—we meaning Lew and I. We set up some card tables with sheets over them outside the new stadium. Lew and his wife and a couple of their friends, and a couple of friends from the Wynkoop, drew up some posters and slogans for the backdrop. Lew sent out a press release. And we waited for the crowd.

Which never came.

But we did get reporters from all three local newspapers, and we had all five TV stations with cameras there. There were maybe ten people total on hand. Lew made me do almost all the talking. I laid out our case. That night we were on every news channel, and we were on the front page of the newspapers the next day. The earth shuddered beneath our feet.

But the Metropolitan Football Stadium District Commission (a nine-member board with one representative from each of the six original Colorado counties, and three representatives appointed by the governor) yawned. They knew public sentiment was against them. They had been going around to the counties gauging public response to the "possible sale" of the naming rights, which they had found was three-to-one against, and still the commission continued right along doing as they pleased.

Things changed in the fall of 2000. For the stadium deal and for me.

As the finishing touches were being put on the new stadium, the commissioners decided to give one of the TV stations a tour. Because almost all the commissioners were from the suburbs and Republicans, they asked the conservative governor, Bill Owens, to be the pretty face of the tour. All well and good.

Except that Denver mayor Wellington Webb caught wind of this and blew a gasket. He had worked his butt off to pass the regional sales tax to build the stadium. Governor Owens had opposed it. Plus, he and Owens had gotten crosswise so many times they couldn't stand to be in the same room with each other. Mayor Webb was seething. He asked his press secretary, Andrew Hudson, "Who's that beer guy in LoDo who is trying to save the name 'Mile High Stadium'? Chickencooper, Hickenpooper . . ."

Andrew knew me well. He was no stranger to the Wynkoop Brewing Company. We had become friends. So while I was not surprised to hear his voice on the phone, I was surprised when he asked if I could join a press conference about the naming rights in the mayor's office the next day. At that very moment, I was leaving a banquet at the Association of Brewers conference in Portland, Maine, where earlier that day I had given a speech on marketing beer. The next day was Sunday, and I said I couldn't make it. I suggested Tuesday afternoon. Andrew asked me to hold on. I heard voices in the background, and then he got back on the line and said, Tuesday afternoon.

I arrived fifteen minutes before the scheduled start. The mayor's spacious office was jammed with probably sixty people. Bright lights on a makeshift stage, maybe eight cameras. Mayor Webb, who is six foot five if he's an inch, and broad across the beam, welcomed everyone. He said he'd been frustrated like so many others that a small group of people had effectively decided to sell one of the most beloved assets of the entire metro area—the revered name of its historic stadium.

He said the Mile High moniker was Denver's identity, not unlike the Big Apple for New York City. He said, "Everything should not be for sale." Talk about marketing; that line was gold. We were both on national news, although I could see his statements were more compact and powerful than mine, that he was painting images with words, while I was less articulate. Wellington Webb was one of the most significant mayors of the latter half of the twentieth century. His natural political instincts are almost unrivaled. He suggested that the name change decision be put to a public vote. The Stadium District Commission refused, but delayed its decision to sell or not sell.

As the controversy grew more intense, the Broncos played a big game of the 2000 season on *Monday Night Football.* For the occasion, we had fifty thousand large placards printed that said SAVE THE NAME on one side and MILE HIGH FOREVER on the other. I recruited Andrew Hudson and the communications director for Denver's tourism office, Rich Grant, and a few other friends to hand them out to Broncos fans as they arrived to watch the team play in the new (and as yet unnamed) stadium. Men were shaking my hands and slapping me on the back. Women were kissing me on the cheek. Little kids asked me to sign autographs.

When we finished handing out the placards, Andrew and I went to a rooftop bar near the stadium to watch the game on television. The first big Broncos play of the game, the crowd erupted. The *Monday Night Football* cameras panned over the audience. Images of that sea of Broncos Nation orange waving our SAVE THE NAME and MILE HIGH FOREVER signs were broadcast to millions of viewers around the country. Andrew and I could hardly believe it. If I recall correctly, the cameras never again turned toward the fans in the stands that day.

The last thing the NFL wanted was to promote controversy over the Mile High sale and deter corporations from buying into stadium sponsorships. At that time, nationwide, more than fifty-nine naming rights deals on sporting facilities had been sold for nearly $3 billion. This was big business, a huge revenue stream for franchises around the country and for the NFL.

In January 2001, *Sports Illustrated*'s Rick Reilly, who also happened to be another Wynkoop regular, dedicated his wildly popular back-page column to the naming rights trend around the country. His column was titled "Corpo-Name Disease: Stop the Plague!" He made the Mile High story and his favorite brewpub owner the centerpiece.

> People across the U.S. are rising up against corpo-name disease. In Denver, a skinny restaurateur named John Hickenlooper heard that the new citizen-paid-for Mile High Stadium was going to become Invesco Field or some such cheesiness and thought, Hey, wait a minute! How much is the name Mile High Stadium worth to this city? How many people hear Al Michaels go, "Live, from Mile High Stadium . . ." and think, I'm going to live there, or I'm going to visit there? He commissioned a poll, which showed that most Denverites agreed with him. Then the mayor agreed. Then Hickenlooper helped pay for 50,000 signs, handed out at a Broncos game, that read MILE HIGH STADIUM: BEST NAME BY A MILE. Now, no corporation with half a focus group will touch it, lest it risk the Oprah of all boycotts.

Rick encouraged citizens and sports fans everywhere to "rise up" and "find the Hickenlooper inside you!" (While this was catchy, for obvious reasons, we never did use it as a campaign slogan.)

Some said that we who opposed that sale of naming rights lost. I say we won. The Stadium District delayed the decision to sell or not to sell for months, and ultimately struck a compromise. They would sell the name to Invesco, but would also keep "Mile High" in the moniker: "Invesco at Mile High." In the end, we kept our stadium Mile High, and no one ever called the stadium by the full name. As far as Coloradans were and are concerned, it was and always will be Mile High Stadium. What's more, *The Denver Post* refused to refer to the stadium by its corporate hybrid form for almost two years. In its newsroom style books and in its pages, it remained "New Mile High Stadium."

The night of that *Monday Night Football* game, as Andrew and I sat in that rooftop bar and watched it on television, he said, "I've never seen someone garner so much goodwill as you have in such a short period of time. You ought to run for mayor." I let out a "Ha!" A day or two later, another friend, Chris Romer, the son of former Colorado governor Roy Romer, suggested the same thing. He pointed out that Mayor Webb, then in his third term, would be term-limited in two years. Chris said I could bring a small-business perspective to the job. I asked him what was he talking about; I'd never even run for student council.

Then I bumped into Chris Gates, another friend active in politics. Chris was the vice president of the National Civic League. He, too, said I should consider running for mayor. Chris and I had a bit of a longer discussion about it. Among other things, he talked about how I could bring common sense to government. With these three smart political veterans all saying the same thing to me, I started to think about it.

The more I thought about it, the more I thought about it.

Ten

"DRINKS ON THE TABLE"

A s 2001 began, I stayed in touch with Andrew Hudson, Chris Romer, and in particular Chris Gates. Chris suggested that if I was fermenting thoughts about running for mayor—and I *was* thinking about it—it might be useful for me to talk with some actual mayors and get a sense of what the job entails. His idea was a brilliantly practical one. I was forty-seven years old—that February I was turning forty-eight—and I had never before run for any elected office in my life, not even high school student council. Here I was considering a run for mayor of the twenty-first-largest city in America and I was completely ignorant of what the job required. I had zero political experience. I didn't know what I didn't know.

In his role as president of the National Civic League, Chris had relationships with many mayors and municipal leaders throughout the country. The National Civic League is a "good government" organization formed by Teddy Roosevelt, Louis Brandeis, and other such nobility. In the summer of 2001, with Chris leading the way, we traveled along the northeastern seaboard, and I visited and talked with current and former big-city mayors or members of their senior staff. Before embarking on the trip, Chris and I discussed some of what I hoped to get out of my visits. It seemed to me I had three questions to answer for myself: Could I make a difference? Would I be good at it? Would I enjoy it?

In the middle of August 2001, Chris met me in New Hampshire, where we stayed a few days with my brother, Sydney, and his family at our extended family's vacation home on beautiful Squam Lake (a beautiful glacial relic of the last ice age, for those of you still following along geologically). Chris and I then headed for Boston.

Tom Menino was running for the third of what would be his five terms as Boston's mayor. With his approval ratings wandering from 70 percent to above 80 percent, Tom was so far ahead in his race that he gave us a full hour at the end of a beautiful late-summer afternoon. He was a lifetime pol, a bare-knuckled brawler—the opposite of what I imagined I might be. My God, he was an impressive man. He shared a dizzying array of war stories with a raw candor that was magnetic. His salty language included explicit directions on how I should deal with the press if I decided to run. I loved him.

We mooched a night's stay with friends in Boston. In the morning, we took Amtrak down to New York City, where we had an uneventful meeting with Deputy Mayor Rudy Washington, who served with Mayor Giuliani.

We hustled back to Amtrak thinking we had plenty of time to make our 3:30 meeting with David L. Cohen, who had been chief of staff to the great Philadelphia mayor Ed Rendell. In planning the trip to Philly we counted on Amtrak being on time. Big mistake. After the train's second long delay we called David's office at the law firm of Ballard Spahr to say we might be a little late. His assistant told us to hurry up, as Mr. Cohen had to leave promptly at 4:30 p.m. in order to pack for his first vacation in almost a decade.

After two or three more delays, we finally arrived in Philadelphia's 30th Street Station precisely at 4:30, blocks from Ballard Spahr, at the height of rush hour. By the time we ran out of the elevator toward his office it was almost 5:00 p.m. Yet David was still there, patiently waiting for us. And darn if he didn't spend the next ninety minutes telling us a whole different side of what running a city could be like.

Whereas Tom Menino had loved the hand-to-hand combat of big-city politics, David waxed rhapsodic about all that a progressive-minded administration could accomplish. David and Mayor Rendell had rescued Philadelphia from the brink of bankruptcy. Their story is beautifully told in Buzz Bissinger's now classic account of their first term, *A Prayer for the City.*

Every few minutes, David's secretary would stick her head in his door and say his wife had called, and David would think of another challenge, another obstacle overcome, that he must share with us. It was starting to become apparent why David had not been on a vacation in a decade. But there was no bragging in David L. Cohen. He seemed totally selfless. Many of the stories he told were about the heroic efforts of junior- and middle-level staff. I was thoroughly inspired.

Chris and I had dinner in Philadelphia with Lee Driscoll Jr., the father of one of my business partners. In 1962, Lee had run for United States Congress and gotten crushed as a liberal Democrat in a conservative district. Instead of advising me to be cautious, he told me in no uncertain terms that if I had a legitimate chance to run for a high office I would be a fool not to do so.

Lee said that while campaigning he had met amazing people, many of whom became friends for life. A campaign was a rare, intense opportunity, he said, to quickly develop deep relationships with uniquely wonderful people you would otherwise never meet. He was perhaps the most motivating person of everyone I talked with.

That night Chris and I took the train out to spend the night with my mother and my stepdad, Bill, in their shoebox of a house that backed up to the local Paoli train that traveled the Main Line. Once again, she prepared a feast for us. I was still the Prodigal Son. I'll repeat here that my mother was a brave but cautious soul, whose instincts were permanently colored by seeing so many of her neighbors lose everything during the Great Depression.

She didn't invest in the Wynkoop, and she was no more enthusiastic about my thoughts of running for mayor. But she liked and respected Lee Driscoll, and she agreed that the opportunity to build unique friendships had value. "Like college," she said to me. Mom was comforted that I wasn't going to "self-finance." In typical Mom fashion, she cautioned that if I was going to do it, don't do it halfway, and don't quit. Just as with the Wynkoop, I don't think she thought highly of my chances.

When we set off on the train to Baltimore the next morning we were well fed and well rested. We spent the better part of that afternoon getting the soup-to-nuts demonstration of Martin O'Malley's seminal Citi-Stat program—a magnificent, data-driven initiative to reinvent good government. At the time of our visit, Mayor O'Malley was doing good works (and maybe a little singing) in his ancestral Ireland, but his brother Peter, a senior staffer, pulled out all the stops for us.

They were measuring everything in Baltimore, from overtime to parking violations to potholes repaired, and mapping everything from lead paint in neighborhoods to trash truck routes and schedules. They were beginning to show how city government could do more with less, tracking public-sector services as if it were a private-sector enterprise, applying private-sector standards and metrics to governance. I was beginning to think one really could make a difference, maybe even the likes of me.

We went down to Washington, D.C., to mooch another night with friends. As you may be gleaning, this was a low-budget tour that for the both of us cost less than $500. My frugal mother would have been proud. In the morning, we met with Stephen Goldsmith, who had recently finished two terms as mayor of Indianapolis. He had challenged his unionized sanitation workers by making them bid, district by district, against private firms. Again, here was a policy rooted in leveraging private-sector economics and competition.

Stephen gave the unionized workers enough advantages that they won most of the district bids, but costs came down, a win for taxpayers. His "Front Porch Initiative" sought to partner with faith groups to enhance the safety and orderliness of many challenged neighborhoods. Stephen had clearly loved being mayor, and his city was the better for it.

That afternoon, we stopped at Union Station in D.C. to meet with David Skaggs, formerly the United States congressman from Boulder, who had filled Senator Tim Wirth's seat. That was the election Eileen and I had worked on fifteen years earlier, in 1986. David, who also happened to be a Wesleyan alum, was equal parts curious and enthusiastic about my potential run for mayor. He described ways he was working in Congress to build bridges across party lines and transcend the intense partisanship that was rapidly growing even then.

It was quite a tour. Because Chris had work to do in D.C., he stayed put while I flew back to Denver. On the return flight, for the first time, I tried to imagine what it would be like to *be* mayor. Not my strong suit. I can imagine warehouse into restaurant, abandoned into vibrant. Give me a geologist's map of rock strata, and with the facts and science, I'd like to think I can make a good guess as to where to set up the drill. But a different future, a different identity from the one I inhabit at the moment, that is more of a stretch for me. Truth was I had no idea what it would be like to be mayor. Considering all that I'd heard during our trip, though, I thought I might like it. I thought I might be good at it. Ignorance, as they say, is bliss. All that I had heard was wonderful and terrifying.

Home in Denver, although exhausted from the trip, I had a devil of a time falling asleep that night in my loft above Table 16 in the Wynkoop. My mind was far from made up. While that tour was excellent for fact-finding, I had much soul-searching left to do. In a few weeks, on September 11, 2001, terrorists would fly planes into the World Trade Center towers, the Pentagon, and a field in rural Pennsylvania. The entire nation would soon be thrust into soul-searching about questions of good and evil, to wage war or not to wage war; the decision I wrestled with would suddenly seem at once inconsequential and all the more profound.

ON SEPTEMBER 11, 2001, I was visiting the intriguing Helen Thorpe in Austin, Texas.

We had been dating long-distance since January—January 27, to be exact. I can be sure that was the date because I had crashed her birthday party in Austin. Well, not a cold crash. It's not like I came through a skylight. I entered by the front door, with an old friend from Wesleyan. My meeting with Helen had been slyly orchestrated by Tracy Killam, the same Wesleyan pal who led me into that pivotal geology class on leach fields many years ago.

Tracy was a Texan, now Tracy DiLeo, married to Michael, a gifted writer. Michael and Helen had become friends working together on the staff of *Texas Monthly* magazine. For months, Tracy had been telling me that I had to meet this friend of hers, Helen. Tracy kept saying how smart and cute and funny and kind this Helen was. She told me Helen was a writer. Tracy knew how much I liked writers. Tracy was one of my dearest friends; no bride bounty could have landed me a better matchmaker. Tracy proposed the idea of my visiting Austin and attending a party for Helen's birthday. I saddled up and headed to Texas.

This wasn't my first time traveling to Austin to meet Helen. I had gone months earlier, only Tracy had not checked with Helen and when I arrived Helen was off covering George W. Bush's run for president for the now defunct *George* magazine. This time, however, we were quite certain Helen would be at her own birthday party. The hostess was a friend of theirs, Kat Jones. I arrived at the party bearing two CDs as gifts: one a Billie Holiday and the other a Louis Armstrong. One was for the hostess, the other for the birthday girl, who naturally got to pick first. Helen chose Billie. A good sign; I would have chosen Billie.

Helen was all of the things Tracy had said, plus she had a tremendously wry sense of humor. Me being me, I "nonchalantly" walked about the room of journalists, musicians, and other creative types and tried to get the scoop on this Helen-writer-woman. I asked a few of her friends how they knew her and heard four different people say, "Helen's my best friend." I thought that was telling in the very best way.

A few weeks after the party, Helen had a reason to travel to Colorado and we went on an actual date, which turned into more dates. That year, I took eleven weeks of vacation and spent much of it courting Helen Thorpe. We clicked. We took a few trips: London, St. Bart's, and Italy. We fell in love.

On September 11, 2001, Helen and I were just getting out of bed in Austin when we heard the news that a plane had crashed into the World Trade Center. We were half paying attention and didn't realize the full scope of what was unfolding. As is typical for me, I was running late, throwing my bag together at the last minute. We raced to the car and Helen drove me to the airport for my return flight to Denver. Arriving at the airport, we heard a radio report about a second plane hitting the towers. A security guard at the Austin airport informed us that all flights had been grounded, the airport was closed.

Back at Helen's house, like most Americans, like much of the world, we tuned to the news, watched the reports, and saw the horrific videos. I became convinced that the media, with all of its speculating and the endless replaying of the unspeakable imagery almost as if on a loop, were unwittingly playing into the hands of the terrorists, intensifying the fear, which was the terrorists' goal.

By that time, Helen and I were very much a couple, and in such a moment I felt all the more fortunate to be with someone I had come to love. In having someone, I could more acutely imagine what it would be like to lose someone. What I could not fathom was the nightmare that the victims suffered, and now the uniquely devastating anguish and trauma that the survivors and all of their families were experiencing and would endure for a long time to come. How would they carry on? Where would we as a nation go from here?

There is something else I remember my mom saying after my father died. During one of those kitchen-counter, predinner talks we had when I was teenager, I asked Mom how she was able to get through it all—this small, strong, quiet woman who had lost two husbands and was matter-of-factly fixing the two of us dinner. Mom did her shoulder shrug and told me that she felt she had no choice; we were obliged to find joy in life; she felt she owed it to Bow and to Hick to seek out happiness for herself and for their children.

Together, Helen and I were happy.

In the fall of 2001, I rented for two weeks an eleven-bedroom hilltop villa in Tuscany from a good friend of my partner Lee Driscoll III. Helen and I hosted many of the chefs and managers from my restaurants for the first week, and many of my oldest friends, like Joyce and Jed, for the second week. There were many conversations around this wild notion of my running for mayor, with mostly skepticism in response. The best part of the Italian retreat was discovering a month later that we were pregnant. The instantaneous joy in both of us was reflective of a deep affection for each other, and we told friends immediately we wanted them to come to our wedding in Austin in two months.

The two of us had many conversations about how challenging a campaign would be for us as newlyweds and as new parents. Having covered politics and campaigns, Helen understood much better than I did what was in store. She was remarkably supportive. Whoever the next mayor was could serve as many as three four-year terms. Helen understood that if this was something I felt I should do, the time to run was now or maybe never.

While I weighed running for mayor, she attended my kitchen cabinet meetings, which were then more like kitchen drawer meetings. In addition to Helen, Andrew Hudson, Chris Romer, and Chris Gates, I was fortunate to have Patty Calhoun, the founding editor of the alternative weekly *Westword*, as a member of our think tank. Patty had been a friend since I'd first opened the Wynkoop, and had covered city politics for three decades.

As the old cliché goes, Patty knew where the bodies were buried. In the early days of our friendship, we developed a trust and shared information about the goings-on about town under the auspices of "drinks on the table." It was our version of way, *way* off the record. I was also lucky to have Allegra "Happy" Haynes on the unofficial Team Hick. Happy was wrapping up her third term on the city council. I met with this group maybe three or four times over the course of several months in 2002. Occasionally, others joined the group. During these meetings, with "drinks on the table," my friends would grill me to see just how much of a fire in the belly I had to run and be mayor of Denver.

In July, I rode the *Denver Post*'s "Cheyenne Frontier Days" train up to the rodeo in Cheyenne, Wyoming, as I had each summer for the previous decade. Good schmoozing always. Donald Seawell, a New York theater impresario who came out to Denver in 1966 to run *The Denver Post* for fifteen years and stayed on to help create the Denver Center for the Performing Arts, was on board and holding court in the caboose. A very young ninety years old, he filled my head with fantastic stories of Old Denver political adventures and hijinks. More important, Dean Singleton, who owned the *Post* and more than 125 other newspapers, cornered me in the Wigwam Bar in the historic Plains Hotel when we arrived, and then again after the rodeo at the old Albany Bar across from the train station before the train ride home.

I didn't know Dean well, but that didn't stop him from advising me. He was adamant, indeed he demanded, that I run for mayor. He had ten editorials' worth of reasons why I would transform Denver politics forever, why I would love it, how I owed it to the city. Dean was easily the most influential media person in the state, as well as one of the most powerful media people in the country. Although he didn't quite get me to commit, my head certainly swelled accordingly. I only found out some years later, after we'd become good friends, that he was embroiled in a bitter feud at the time with Denver auditor Don Mares over the management of the Winter Park Ski Resort, owned by the City of Denver. Dean wanted anyone but Don Mares to be the next mayor. He thought I was the only hope of preventing a Mares victory in nine months.

As a part of my decision-making process I went on a Leadership Exchange trip. Every year, the Denver Metro Chamber of Commerce arranges one of these LEX trips where Denver sends a small battalion of civic leaders to learn about programs in other cities. I had been invited because I had served on the boards and committees of more than forty civic and nonprofit organizations since I'd opened the Wynkoop in 1988. In mid-October 2002, my LEX trip was to Atlanta. All the top mayoral candidates went along.

At the end of the weekend, after the final session, Denver's legendary community organizer and my good friend John Parr somehow persuaded the Chamber brass to ask each of the potential mayoral candidates what they had learned from Atlanta, and how it might enhance their vision for Denver. I'd not publicly made any mention of how inclined or not I was to run, but there were many rumors, and I was asked to speak. One of six candidates on the trip, I was the second to speak.

While I tend to run my mouth off and enjoy telling a story—as if you hadn't figured that out by now—official public speaking is another matter. I had taken a class a few years before to help me with quarterly employee town hall meetings as well as with presentations to potential customer groups for the brewpub (Historic Denver, Colorado Homebrewers, Beer Can Collectors of America, etc.), but it hadn't helped much. To this day when I ask old friends if my public speaking has improved, they fidget and generally smile uncomfortably, and say that at least I'm "authentic." That day, I was caught completely off-guard, utterly unprepared. My breathing quickened, my chest tightened to the point where I could take only short, quick breaths, my armpits became swamps, my stomach churned into knots. I hadn't been this scared since standing on the bridge in Middletown with Angela.

The room held 150 of the top civic leaders from the Denver community. You could hear a pin drop. I remembered to smile, which might be about the only thing I did right. I stammered something about how I was only vaguely considering a run, and mumbled something about collaboration and public-private partnerships. After two or three minutes, my voice trailed off without even any conclusions; certainly, I offered no vision. In the moment, I could barely see clearly myself. If there had been something in the room I could have crawled under, I would have.

Later, no one came up and patted me on the back; even my friends kept their distance. Within a week, four of the candidates had called to meet with me. One by one, they met with me and explained why they could deliver my objectives of good government without my having to get my hands dirty, and that I should throw my support behind them. In their voices, perhaps unfairly, I heard a tone of, *Come on now, John, you don't belong in the game.* I was in an absolute funk until after the fourth meeting, which occurred in late fall 2002. I don't know why exactly, but I felt like I did when I was warming up to pitch in high school and everyone was hanging on the chain-link fence around the batting cage, talking smack at me. I got this warm feeling. I decided I was going to do this, and do it my way.

Toward the end of 2002, I hired my campaign manager, Paul Lhevine, and communications director, Lindy Eichenbaum Lent, both veterans of U.S. congressional campaigns. They were both young and, since I had not yet raised any money, willing to work cheap. After all, it would only be a six-month campaign.

On January 28, 2003, I officially declared my candidacy for mayor.

I stood on the Millennium Bridge, a modern walkway just west of Union Station, a stone's throw from the Wynkoop and the now bustling former ghost town that was LoDo. The crowd was not as large as I would have liked.

Local businessman Sid Wilson and nonprofit agency leader Lisa Flores introduced me. "I'm amazed and inspired by how he's chosen to live his life," Flores said that day. "I have never so strongly believed in the ability of a candidate to lead our city." Flores was a respected community leader, committed, knowledgeable, and selfless. Hearing her say those words, and so publicly invest her faith and trust in me, I felt the potential responsibilities and expectations become all the more real and solemn.

It was my turn to speak.

The first official speech of my political career.

My mouth dried, my stomach again knotted. Yet I spoke without a major rhetorical flub. I felt a surge of something that almost felt like confidence. I believe that was because Helen was at my side, holding our infant son, Teddy.

Helen's theory about me, as you may recall, is that a large portion of my heart shut down when I was a small child and my father died. Unpleasant as it is for me to confront that observation, I think there's truth in it. Hearing Helen's take, a friend who visited my extended family's vacation home on Squam Lake in New Hampshire put it another way. The lake house, which has never been winterized, has a large wraparound porch. Naturally, at the end of every summer, when it's closed up, of course, it gets dark and chilly in there. At the beginning of every summer season, as we open the doors and windows, piece by piece, light pours in and warms each section.

According to my friend, when I was eight and my dad died, a piece of my heart was closed up for that sad season, and it stayed closed up. Closed off, damp and dark, maybe even with a few cobwebs. This analogy, I think, makes it easier for me to explain how Helen and Teddy affected me.

When I met Helen, I tend to think, my heart opened and some desperately needed light and warmth got in. With Teddy's birth, more sunlight filled my heart. I know when I took Teddy in my arms for the first time in July 2002, I felt a warm glow I had never before experienced and that has never since dissipated. As I said, I'm not a gifted public speaker; that day on the Millennium Bridge, I was not remotely eloquent. I merely spoke from my heart, but because of Helen and Teddy, there was more of my heart to give.

Standing on the bridge, I explained how I had come to decide to run: I talked about the Mile High Stadium campaign and the friends who had put the idea in my head. I said I'd done my homework; I'd talked to mayors both in metro Denver and around the country, and having weighed all that I could weigh, I believed I would be a good mayor, that I would have fun, and that I could make a difference. I said I would bring a small-business perspective to city government and to a city where the economy was stagnating.

"I spent the last two decades building not only my own business, but those around me as well," I said, referring to the development of LoDo. "Economic development is not a catchphrase I picked up on the campaign trail—it's what I do."

The other thing that happened to me when Teddy was born is that I started to become more conscious of the long view. As a young(ish) childless bachelor, I had lived almost always in the moment. I was inclined to throw caution to the wind without much regard for where I or the world would be in ten or twenty years. As just about any parent will tell you, that perspective changes when you have a child of your own. With an infant son, I saw the world, life, everything, with more of a geologist's eye, which is to say I more carefully examined the lay of the land around me, took more time to scratch beneath the surface to see the layers, and I considered what sort of future that I, *we*, could build upon what was there.

In that spirit, on the bridge, I said, "Twenty years ago, Denver mayor Federico Peña asked us to imagine a great city. Over the past twelve years, Wellington Webb has helped build a great city. But now we have to *become* a great city. I believe that with the right leadership and the right vision, we can truly become a city that is Mile High, not just in name, but in achievement."

Like I said, I'm not a great orator, I didn't kick off our campaign with a Gettysburg Address, but I meant every word.

Eleven

HICK TOWN

Here begins the part of the story where I ride into Denver city politics on a moped.

In order for you to better appreciate the trip, I'll share with you some basic road rules. Denver is a consolidated city and county—one of Colorado's sixty-four counties—and the mayor is elected on a nonpartisan ballot in a runoff election. Although party affiliation is technically a nonfactor, and political parties are not permitted to be involved in the mayoral or city council races, make no mistake, Denver is a Democratic town. If you gathered together all of the city's registered Republicans you might have enough people for a softball team. Going into that 2003 campaign, Denver voters had elected a Democratic mayor in every election since 1963. For the record, I was and remain a registered Democrat, although based on some of my decisions my party affiliation has often been disputed, sometimes by my own staff.

Denver's mayor governs in cooperation with a city council comprising thirteen members, and all are closely monitored by a city auditor. The city council represents eleven districts, with two at-large members. All of these elected officials serve four-year terms, with a maximum of three terms.

Denver is a strong-mayor-weak-council form of city government, indeed the strongest "strong mayor" office in the country. Council is the legislative branch, passing and amending all laws, resolutions, and ordinances. The mayor hires all of the cabinet and city leadership without needing council's approval and, most important, crafts the budget. If council wishes to override a veto or make changes to the budget it needs a supermajority minimum of nine of the thirteen member votes, which is almost impossible to achieve. It is the mayor who signs all bonds and contracts. The city auditor is the alert but somewhat toothless watchdog. With such power residing in the office, an open mayoral seat generally means a hotly contested, bare-knuckled brawl.

I joined a crowded field of six other candidates for mayor. The two front-runners were city auditor Don Mares, Dean Singleton's nemesis, and former Denver police chief Ari Zavaras. The first poll found its way into the media in early February, showing Zavaras with 20 percent of the vote and Mares with 14 percent; I was pulling a whopping 4 percent. I'll leave it to you to guess who gave that poll to the media. (Hint: he was in the lead.)

On the upside for me, 41 percent of the voters surveyed were undecided. The first of the two runoff elections was on May 6; if no one got a majority, the big showdown between the final two would be June 3.

As it goes with any mayoral election in a major metropolitan area, there were many challenges the new mayor would have to confront. The most significant and pressing issues were the city's struggling economy and the budget.

In his twelfth and final term-limited year in office, Mayor Wellington Webb presided over a city limping out of a recession and into difficult financial times. Mayor Webb had been one of the great American mayors of the previous decade, but the good old days of the nineties boom were gone. In the wake of the burst dot-com bubble the inflated stock market quickly deflated. In March 2001, the country entered into a recession. During the last eighteen months of Webb's final term, the city lost more than *seventeen thousand* jobs, with one estimate putting it as high as thirty thousand jobs. Downtown office buildings were struggling to find tenants. It wasn't as bad as the 1980s, but it wasn't much better.

As a result, the city's $740 million budget was in dire straits. Because of the ailing economy, sales tax revenues, which make up 55 percent of the budget, were in steady decline. Sales tax collections from January through June 2002 were down 6 percent from the same period the previous year. At the same time, the large unionized part of the budget, the Department of Public Safety, which included the police, firefighters, and sheriffs, almost 60 percent of the total budget, was contractually guaranteed raises of 3 to 5 percent.

For a while it looked as if budget cuts might result in laying off police officers, closing down libraries, and mandating weeklong unpaid furloughs for all city employees. Webb managed to stave off those drastic moves, primarily with three basic strategies: First, he trimmed larger agencies, like public works or parks and recreation, up to $1 million, and held open a dozen positions here or there, where replacements for normal attrition had not already been hired. Some street maintenance would be delayed, and the police helicopter and mounted patrol would be grounded. Second, his administration raised fees for everything they thought wouldn't provoke outrage, like building permits or zoning changes, and even raised parking meter rates downtown by 50 percent. (I had visited the mayor's office with a group of downtown retailers trying—in vain—to dissuade the mayor's team from the latter.) Last, his budget director had projected a sudden and dramatic turnaround in sales tax revenues, an increase compared with the previous year of 3.1 percent in

2004, and 3.5 percent in 2005. So they anticipated all this new revenue, but there wasn't much evidence for it. I spent much of my time out talking to small-business owners (I hated knocking on the doors of people's homes), along commercial strips in the neighborhoods as well as downtown, and literally all of them told me they thought their businesses would be flat at best in 2004, not up.

Meanwhile, critics of the administration, including the local newspapers, the *Rocky Mountain News* and *The Denver Post*, pointed out that the mayor's staff had expanded and received steady pay raises. One story reported that the mayor's fifty-one-member staff had grown from forty-one members in 1999 and seen its salaries increase roughly 52.2 percent, from $2.9 million to $4.4 million. Seventeen staff members made more than $100,000.

One council member said, "It's just staggering that the mayor would have salaries like this when the city's in this situation. This is a slap in the face to taxpayers." City auditor and mayoral candidate Mares suggested the mayor and his senior team should take a weeklong unpaid furlough. Mares and Webb had long been at odds. No surprise there. Webb had been auditor under Mayor Peña, and had nipped at Peña's heels the way Mares was nipping at Webb's. The auditor position was considered a prime launching pad for mayoral wannabes. Webb's spokesperson, my pal Andrew Hudson, dismissed the auditor's suggestion as a political play made by a mayoral candidate. Still, many people were wondering why in such trying times there were two scheduled raises to begin with, and how it could be that the size and compensation of Webb's senior staff had grown as they had in the face of such economic distress and hard choices.

In March 2003, with the campaign under way, the Webb administration presented city council with a budget of about $740 million, with a projected deficit of $50 million over the course of 2004 and into 2005.

Even with the budget director's rosy increasing revenue projections, city budget officials predicted deficits would likely grow over the next three years and cause a drop in the reserves that would jeopardize the city's bond rating.

So the most pressing issue of the 2003 mayoral campaign was the budget, and none of the other candidates appeared to have even looked at the storm clouds gathering on the near horizon.

Fortunately, I had David Kenney and Michael Bennet on my campaign team.

I CAME TO KNOW David Kenney over the years, seeing him around town. I saw him right after the LEX trip, and asked him if he was committed to any of the already announced candidates. He wasn't. David was a seasoned veteran of Denver city politics. He had worked with Wellington Webb, and considered Webb a mentor. He understood this particular political game from the inside out.

Michael Bennet had some politics in his résumé as well. After college, he had worked for a while as an aide to Ohio governor Richard Celeste. After Yale Law School he served as a law clerk for the Fourth Circuit Court of Appeals and counsel to the deputy attorney general during President Bill Clinton's administration. Michael had zero political experience in Denver. However, the guy sure knew how to reverse engineer budgets for vast and distressed enterprises.

In 1997, I had received a letter from Michael. He wrote that he was a Wesleyan alum who had recently graduated from Yale Law School. He was new to town and had heard about me through the Wesleyan alumni network, specifically from the aforementioned Congressman David Skaggs. Michael had come to town because his fiancée, Susan Daggett, whom he'd met at Yale Law, had accepted an offer to work for the Earth-justice Legal Defense Fund in Denver. He was jobless and wanted to know if there were any opportunities with the Wynkoop.

Michael had also written a letter to Phil Anschutz, the billionaire investor and CEO of the Anschutz Company, which had a tremendously diverse portfolio of investments and companies in industries such as oil and gas, railroads, media and entertainment, and real estate. In what turned out to be further evidence that Phil Anschutz is a far smarter man than I am, he responded to Michael's letter and hired him, despite Michael's lack of business experience.

Phil insisted that the young lawyer take night classes to learn account-ing and business basics. Michael not only learned them, he mastered them. Within a few years, Phil appointed Michael to be the managing director for Anschutz's private equity division, overseeing billion-dollar deals like the merger of three bankrupt movie theater chains into Regal Cinemas. Michael developed into a meticulous and metric-driven execu-tive. He implemented systems such that he could tell you how much liq-uid butter the Regal movie theater in Wichita went through the previous weekend.

On the job for Phil, Michael had gone under the hood of countless companies to evaluate them for potential Anschutz deals. He developed an expertise in valuing distressed companies. That business is all about seeing value where others see red ink. As it goes with much of life, seeing that value requires the ability to see around corners. If you can accu-rately predict a projected decline in revenues when others are counting on an increase, well, that changes things, doesn't it?

Over time, Michael and I became friends. He and his wife were among my first campaign donors, and early on Michael had become one of the most valued members of my campaign team. Of course, he never did let me forget that I had not responded to his letter. Anyhow, Michael and David, who had never before met, graciously agreed to work together and examine the city budget.

Looking at three-year economic trends and my admittedly anecdotal field surveys, it appeared that the Webb administration's tax-revenue projections for the next two years were overly optimistic. We agreed that it would be more prudent as well as more accurate if we estimated that the 2003 revenues would be flat and would grow only 1.75 percent in each of the next two years. Based on these numbers, over the next two years, the deficit would be more like $70 million. Behind the scenes, they ran their math by one of Webb's senior budgetary officials, who agreed that, damn, wouldn't you know it, we were right.

All in all, the Webb administration's budget and predictions were too rosy. The city needed to do more, much more, to control its spending and to plan conservatively for the future.

In debates and media interviews, I made our assessment of the budget the cornerstone of my campaign. I was careful not to attack the Webb administration. As far as I was and am concerned, Webb was one of the best big-city mayors of the last fifty years. Besides, as I had learned in the restaurant business, there's no margin in making enemies. During the campaign, when one of the papers was trying to bait me into critical comments, I put it this way:

"When Leo Kiely came in to take over Coors he in no way criticized the people ahead of him. He was a revolutionary in how he changed the culture, the way they approached their business, but he didn't say anything negative about anybody ahead of him. I don't think that's productive to go after someone. I want to look at innovative ways of approaching government."

Of course, before you can innovate, you've got to stabilize what you've got. I proposed pragmatic, albeit austere, solutions. I would temporarily freeze pay for city employees and end a lucrative program that allowed some city workers to collect their pensions while still on the job, and I would make even more and deeper cuts.

I said that if I was elected, the first financial cuts would start with my own salary. I would cut my own salary by 25 percent. When it came to the mayor's sixty-three political appointees, including twelve cabinet members, I committed to slashing total pay by 25 percent and I would also eliminate entirely at least ten of those senior-level positions. "In business," I told one of the local papers, "you never ask your employees to take a hit you don't take first."

I said, "The thing I don't like about budgeting is that it's always a matter of looking at last year's budget and trying to grow it. I'd rather focus on outcomes. That's what you do in business. You say, 'What do we want to accomplish?'"

Not exactly a message of rainbows and unicorns. It certainly didn't do much to improve my polling, and it seemed to bolster the campaign donations to the front-runner, former police chief Zavaras. According to the March campaign finance disclosures, Zavaras jumped way out in front with $840,000; Mares and I had about $450,000 each, and both of us had already loaned our campaigns money. I was still a long shot, maybe now even more so. I could sense morale throughout my campaign operation go flat. Warm and flat was where it was at for Russell's beers; not so great for a campaign.

We had seventy-five campaign debates or candidate forums that spring. With so many candidates, they were brutal. Every time you came up with a good idea or a good line, someone else would claim it, and the chances were they would go before you when the same question was asked in the next debate. One particularly grim Saturday afternoon, after we had not one but two difficult debates, I stopped by my campaign headquarters to visit with our volunteers, to thank them for all they were doing. They kindly got up and gathered around me. It was obvious they were feeling down. Something else I had learned early in the restaurant business was that if you're the boss, your mood often has a tremendous influence on your team and employees; and the mood of your employees influences the mood of your customers. If I came to work in a funk, pretty soon the waiters and the bartenders were in a funk, too. Which has all the makings of a disaster. Who wants to have a beer and a burger in a brewpub where the vibe is a downer? Bad morale is bad for business. It's critical for a leader to be candid, but equally important that the leader also be optimistic.

Sensing the gloom among my volunteers, I talked about some of the dark days when we were launching the Wynkoop. I talked about the time we couldn't muster the funding to get the Pony Express building; the day I learned the main sewer line needed to be replaced and I thought we were sunk; when I didn't think I was going to be able to make payroll. I shared with them each of these times when it seemed all was lost, that there was just no way, but, I pointed out, we persisted and the skies cleared and we won the day.

I told them about a newspaper article I had carried around for the longest time. At least, I told them how I remembered it and, really, adapted it. It was a tiny story, not even a story, really, but rather a snippet, published in the *Rocky Mountain News* in 1999:

A professor had come to visit a faculty friend at one of the rural community colleges. The theology professor, a woman, agreed to teach a class. Standing before the students, she began by asking them, "What is the opposite of joy?"

"Sadness," one student said.

"And the opposite of depression?"

"Elation," said another.

"And how about the opposite of woe?"

A tall young man raised his hand.

"I believe," he said, "that would be 'giddy-up.'"

All of the volunteers cracked up. Watching their faces, I could see them think through the joke to the message.

Eyes and spirits brightened.

Vonnegut had once told me we have to be careful who we pretend to be, because that is who we become. But in the same breath he advised that if sometimes you can't quite be that person you aspire to be, you can fake it until you make it, that sometimes that works. And it does.

IN EARLY MARCH, talk of weapons of mass destruction, yellowcake uranium, Saddam Hussein, and war with Iraq was in the air. Any moment, almost certainly, the United States would bomb Baghdad. Way, way down at the bottom of the list of questions about what this incipient war would mean was the footnote of a question that made for big news in Denver: what impact would the war have on the mayoral elections? All of the political analysts in town agreed that the front-runner, Zavaras, would benefit. "A war impacts the ability of a dark horse to come from behind using newspaper and television coverage," one local pundit said, summing up the consensus. "The war hurts everybody but Zavaras."

Dark horse. That was me.

Sometime in mid-March, I met with my campaign manager, Paul, and communications director, Lindy, along with David and Michael at Michael's home. Mom's Depression-era training paid dividends again, just as it had when we opened the Wynkoop. Our campaign financial "burn rate" was almost half that of our major competitors. Although we'd raised only $430,000, we had spent only $110,000. We had $320,000 "on hand," almost as much as Zavaras. We had decided to spend $60,000 on a couple of television ads, shot and in the can, and were deciding when to put them on the air. We had spent the majority of the campaign funds on these ads. I had decided we would not "invest" in mailings because as far as I was concerned they were pointless. No one ever reads them. Do you read them? No. No one does. Waste of money. I wanted to use $100,000, which along with the production costs would be half what little cash we had left on hand, to buy airtime. But only two weeks of airtime.

I wanted to put the ads up now. David cautioned that we should wait. The conventional wisdom widely held by sensible political strategists like David was that you don't want to put the ads up too early and not have enough money to keep them up for the entire campaign. As of the moment, we had enough money to keep the ads up for only a couple of weeks at most. David's concern was that if we put the ads on the air too soon and had to pull them down for lack of funding, it would look as if the campaign didn't have the financial support; therefore it would seem like we didn't have the voter support.

I was of the mind that this was like advertising a product, a business; you put up the ads and if people like what they see you earn their "business"—in this case, more donations that would enable us to buy additional airtime. Or maybe the ads wouldn't resonate and we'd simply take them down. Maybe that would be that. No other candidate had yet aired a television ad. I saw an advantage to being first. I'm an entrepreneur; we call it being the "first mover." Like opening the first brewpub restaurant in Colorado, it was a gamble.

Most entrepreneurs are used to being the dark horse.

I decided it was time for the dark horse to giddy-up.

The first of our two thirty-second ads aired on Tuesday, March 18, 2003. Just as the ad hit the air, a snowstorm hit Denver. Over three days, almost three feet of snow brought the city to a standstill. Denver International Airport canceled all flights. Schools were closed. A lot of people were snowed in. A lot of people watched a lot of television. In other words, a lot of people saw our first ad.

Did I mention that the ads themselves were rather unusual?

We called the first one "Suit."

The opening shot is of me in a clothing store in a western shirt trying on a cowboy hat; then I enter and exit a dressing room a number of times trying on different clothes, different suits. All the while a voiceover. My voice. "Everybody says I need better clothes. They want me to look more mayoral. The fact is, I'm not a professional politician." I continue to narrate, pointing out that I was a laid-off geologist and after that I spent fifteen years "making beer, building restaurants, and creating jobs in Denver. For me, economic development isn't a campaign slogan. It's what I do."

Cut to an exterior shot of a vintage clothing store, filmed from across the street. A black Mercedes convertible is parked out front. I exit the store wearing a dark suit. I stop behind the car, standing on the driver's side. It appears I am about to get in the Mercedes. Only I don't. I put on a helmet. Next thing you know, I'm driving from behind that Mercedes on a moped. Me, voiceover again. "And right now, we have to find a way to get the job done for less money." I drive off on the moped, in my suit, but with the tag still on it, attached to the sleeve, blowing in the breeze.

Everyone loved it. People were buzzing about it. The *Rocky Mountain News* interviewed two local advertising executives. They called it "fresh," "unique," an ad that "respects the voters." One of the executives said, "It makes me smile." A spokesperson for the Zavaras campaign said they were waiting to see what happened with the war before deciding what his ads would look like. Mares's campaign said his ads were in preproduction.

The dark horse was out of the barn, on a moped.

Two days later, on March 20, President George W. Bush informed the

American people that the United States military had bombed Baghdad. The war had begun. And it was still snowing. Everyone was home in front of their TVs. President Bush called his military strategy a campaign of "shock and awe." The local press described our television ad campaign as "shux and awe."

Against the somber backdrop of the war, I called a press conference at the Wynkoop and presented to the media my six-part economic strategy. "When we first opened this fifteen years ago," I said, "this was a forgotten part of the city." I didn't need to say that now LoDo was a thriving mix of lofts, condos, restaurants, and nightclubs. What I did say was that the city's stagnant economy needed that same kind of transformation.

I noted that the languishing job market might get worse with the recent bankruptcy of United Airlines. If United went under, it would leave an additional seven thousand residents of the Denver metro region unemployed. "We can't just wait to see if that happens and be in a tizzy."

My plan targeted six areas:

Efficiency. I would create a cabinet-level economic development administrator tasked to improve efficiency in city departments.

Job creation and training. I would push everything from workforce training to programs aimed at helping people start home businesses, and reduce the red tape and promote bike trails and live music that would attract entrepreneurs and young talent.

Retention and development of businesses. I pointed out that 80 percent of the jobs in the city were the result of small businesses, and vowed to make Denver more responsive to the needs of local companies.

Helping disadvantaged neighborhoods. I wanted to offer tax incentives to spur businesses to locate in downtrodden areas.

Recruiting and marketing new businesses. I would host a marketing summit aimed at defining the city's brand and attempt to coordinate the efforts of more than fifty groups that were, in one form or another, trying in uncoordinated ways to sell Denver to tourists and businesses.

Major projects. I would do all I could to make sure Denver was the site of new, high-profile, revenue-generating developments.

In an interview with the local media, Mayor Webb endorsed my budgetary strategies. Whether or not this would help or hinder my success at the polls I wasn't sure, but I was grateful all the same.

Within days of that press conference I got a call from my sister Betsy informing me that Mom had had a major stroke. All of us kids flew home. Betsy arrived first, then Sydney, then me, and finally Tad from Britain. We gathered around her bed inside Bryn Mawr Hospital, where I was born and where we had gathered around Hick's bed days before he died. The day Mom suffered her stroke, she had woken up, sat up in bed, told Bill she had a splitting headache, and then fallen back onto the bed.

When I walked into her hospital room, she had just come out of her coma. She greeted me warmly. She said I needn't have come and asked how my trip was. I said my flight landed ahead of schedule. She looked a little startled, and asked why ever did I fly. We figured her mind must have been in the wrong decade.

All four of us kids had dinner with her and Bill in the hospital room. Mom was wonderfully lucid. My siblings and I and Bill went back to Mom and Bill's home. By the time we returned the next morning Mom had slipped back into her coma. Two of her doctors made a pretty firm pitch for surgery that would send a "tool" from her thigh up into her brain, where they would remove as many of the tiny blood clots as possible. They promised a 65 percent chance that she would be able to get 65 percent of her faculties back. It would mean six to nine months of recuperation and rehab. Did we want the doctors to go ahead with the surgery?

We all knew the answer.

Mom had always been very clear that if she was ever in such a way she didn't want any heroic efforts to attempt to "save" her if there was a chance that being saved meant barely living a life. Her mother, my grandmother, had had a series of strokes over seven or eight years, and Mom and her sisters rotated duty at the nursing home, which of course had minimal attendant support, so they cleaned a lot of bedpans. Mom thought it was thoroughly demeaning for her mother, and she was determined never to be that kind of a burden to all of us. Not that she would have been a burden. If that's what she wanted, it would have been so. But that is not what Mom wanted. And all five of us knew it.

Without discussion, we informed the doctor there would be no surgery.

I FLEW BACK to Denver without the slightest doubt we had made the right decision by honoring Mom's wishes. She had earned the right to live and die on her own terms. I returned to the campaign somber but focused on what would come next, as I knew my mother would expect. I was concerned that perhaps there were too many people in Denver who viewed me as the P. T. Barnum–style entrepreneur on Eighteenth and Wynkoop, just a Mile High Stadium crusader who might know the beer business, but who had no business running for mayor. In my dream scenario, one of the two major newspapers would help establish the legitimacy of my candidacy by endorsing me. A few days after I returned from Philly, the *Rocky Mountain News* invited me in for a long, grueling interview by their editorial board.

A few days later, on April 2, we got a call from the *Rocky*. Editor and publisher John Temple and editorial page editor Vincent Carroll were thinking about having the paper endorse me. We met at a restaurant in LoDo. With me I had another seasoned political adviser, Mike Dino, who chaired my campaign committee. Temple and Carroll said they liked my ideas; they believed I was the best candidate, but they were concerned that I didn't have a chance to win and that their endorsement would be wasted.

Dino made the case that I was the populist favorite; that I had the momentum; that I represented a movement rather than the perceived machine politics common to most big cities. He said that if the paper endorsed me they would be the tipping point and could take credit for being ahead of the pack while making what they, and so many others, already believed was the right, responsible choice. Dino brilliantly and subtly dared the newspapermen to follow their convictions and make the difference. The implied nudge was: isn't that what a newspaper endorsement is supposed to do?

As we wrapped up the conversation, Dino encouraged Temple and Carroll on their walk back to the *Rocky* offices to ask people on the street and in their own newsroom what they thought about me. Dino bet them that everyone would be talking about me in no small part because the second of the two ads had begun airing on television that morning. Dino was right.

We dubbed this one "Change."

This ad opens with a close-up of a change belt on my hip. Camera pulls back to show me on a downtown sidewalk, in that same suit from the last ad, walking along parking meters, clicking on the change belt, popping out coins and handing them to people. A voiceover, me: "I'm John Hickenlooper and I'm out to make change in Denver. These parking meters are just one example of what I call the fundamental nonsense of government." I explain that the city has raised parking-meter rates while businesses are suffering and city tax revenues are in decline. There's a bit of a showdown between me and a city parking attendant. Just before he gets to writing a ticket, I drop a quarter in the meter. Voiceover: "I know

I can make positive changes for Denver's economy and solve our water and traffic problems. Now that's the kind of change people can get excited about."

The next day, the day after our meeting, the *Rocky* published a story about local ad executives raving about the "Change" ad, calling it "outstanding." One of the two executives, Ed Kleban, said the public usually dreads political ads, but he expected voters to enjoy and even look forward to mine. He said my ad strategy could signal a change in the tone of the future of political ads in Colorado.

This was especially gratifying to read. And I daresay, win or lose, changing the tenor of political campaigns was indeed one of my goals. Attack ads are almost unique to politics. And they are as effective as they are destructive. You rarely see it in private industry. Coke doesn't do venomous attack ads against Pepsi because then Pepsi would attack Coke, and then Coke would counterattack. In the end, they would drive down not only their sales, but the sales of all soft drinks. It would diminish the entire product category of soft drinks. If you ask me, candidates who release attack ads in an attempt to elevate themselves diminish and denigrate the product category of democracy. This is our great experiment, the world's great experiment. Our democracy and our voters deserve better.

In that very same issue of the *Rocky* with the ad executives' kind reviews of our second commercial, the paper also published its endorsement of me for mayor. It has to be one of the most glowing endorsements in the history of newspaper political endorsements. Just so you see that I'm not exaggerating, I'll share a bit of it.

Under the headline "HICKENLOOPER FOR DENVER MAYOR—THE BEST CANDIDATE FOR UNCERTAIN ECONOMIC TIMES," there were lines like: *"Hickenlooper ... has actually done what all of the other candidates say they want to do as a top priority: create an impressive number of private sector jobs. . . . But Hickenlooper's boot strap success story is hardly the only reason we are endorsing his candidacy for mayor. Some business leaders make the transition to the political world with ease, while others don't have a clue regarding public policy. Hickenlooper, however, is no John-come-lately to civic affairs. Even as he was creating a business from scratch, he was plunging into the worlds of nonprofits and neighborhood affairs, serving on boards as varied and as staid as the Denver Art Museum and Convention and Visitors Bureau, to the edgy Chinook Fund, which funnels grants to maverick activists. . . . He wouldn't come into office with any fixed idea that 'this is just the way things are done.' Listening to Hickenlooper talk about his upstart businesses, you realize that he is always challenging and rethinking the way he operates. Otherwise, he wouldn't survive. He brings the same restless curiosity to his discussions of city affairs . . . the first candidate to talk seriously about the need for the city to get a grip on its soaring personnel costs. . . ."*

It was one of the most bittersweet days of my life. Just an hour after we opened the newspaper, I got a call my from stepdad, Bill. Mom had died.

I wasn't immediately overwhelmed by grief. I didn't acutely feel Mom's absence during her funeral services. By her example, she had taught me to keep working despite any intensity of grief.

The loss hit me on June 3, when I won the mayoral election.

A few months earlier, Mom had talked with a local reporter who was writing a profile of me. Referring to me, she said, "He was never the best. He was always the 'player who improved the most' or the one who tried the hardest." I wish Mom could have witnessed the election. Maybe she would have felt that all of the time and energy and love she had invested in her prodigal son were worth it. Maybe she would have told me she was proud. Maybe she would have told me that Hick would have been proud. In truth, saying anything of that sort would have been out of character for her. I imagine she would have said something along the lines of, "Congratulations. Good job. You've got a lot to do. Now get to work."

AS THE *Rocky Mountain News* reported it, Denver was now "Hick"-Town. I was elected Denver's forty-third mayor in a "historic" and "stunning landslide." I received 65 percent of the vote, with Mares getting 35 percent. The early front-runner, Zavaras, had not survived the first round. My margin of victory surpassed what had been the precedent-setting blowout election of 1991, when then–city auditor Webb was first elected mayor with 58 percent of the vote.

Such a convincing victory, this dark horse knew, amounted to a mandate from the voters to deliver on the plans and promises I'd made during the campaign. Just in case I had missed this fact, the day after my win, the *Rocky*, which had given me that campaign-altering endorsement, published an editorial headlined, "THE HONORABLE MAYOR LANDSLIDE—HICKENLOOPER HAS A MANDATE, NOW HE MUST USE IT."

In the column, editorial page editor Vince Carroll highlighted that voters expected me to overhaul the city's personnel system. He also pointed out what to me was an obvious reality: in order to achieve this reform and implement the rest of my vision, I must build a coalition of allies, beginning with city council. "But then," Vince wrote, "Hickenlooper did insist throughout the campaign that he is a good listener, negotiator and coalition builder, and now he has a chance to prove it."

Years later, on February 27, 2009, the *Rocky Mountain News* would fold after a 150-year run, leaving Denver a one-paper town, with *The Denver Post*. That was a sad day for our city. Many journalists lost their jobs and Denver lost many journalists whose reporting had kept the citizens informed and had gone a long way to holding people in positions of power accountable. The competition between the two papers had motivated journalists on both teams to work harder.

These days, as the journalism industry struggles to find a viable business model and more and more newspapers fold, cities throughout the nation lose more and more journalistic watchdogs, veteran reporters who have developed both a historical knowledge and deep affection for their communities. This is a troubling trend for our democracy. The Fourth Estate, as I came to more fully appreciate during my own election, and in the years after, is essential to maintaining an informed society, to helping voters make sense of what really matters; ultimately journalism plays a critical role in effecting change.

In writing that column, I think, Vince knew he was doing me a favor; really, he was doing the city a favor. The people of Denver had elected not only me, but also ten new city council members and a new city auditor, Dennis Gallagher. While Vince wrote that editorial directed at me, as if he were preemptively holding my feet to the fire I had ignited, I think he was addressing everyone in the city—the new city council members, and business and civic leaders.

He was making sure they understood that the pronounced margin of victory was a referendum on the ideas I had presented in the campaign. I thought Vince was saying, in this moment of a fresh start, that everyone was obliged to work together to help this Hickenlooper guy because the voters were expecting it. There's the old reporter axiom that goes, "We don't make the news, we just report it." The way I see it, some of the most responsible journalists, like Vince, sometimes nudge the news by how they report it.

Vince, of course, was correct in noting that I would need to build a coalition of allies. During my "due diligence" period, and even more on the campaign trail, I had learned that there was tension between Denver and the mayors in the surrounding cities and suburbs. Frankly, many of those mayors whom I talked with before and during the campaign felt ignored and disrespected by the Webb administration. Many of them told me they felt as if the Webb administration had thought only of what was in the best interest of Denver, and often at their expense.

Just as when we launched the Wynkoop and I believed that the merchants of Lower Downtown needed to work together to get people off of their couches, out of their homes, and into LoDo so that we all might benefit, I believed that Denver and the surrounding counties needed to work together. It did not serve any of us well if Denver was too Denver-centric; we had an alignment of self-interests. There was no margin in making enemies among ourselves.

With issues like water, public transportation, and the economy, I believed collaborating—regionalism—was the key to all of our communities' surviving and thriving. I wanted to do all I could to bring together constituencies that historically had been at odds, who often shouted at one another across the city and rarely came together and talked like neighbors.

During the six-week transition before the inauguration, we enlisted 450 volunteers to serve on committees that analyzed every agency and every function of the city. We emphasized this "new regionalism" at every meeting. On the Saturday night before my Tuesday inaugural, I hosted a reception at my spacious penthouse loft (part of my last private-sector project) for all of the city council members and mayors and county commissioners in the entire Denver metropolitan area. For the vast majority of them it was the first time they had ever been invited to a City of Denver political event. That night the crowd seemed almost frenzied, and I interrupted to give a three-minute speech. I said that the days of Denver's making decisions solely for its own benefit were over. Denver could never be a great city without great suburbs, and I pledged that if we couldn't find solutions that helped our suburbs as much as Denver, well then, we'd just work on another problem. There was a pause, and then uproarious shouting and stamping. There was an appetite for working together all right, it just hadn't been fed in a while.

I held a separate event at my loft where I hosted leaders from the environmental community and real estate developers. As a real estate developer myself and as an environmentalist, I felt it was important to bring these typically opposed camps together to hopefully begin to talk and see that their goals were not mutually exclusive.

One last thing about that postelection editorial in the *Rocky*. Vince also correctly noted that because of my lack of political experience, it was especially critical for me to surround myself with top-notch, experienced professionals. However, the first person I hired, like me, also had zero political experience: I appointed Michael Bennet my chief of staff.

Funny story: Before offering Michael the job, I ran into Phil Anschutz at the gym and gingerly floated the possibility that Michael might join my administration. Phil said, "Michael. Bennet. Will. Never. Work. For. The. City. Of. Denver." I didn't have the heart to tell Phil that Michael had already come to me and discussed becoming chief of staff.

When Michael gave Phil the news he was supportive, albeit also understandably a bit shocked. Michael walked away from Anschutz only a couple of years shy of having his last shares vest in the Regal deal; he stood to make millions of dollars' worth of publicly traded shares. But Michael already had made a few million dollars, more money than he ever imagined. He was never going to have any problems paying his bills, and he had been vigilant for the right opportunity to make the transition into public service.

In Michael's family there was a strong tradition of choosing careers rooted in public service. His father, Doug, worked in numerous congressional offices and federal jobs before becoming president of NPR and then president of Wesleyan University. Michael's mother, Susanne, escaped the Holocaust in Poland, emigrated with her parents, and later studied art history. Michael's younger brother, James, worked as a journalist, covering the Middle East for *The New York Times*, and went on to become copresident and editor in chief of *The Atlantic*.

Thanks in no small part to Michael's political instincts and raw intelligence, I had been elected, and my administration had the overwhelming support of the people; Michael felt this was his time to enter the public sector and make the most impact.

Before he accepted the position, Michael and I had a candid discussion over at the Wynkoop. In his humble, soft-spoken, yet assertive manner, Michael said he'd done some due diligence on me and heard that I sometimes second-guessed the decisions of the people who worked with me, perhaps especially the senior-most people. Michael said he wanted to be part of a team that worked together. He said he would never surprise me and would keep me informed at all times, and in return he would expect my trust and support. If we had differences, he expected that we would discuss them privately.

What Michael had heard was not an unfair rap against me. I can be demanding, exacting, and hard on my staff. The entrepreneur in me dreams big, has high expectations. As you now have seen, I often, almost always, have multiple plans in play. Sometimes I focus too much on meeting the bottom line, achieving the goals, and I fall into thinking I would have or could have done something better.

This is a character flaw. I know this about myself. However, I would like to think that I am fair and reasonable. I try to surround myself with at least one or two people who I know will rightly pull me aside and tell me when I'm behaving like an ass. When I have indeed been a jerk, I have acknowledged it. I say I'm sorry, and I mean it, and do my very best to make amends and do better. I had my share of bad bosses at Buckhorn. I don't want to be that guy.

I shared some of this with Michael. I assured him that I respected and wanted the best possible talent and I recognized the need to delegate. In the business world, I learned how important it was to have the right people in the right jobs at the right time, and then let them do their jobs. If my administration was to achieve success and effect change for the city of Denver, we needed top talent; we needed a strong team—emphasis on *team*.

I was glad Michael raised the issue—typically forthright and smart of him. I told him he would indeed have my trust and support. If he upheld his end of the bargain—no surprises, kept me informed—we would never have a problem. I'll say right here, before we get into what Michael and I and our team accomplished together: he and I never, not once, broke that agreement we made that day at the Wynkoop. During my first few years as mayor, before many of our biggest decisions, Michael and I would stand in my office at the City and County Building and play catch with a hardball and two old gloves I kept around. All the while, he'd throw his ideas my way and I'd throw mine back.

Immediately after Michael shook hands and he signed on, we began discussing our front-burner issues: reforming the personnel system, doing all we could to foster economic growth in the city, and resolving the United Airlines bankruptcy situation, which was now intertwined with issues involving Denver International Airport and Frontier Airlines. Of course, Michael and I would have to hire the rest of our staff. We hired Happy Haynes to be our liaison to city council. That election, she was term-limited out of council. With twelve years of council experience and her prior experience as an aide to Mayor Peña, she brought a wealth of institutional knowledge and political savvy. We hired the amazing Lindy Eichenbaum Lent as our director of communications.

But before we could get to our existing pressing issues, another was added to the mix.

ON JULY 5, 2003, Denver police officer James Turney responded to a police radio dispatch report of a teenage boy attempting to stab his mother. Officer Turney was the first cop to arrive at the home in northeast Denver. He ran to the front door with his pistol drawn. He ushered out the teen's mother and sister and cleared the house of visitors. He then turned his gun on the teen, fifteen-year-old Paul Childs.

Childs stood less than twelve feet from the officer. Childs was crying and clenching a kitchen knife under his chin as if he were carrying a candle. Several times Officer Turney ordered him to drop the blade. Childs took a step, and Officer Turney shot the boy four times.

Paul Childs was developmentally disabled, enrolled in special education classes and on prescribed medications. As the details of the case emerged in the news, the public was outraged. There was already a populist sentiment throughout the city that the Denver Police Department had been operating unchecked. A "crisis in confidence" was a phrase that often appeared in the media.

A couple of recent high-profile controversies had fueled this widespread frustration. One concerned "spy files." For years, the DPD had been monitoring protests throughout the city, keeping "intelligence files" on citizens the department deemed "criminal extremists." Many community leaders were incensed that the department had been monitoring peaceful citizens and collecting these dossiers.

There was also the fatal shooting of Ismael Mena. In September 1999, Denver police launched a middle-of-the-night, no-knock raid—meaning a bust-down-the-door raid—on a home in which SWAT officers killed Ismael Mena, a forty-five-year-old father of nine. The warrant was based on a tip from an informant who claimed there were drug dealers in the house. Police maintained that they shot Mena after he fired a gun at them. There was evidence to suggest that Mena may have fired a gun multiple times at police, but it was circumstantial, and there was absolutely no evidence of drugs or drug dealing found in Mena's house. An autopsy revealed no drugs in his body.

Childs had been killed only four weeks after I was elected, and three weeks before I was even officially sworn in as mayor, on July 21, 2003. I attended Paul Childs's funeral, alongside Mayor Webb and his wife, Wilma. I chose not to politicize the tragedy or to interfere with the district attorney's investigation into the shooting, but closely monitored the matter, anticipating that we might have to deal with the issues around the fatal shooting and fully aware that we would need to address issues swirling about the Denver Police Department.

Meanwhile we moved quickly to address the budget. Within days of my being sworn in, we presented a plan to overhaul the city's personnel system. Among the changes we outlined, we wanted to strip the Career Service Authority—that board of four mayoral appointees—of its power to set salaries. Instead we wanted that responsibility to rest with city council. Our plan, which we dubbed "SmartGovt Inc.," would require amending the city's charter, which required a vote of the people at the polls that November.

We slashed another $14 million from the budget. Adhering to our promise, we started with me and my staff. I took a pay cut, cut the size of my mayoral staff, and trimmed the salaries for remaining positions by 25 percent. The savings of more than $1.6 million were a drop in the bucket in the overall budget, but, as I said, it was important for us to walk the walk before we asked our city employees to do the same.With Michael as my administration's chief negotiator, we set about getting concessions from the city's safety workers—the firefighters, sheriff department, and police. Michael and I spent hours playing catch in my office discussing strategy and he spent hours at the negotiating table. We were successful with two of the three. Representatives of the firefighters' union came to the table and began the discussions saying to Michael, "We know the city has severe budget problems and we want to be part of the solution." The firefighters showed selflessness beyond selflessness by agreeing to concessions that saved the city millions of dollars. Our sheriff's deputies did the same. The meeting with representatives of the city's police personnel was short and anything but sweet. They said they would not make any concessions and got up from the table. With the concessions and cuts we were able to make we presented the leanest budget a Denver city council had seen in five years, $712 million.

One day while we were working through the contracts and personnel issues and still unpacking our offices, I mentioned to Michael that while I was in D.C. for the U.S. Conference of Mayors I would make a trip to Maryland to try to secure the collection of Clyfford Still. Michael looked at me as if I were nuts. Surrounded by binders and spreadsheets and contracts, he looked up and asked me what in the world I was talking about. I explained that Still was one of the first great abstract expressionist painters, regarded as one of the seminal artists of the late 1930s and early 1940s, along with Jackson Pollock, Mark Rothko, and others.

Unlike the works of Pollock and Rothko, however, Still's work was not on display—anywhere. In protest of just about everything, he'd kept his work to himself. He died in 1980. His widow, Patricia, lived at the rural Maryland farmhouse where Still's collection of works, rumored to be north of two thousand paintings, was stored. Still's will stated: "I give and bequeath all the remaining works of art executed by me in my collection to an American city that will agree to build or assign and maintain permanent quarters exclusively for these works of art and assure their physical survival with the explicit requirement that none of these works of art will be sold, given, or exchanged but are to be retained in the place described above exclusively assigned to them in perpetuity for exhibition and study." Over the years several cities had tried and failed to acquire the collection: Atlanta; Baltimore; Santa Ana, California; Chicago; New York; Worcester, Massachusetts.

Michael said, "And?"

And, I said, I wanted to try to get it for Denver.

Michael said, "You've got to be kidding me. We've got all of this work to do and you're going to go off to Maryland and try to get some artist's widow to give his paintings to Denver? We don't have enough money in the budget as it is. If you do get the artwork, where exactly are you planning on putting it all? We can't build a museum."

I told Michael not to worry about it. We had to try. Lew Sharp, the head of the Denver Art Museum, thought we had a shot and that Chris Hunt might lead the fund-raising. It was worth an hour-and-a-half drive out of the way. This was an opportunity to perhaps land one of the major developments for Denver that I had talked about in the campaign. Art and culture were essential to the city. Off I went. I had the ideas of author Richard Florida in my head. Richard had just written *The Rise of the Creative Class* and I agreed with his findings that the Creative Class, which includes young coders and entrepreneurs, along with artists and writers and musicians, would be attracted to cities that embraced music and culture. And when these young hipster innovators came to town, they brought new ideas and the possibility of new companies and new jobs with them.

On the way, I rehearsed my sales pitch: Still was a Westerner; he grew up in rugged Grandin, North Dakota. Denver was a city he would have liked. It was rugged, too, still a work in progress. Denver is a city that is more about the future than the past. Denver wanted to be a new kind of city. Denver was no New York, which in Still's view was pretentious and phony, full of itself and full of bad art, preoccupied with labels and pedigree. In Denver, in Colorado, we don't care about pedigree; we celebrate the risk takers, the courageous, those who follow their heart and try new things, who innovate. Still was all of that. In his work, that's evident. Denver was a place that would uniquely appreciate the hard work and creativity that infused his masterpieces.

I arrived at Patricia's farmhouse with her nephew, Curt Freed, a Denver neurosurgeon, and a very small group from the city. Inside, we saw hundreds, maybe thousands, of paintings rolled up in the corners of rooms, lying against the walls. I made my pitch. Patricia stunned us all; on the spot she said, "That all makes a lot of sense."

Meanwhile, out at DIA we also resolved a potentially devastating dispute between United Airlines, Frontier Airlines, and the airport. The disagreement was over which airlines got which gates—location, location, location—at what price and for how long. We wanted to do all we could to assist United, which was in bankruptcy, to recover and sustain those jobs. Yet we did not want to lose Frontier's business and jobs.

If it didn't get what it wanted, Frontier threatened to open a hub elsewhere. Lawyers for both airlines, doing what they needed to do to advocate for their clients, presented threats here and there and more or less tried to intimidate us. But we didn't budge. I gave Michael and John Huggins, who had joined the cabinet to consolidate all of the economic development function into one agency, only two directives: preserve the interests of DIA and create a climate where United, Frontier, and the other airlines could grow and compete fairly. When the airlines competed, prices dropped and the whole region benefited. Michael and John accomplished all of that, and ultimately preserved ten thousand metro-area jobs.

In October, Denver district attorney Bill Ritter announced that his office would not criminally prosecute Officer James Turney for the Childs shooting. Many citizens were outraged, especially in the minority communities. I met with representatives of the Greater Metro Denver Ministerial Alliance. Some members of their leadership wanted Turney fired, and told me they feared that "the city and in particular the black community could go the wrong way—violence." It would be an understatement to say that this was the most troubling matter I had yet faced. I said I felt we had a moral obligation to do everything we could to make sure this did not happen again.

The day before I was sworn in, Mayor Webb invited me to his office. He offered me his candid appraisals of every city agency. He said if he had one regret, it was that he hadn't pushed harder for protocols to make the police department more accountable and to reform police procedures.

Working with our manager of safety, Al Lacabe, and our city attorney, Cole Finegan, we pledged that every officer would be trained in "crisis intervention," and that nonlethal Tasers, as well as nonlethal beanbag shotguns, would be issued to all patrols. We announced that we were working toward establishing an independent police monitor who would work with a civilian oversight board and make the investigations transparent to the public.

However, we were still within my first hundred days in office, and the way I saw it, we were already in the midst of some rather seismic changes. That November 2003 voters passed our ballot measure for personnel reform and our proposals for a bond measure and a tax increase, both to help improve Denver Public Schools. I campaigned hard for all those ballot initiatives. I figured if I was going to use my honeymoon-period political capital, these were the issues. We would get to the police reform; I needed to wait for the right time. Advocating for too much change all at once might undermine our progress. Intellectually, I knew this.

But I couldn't help myself. There was too much at stake.

I just felt it was time to giddy-up.

In January 2004, I visited the Cole Middle School, which has a high-poverty student population. I was there for a test-score rally, to try to provide some inspiration and enthusiasm, to let these kids know we cared. From the time I was elected, I had been talking to business leaders about forming a privately funded scholarship fund that would provide college tuition for any Denver student who worked hard and made the grades.

The idea was rooted in my belief that lack of money should not prevent a motivated, hardworking student from attending college and benefiting from all the opportunities that go along with it. I believed, and believe, that if every kid, no matter how poor his or her family, believes he or she really can go to college, kids will work harder in the classroom, which would enable teachers to be more effective; the culture in classrooms and schools throughout the city would improve. In truth, the day I visited Cole the plan was far from fully baked, but I was so moved by what I saw in the kids that day, I told them that if they graduated from high school and earned the grades, "I guarantee we will find the resources and you will go to college. If you go to college you can do anything you want." My communications director, Lindy, just about had a heart attack. What can I say? I believed we were far enough along to put it out there and get it done. And we did. A year later, thanks in large part to the extraordinary generosity and efforts of Tim Marquez, a successful oil and gas businessman, and his wife, Bernie, the Denver Scholarship Foundation was born.

A MONTH LATER, in February, at a University of Denver diverse housing conference, I rolled out our plan to cut bureaucratic red tape in order to make it easier for developers to build affordable housing. In 2001, I had codeveloped thirty-two lofts on Osage Street in the Lincoln Park neighborhood. The city's approval process took about eighteen months, almost twice the ten months expected.

In announcing our plan to streamline the process, I said, "Sometimes city workers in the bowels of bureaucracy don't recognize that if they keep asking for more information and postponing meetings and getting cross-wired with other people in other city departments, it costs builders and developers a lot of money." The policy we implemented was relatively simple: adopt the International Building Code, which would cut costs by 1 to 2 percent because developers wouldn't have to deal with quirks specific to a Denver code.

In April 2004, after the Denver Police Department had completed its own civil (internal) affairs investigation of the Paul Childs shooting, I consulted with our manager of safety, Al Lacabe, who was a former police officer and a lawyer. It was clear that Officer Turney had violated the police department's "efficiency and safety" rules when he shot Childs. We suspended him from the force for ten months without pay. When he returned to work, he would not return to the street; he would be assigned to administrative duties.

The next day, hundreds of police officers and their families protested outside my office at the City and County Building, chanting "Chicken-looper." While I understood the officers' desire to rally to support their brother in blue, the facts were the facts. It wasn't as if I wanted to be perceived as taking on the Denver Police Department my first year on the job, and while there might not have been a political margin in making enemies of those officers, I believe it was the right thing to do. Shortly thereafter, we settled a civil suit filed by Paul Childs's mother for $1.3 million.

That summer, we made all five decades' worth of the police department's "spy files" public and turned them over to the city's central library, and we formally proposed establishing the Office of the Independent Monitor to oversee police investigations. That, too, like the proposed civilian oversight board to replace the city's woefully ineffective Public

Safety Review Commission, required amending the city's charter, which meant another ballot referendum on my administration's policy.

That summer, we also began to campaign to pass FasTracks, the most ambitious transit initiative in U.S. history, 119 miles of light rail and commuter train lines, connecting Denver County and seven surrounding counties. The project would take twelve years to complete at a budget of $4.7 billion. Our hope was that it would be financed through a .4 percent increase in a regional transportation sales tax shared by all of metro Denver. I believed a modern public transit system connecting Denver with its suburbs and eventually to Denver International Airport was necessary for Denver to become a world-class city, and, more than that, flat-out necessary in any case. Demographers projected that over the next twenty years, the Denver metro area would grow by nearly 1 million people. We were already struggling with traffic. We needed to do something to provide alternatives to alleviate traffic congestion and help all of us to grow.

A handful of mayors from surrounding towns and cities initially refused to support the initiative. They didn't see why their constituents ought to fund FasTracks when they had no rail stations in their communities. That concern was rather easily addressed with facts. We had studies on commuter patterns throughout the region. The majority of their commuters drove to and from jobs in the Denver metro area and spent twenty to fifty minutes driving each way.

Even if these commuters never took a train, FasTracks would take enough drivers off the road to save their constituents who did drive an average of about twenty-four minutes round-trip. I said, "FasTrack will provide incentive for drivers to get out of the way of your citizen-drivers to make their commute more pleasant and quicker." In the end, we achieved the unthinkable: we got all thirty-four metro mayors, two thirds of them Republicans, to unanimously support FasTracks.

This was yet another initiative, along with the police reform measures, that would go to the voters to decide on the ballot in November. That July, we had completed one year in office. After all that we had already been through, polls showed my approval rating in Denver was 83 percent. That same poll showed my approval rating in the largely Republican suburbs was at 67 percent.

As the *Rocky* reported on the polling numbers, they wrote, "He has tamed an out-of-whack budget without slashing jobs, remolded Denver's economic efforts, cut back on the size of his top administration, campaigned for two school bond issues [totaling $200 million] approved by voters, forged new lease agreements for Frontier and United Airlines, and dealt with the incredibly divisive fallout from a police shooting that left a teenager dead."

The paper mentioned some of the other things we'd accomplished, like beginning to overhaul the personnel system, teaming with the Denver Metro Convention & Visitors Bureau to help lure three major new conventions to the city, with a total economic impact estimated to be worth $43 million, and cutting the red tape for developers in the hopes of prompting construction of more affordable housing.

"We have a person that's been on a very long honeymoon," the paper quoted Floyd Ciruli, who had conducted the survey for a group that was behind a campaign for a new scientific and cultural tax. "Denver mayors are almost never beloved by the suburbs. Historically they've always felt that Denver took care of Denver first."

Come November 2004, with these next two ballot initiatives regarding police reform and the FasTracks tax, I would be investing the capital of that support. I actively campaigned for both, and served as the main pitchman for FasTracks. One morning, I was talking to *The Denver Post* about the initiative and the reporter said she had heard that I was thinking of changing the holiday lights display at the City and County Building.

It was true, we were. For decades, the message in lights atop the building had been "MERRY CHRISTMAS." We had decided we would change it to the nonsectarian "HAPPY HOLIDAYS." The sign was being replaced anyway because it was so old and I had been assured this new message wouldn't cost any more. But when the reporter asked me about it, I had not yet discussed it with Michael and Lindy. Frankly, I didn't think it was a big deal. I thought it was more inclusive. I told the reporter that yes, it was true we were going to make the change.

Michael and Lindy were seated nearby. They both overheard the discussion and their heads popped up and their eyes opened wide. When I hung up the phone, they both insisted this was going to be trouble. I told them they were both being ridiculous.

The next morning, it was all over the front page, and the scandal of talk radio. Lindy came into my office and told me that on her drive in she had been listening to Peter Boyles, the host of what was then a widely popular local conservative talk radio program, and he was eviscerating me over the decision, and so, too, were his listeners who called in. I tuned in for a few minutes. Indeed, Lindy was correct. I asked her to call in to the studio and see if Peter would talk to me. She asked me why and I told her I was going to call him and apologize for the decision and say that I was going to revert back to "Merry Christmas." She advised me to think twice, that if I changed it back now I would seem weak. In the end, we agreed to change it back.

Within minutes I was live on the air with Boyles. He asked if I was going to remove the "Merry Christmas" sign, and I said yes, but after listening to his show and the voices of so many angry citizens, I was changing it back. He was stunned. He asked if I was serious. Yes, I said, I am serious, and I went on to apologize and explain my initial reasoning, that I thought it was more inclusive. Lindy slipped me a note with a witty sentiment. I said, "Just because there's two *o*'s in Hickenlooper doesn't make me a Scrooge." Boyles commended me for the decision to restore Denver's "Merry Christmas," and when I hung up the phone he and his listeners spoke favorably of my decision. How refreshing, Boyles said, to hear an elected official own up to a boneheaded mistake and not try to defend it. With the best of intentions, I had made a mistake. I admitted it and corrected it. To me, it was as simple as that.

Come November, both the police reform and FasTracks initiatives passed with overwhelming support. My approval ratings skyrocketed to 92 percent. The following April, *Time* magazine picked me as one of "The 5 Best Big-City Mayors," citing the FasTracks effort and the spirit of regionalism that supported it. I figured it was a slow year for mayors. *Esquire* put me in a fashion spread of politicos, dubbing me one of the "best-dressed mayors in America," which, as anyone who has ever laid eyes on my everyday wardrobe, or for that matter even my best-day wardrobe, would have told you, was rather comical.

The honeymoon continued through 2005 and into 2006. There was a grassroots movement, complete with a Web site created by an anonymous group, that tried to coax me into running for governor in 2006. I gave it some thought but decided against it. Heck, I'd only been mayor for two and a half years. I thought the best way to make use of my popularity, given what in political-speak had become my brand, was to advocate for more change, continue to balance and eventually grow the budget, and when necessary campaign for ballot initiatives so that we could invest in desperately needed improvements in education, transportation, and health care. Between 2005 and 2007, we did all of that. In 2007, with 87 percent of the vote, I easily won a second term.

The biggest issue of my second term was the dominant historical event of 2008, the presidential election. I spent much of 2007 and 2008 leading the effort to persuade the Democratic National Committee and its Convention Selection Committee to choose Denver for the Democratic National Convention, and when they did, I spent an extraordinary amount of time engaged in ensuring that the city was prepared and our residents would be able to enjoy the events if they chose to, without being unduly inconvenienced.

It was remarkable to watch a freshman United States senator from Illinois, Barack Obama, stand in the middle of Denver's Mile High Stadium—still Mile High Stadium—and accept our party's nomination for president of the United States. A freshman United States senator. A guy who before that had been a community organizer in Chicago. The first African-American major-party nominee for president.

Our nation was still mired in the wars in Iraq and Afghanistan; Osama bin Laden was at large. Our country was in the midst of the worst economic downturn since the Great Depression. This time, we were calling it the Great Recession. Wall Street, the banking industry, and the automotive industry were all in need of bailouts.

"Change happens," Senator Obama said on that night of August 28, 2008. "Change happens because the American people demand it, because they rise up and insist on new ideas and new leadership, a new politics for a new time.

"America, this is one of those moments.

"I believe that, as hard as it will be, the change we need is coming, because I've seen it, because I've lived it."

His was perhaps one of the most American of American stories.

Change.

Like many Americans, I felt inspired. I confess, I allowed myself to feel proud.

I could not help but think of the lame speech I had given five years earlier, on the Millennium Bridge. I had said then, "I believe that with the right leadership and the right vision, we can truly become a city that is Mile High, not just in name, but in achievement." Watching this history unfold in Denver, I felt the city had reached a moment that truly was worthy of being considered a Mile High achievement.

Change.

With the FasTracks project, the budget, the local economy, and all else in the city on track, I was finally settling into the job.

In early January 2010, Democratic governor Bill Ritter stunned the Colorado political world when he announced he wouldn't be running for a second term.

Change.

I realized that the change for me might be running for governor.

Twelve

CALLED

I t was a given that Colorado's Democratic governor, Bill Ritter, would run for a second term. Until it wasn't. I was stunned when he called to give me the news on January 5, 2010, that he would not seek reelection. The all-consuming nature of the job had taken too much of a toll on him and his family, Bill told me. He said that if I thought I was prepared to weather the storms of the governor's office—and Bill said he would be happy to talk with me about just how stormy it could get—I ought to run to succeed him. I thanked Bill for the heads-up, and for the vote of confidence, and said I just might take him up on his offer to talk about what it was like to be in the governor's seat.

Five years earlier had not been the right time for me to campaign for governor; now my instinct was that the time was right. The day I got the call from Bill, I asked a few members of my senior staff to join me at my house that evening to discuss the news and to brainstorm ideas for a campaign. The first call I made was to my chief of staff, Roxane White.

I was fortunate to have the chiefs of staff I did. After Michael Bennet and Cole Finegan, there was Kelly Brough, who served in that role from

2006 until 2009. In the winter of 2007, when a snowstorm hit Denver and we didn't move swiftly enough to clear away the snow and ice, Kelly made the decision to welcome the media into the process, to let the press and thereby the public see that we were doing all we could. That transparency went a long way to keep our administration from being buried in a storm of bad press. Her organizational skills and grace under pressure were instrumental to all of the city's preparations for the 2008 Democratic National Convention.

All of my chiefs of staff were truly gifted leaders and managers. Each was integral to our administration's success, and all of them went on to impressive next acts. Kelly became the head of the Denver Metro Chamber of Commerce. The international law firm of Hogan Lovells hired Cole as a managing partner. And Michael, holy cow. After serving four years as DPS superintendent, during which time he dramatically improved Denver's public schools, he was appointed a United States senator.

As impressive as those chiefs of staff were, just between us, Rox was the best of them all. She accepted the job after Kelly departed to lead the Denver Chamber. One of the many honors Roxane received over the years was a plaque with the Shakespeare quote, "And though she be but little, she is fierce." That's about right. In heels, Rox might be an inch or two taller than five feet, but I don't think I have ever met a more compassionate and selfless person, or a more tireless worker, than Roxane White.

At the city, Rox made sure we never forgot our constituents, who, as she put it, were "the last and the least." She was one of my first hires as mayor. Although she was relatively inexperienced, I picked Roxane to lead our Department of Human Services, partly because during our interview we discovered we shared a commitment to address Denver's chronically homeless population. I had gotten to know several chronically homeless individuals while first building the Wynkoop. These were mostly men who had been sleeping and living in the abandoned alleys and doorways of LoDo. We sometimes hired them to paint walls and sand floors, and, unsuccessfully, tried to help them get their lives together. After several good weeks, they would disappear for a week or two, bingeing on whatever, and then return more broken that they'd started. Very frustrating, but we didn't understand the issue. Roxane did.

Soon after Rox arrived, she brought in Philip Mangano for a meeting. Philip was a Boston crusader who had persuaded President Bush to appoint him the executive director of a new creation, the U.S. Interagency Council on Homelessness. This new position would control all the different federal sources of funding being used against homelessness, whether from HUD or the Veterans Administration or Health and Human Services or wherever, and for the first time integrate them and award funding to cities based on results-based outcomes. What a concept! We were one of the first cities to commit to Philip's vision, a ten-year plan to end homelessness. We called it "Denver's Road Home."

Part of Roxane's genius was to design an eighteen-month process for creating the plan that involved literally all the civic leadership in the region. We aligned the self-interests of restaurant, hotel, and other downtown retail operators, long frustrated by panhandlers hurting their businesses, alongside the ethically driven faith-based and social welfare organizations. Even our professional sports teams, which all played their games downtown, chipped in more than $1 million. Unheard of.

Part of this alignment of self-interests was possible because Rox, as always, made sure there were clear goals, deliverables, and metrics to track our success. Sadly, the city had too often treated the indigent like criminals; our homeless citizens were arrested and imprisoned. That is incredibly expensive and solves nothing. The only way to come close to meaningful and enduring remedies was to provide our city's homeless not only with shelter, but also with wraparound services such as medical attention, counseling, and, where necessary, medications for addiction, and always job training. These individuals were almost always emotionally fragile, and desperately needed the structure and social support of a consistent workplace.

In 2005, using a three-year average of various factors, we estimated there were 942 chronically homeless people in the City and County of Denver. Four years into our program, in 2009, the data showed 343 chronically homeless, a reduction of 62 percent. In 2010, independent researchers found there were 310 chronically homeless individuals, a reduction of 67 percent, with all signs trending toward a 75 percent reduction. That same year, the U.S. Department of Housing and Urban Development highlighted Denver as a national model for helping people who are homeless access benefits and services.

When I told you that I am aware of many of my shortcomings—sometimes impatience with project delays and long meetings, or frustration with too much detail, or the occasional empathetic blind spot—and I said that I try to hire people who balance those weaknesses, well, I meant people like Roxane. Of course, there's nobody like Roxane.

She was born on a farm near Missoula, Montana, and raised to work hard and put herself second. On her family's farm, the rule was that nobody got fed until the animals got fed. In addition to being farmers, her mom, with three master's degrees, was a teacher, and her dad was a professor at the University of Montana. In Rox's childhood home, time was not meant to be wasted; it was meant for getting things done. The best thing you could do was be of use. My mom would have loved Roxane.

Rox and I shared something in common. Her father died when she was young, only thirteen. In the wake of her dad's death, part of what Rox realized was that she didn't want to die in small-town Montana. She graduated first among her eighty-two high school classmates, earning a debate scholarship to Lewis & Clark College in Oregon. (Trust me, you do *not* want to debate Roxane, though I tried many times.) She earned master's degrees in social work and divinity from San Francisco State University and San Francisco Theological Seminary, where she came to admire and study Gandhi, Pope John Paul II, and the Dalai Lama. If you're looking for role models, you could do a lot worse than those guys.

In 1994, after graduate school, Rox moved to Denver and sought a career working on behalf of society's least fortunate. She was appointed the executive director of Urban Peak, a nonprofit for the homeless and runaway teens. She led the organization into an unprecedented expansion, which was a big reason why, when I was elected mayor, I hired her to head the city's Department of Human Services. Rox wasn't born to work in politics, which made her all the more perfect to be my chief of staff; that, and she read and utilized just about every managerial book written.

Rox liked to know everything before anyone else. Make that, Rox *insisted* on knowing everything before anyone else, especially before me. To be fair, that's a job requirement for a chief of staff. I often poked fun at her for being a control freak. I came up with a knock-knock joke that I took great joy in sharing with her.

"Knock-knock," I said.

She rolled her eyes, as if to say, Okay, I'll go along. "Who's there?"

"What do you mean who's there?" I said. "Why don't you know who's there?"

This news of Bill Ritter's not running, however, was one of the few times I knew the scoop before she did, which I pointed out to her when she arrived at my home that night. Rox brought with her our senior legislative aide, R. D. Sewald. The two had been at a Denver Nuggets game. Also on hand was my communications director, Eric Brown. Eric had been the city editor at the *Rocky Mountain News*; we hired him not long after the paper folded, and he took over after Lindy Eichenbaum Lent left. Having gone way above and beyond the call of duty since the campaign days, throughout my first term as mayor, and into my second, Lindy moved on to run the nonprofit Civic Center Conservancy, building upon urban place-making interests and allowing her a better work-life balance with her young child.

We gathered around the island in my kitchen. With this tight-knit group, it was always understood that beers were on the table. Rox, of course, had prepared a list of topics to discuss. It included a timeline. We talked about how and when all of the necessary steps would occur. Informing staff, announcing, filing, and so on. There was also the question of who else would run. Former Colorado speaker of the house Andrew Romanoff? (We accurately guessed no. He was committed to his run for the U.S. Senate, challenging and eventually losing to Michael Bennet.) Former U.S. senator and current secretary of the interior Ken Salazar? I had already called him after Bill Ritter had called me. He would have been a great governor, and I would have supported him, but he felt it was too soon for him to leave his still-new job running the Department of the Interior.

Another issue was my day job: How would we manage Denver if I was campaigning? That was relatively simple. If I was off campaigning in a town like La Junta or Buena Vista and there was a pressing issue developing in the city, I'd immediately return. We accepted that it was almost inevitable some political operative on the other side would use the fact that I was mayor of Denver to paint me as a city slicker who didn't really care about Colorado's rural communities. After all, there were reasons why it had been 125 years since a Denver mayor had been elected governor. But, hey, political operatives are paid to promote nonsense and attack. What was I going to do? It is what it is.

Denver deputy mayor Bill Vidal was an experienced pro, and with Rox as chief of staff the city would be in good hands during those brief times when I was away, and really I would never be far or without my mobile phone.

I felt we had accomplished much of what we had set out to do in the city. We dared to believe we could take the core principles I'd learned in the restaurant business and that we applied so successfully to city government—talent and teamwork, truly serving our constituents and one another, the alignment of self-interests, no margin in making enemies, eliminating red tape and the fundamental nonsense of government— and apply them to state government. We had a formula and an ethos—a culture—that could make the state run more efficiently. I believed our collaborative, common sense–driven style of governing would be a good thing for the state, and just maybe a good thing for the country. If, in Colorado, we could show that a democracy can and does work, well, maybe, dare I think it, that might just provide a model and motivation for D.C. and states around the country.

With her master's degree in divinity, my resident "God" person, as I liked to refer to Rox, looked at me and said: "John, is this what you feel you are called to do?" Rox very intentionally invoked that word "called." In religious vocations it means that one is not so much making a choice as that one feels one has no choice. I turned it back on her, asked her the same question. She said yes, she felt called. Perhaps being crass, or maybe it was shrewd—it was definitely smart—I asked her if she'd commit to all four years of the term. And she said yes. And she did.

In addition to the wars in Iraq and Afghanistan, our nation was in the midst of the Great Recession, the most dramatic economic downturn since the Great Depression. There was the mortgage meltdown. The automotive industry was on the verge of collapse. So, too, was the nation's banking system, thanks in large part to the mortgage industry house of cards. The U.S. Congress couldn't seem to get beyond its partisan pettiness and was grinding more and more into gridlock. Just about every poll showed Americans had lost faith in our political system and with elected officials in particular.

"John, you still haven't answered my question—the question you need to answer for yourself. Do you feel called to do this?"

"Yes," I said.

SEVEN DAYS AFTER Governor Bill Ritter called to tell me he was out, I was all in.

I announced my candidacy for governor on Tuesday, January 12, 2010, at a press conference on the west steps of the Colorado State Capitol. Off in the distance, directly across Broadway Street, was Denver's Civic Center Park. Immediately on the other side of the park was the City and County Building—Denver's city hall, my mayoral office. Beyond that, the backdrop of the Rocky Mountains. When I look up and see those spectacular mountains, under that limitless sky, it's mighty easy to feel inspired and awfully hard to have a bad day.

As a geologist, I think it's fair to say I have a keen appreciation for the omnipotent natural forces that over millions of years birthed those mountains. Seeing them, I can't help but feel small and humbled. For me, those sublime Rockies offer perspective: they stand as a reminder that our time on this earth is fleeting and that true power rests not with any one person or political party—thank goodness—but with Mother Nature. And soon, all of us in Colorado would see ample evidence that indeed she giveth and she taketh away.

"I love Colorado every bit as much as I love Denver," I said to the crowd gathered that day. Unlike seven years ago, when I had stood on Millennium Bridge and launched my run for mayor, this time there actually was a crowd. *The Denver Post* reported the press conference as being "packed." I don't know about *packed*, but I was grateful to see so many familiar faces and so many new ones.

We had been deliberate in selecting the timing and location for the press conference. The media were already focused on the capitol building. The next day, the Colorado General Assembly would kick off its legislative session, and the day after that Governor Ritter would give the annual State of the State address. Bill stood right behind me on the steps. It meant a great deal to me that he endorsed my run and told the media he thought I had a clear vision for how the state should move forward.

Days earlier, I had taken Bill up on his offer to tell me about his time as governor. Helen and I met with him and his wife, Jeannie, at the governor's mansion. Bill said he loved being governor, but the schedule was often a grind on him and his family; commitments compelled him to keep long days, and Jeannie and the kids often understandably felt frustrated by his absence.

After the meeting, Helen and I discussed what Bill and Jeannie had shared with us. We understood. Helen and I were then in the midst of our marriage therapy, talking about our struggles with similar challenges, balancing my mayoral and family responsibilities. We were trying to figure it out, as they say, but our love and respect and support for each other were never in question. We would try to make the campaign an opportunity to somehow reinvent our relationship. Helen told me she thought I would be a great governor for the people of Colorado and she encouraged me to go for it. She joined me on the west steps as I kicked off my gubernatorial campaign.

The agenda I broadly presented at the press conference was relatively straightforward: The state was in very similar circumstances as the city was when I first ran for mayor. Colorado was feeling our nation's economic downturn. The unemployment rate in the state was headed toward 8.9 percent. I would focus on jobs. I would do all I could both to support the state's existing businesses and to lure new businesses to Colorado. Only a vibrant private sector can preserve and create jobs.

I talked about our track record at the city, how we had done more with less, and actually had used the retirements of baby boomers to end up with 7 percent fewer city employees than when we started. I promised that I would collaborate with all parts of the state—rural and urban—and that I would not attempt to be a top-down governor who tried to impose policy.

The rest of my speech was not so much a speech as just me talking. I talked about many of the same things I'd talked about on the Millennium Bridge in 2003. I spoke about the time when I was laid off from my geologist job; how I'd experienced a downturn and witnessed firsthand what a souring economy can do. I did my best that day to begin to introduce myself to the rest of the state. Maybe some political consultants would have told me there was a better "campaign narrative" I could have or should have told, but I only know how to be me; my story is my story.

I was the only Democratic candidate in the race for governor. On the other side—well, there were two other sides, and soon, there were *three* other sides. Dan Maes had been the first contender in, announcing his bid in March 2009. Maes was a former Kansas law enforcement officer who then had a career as a telecommunications executive. He was the Tea Party candidate. Two months later, in May, Scott McInnis announced his bid. McInnis was a six-term United States congressman from Colorado, in office from 1993 to 2005. He was the Republican establishment's candidate.

The Tea Party's popularity was just emerging. In 2008, these far-right conservatives had coalesced around their objection to President Obama's policies of providing relief to Americans who were on the brink of losing their homes in the mortgage meltdown. Two years later, the Tea Party had become a political force. Its message resonated with many Coloradans, who have long held fast to their roots of rugged individualism.

The divide between Tea Partiers and the traditional Colorado Republican Party was tearing apart the state GOP. In May 2010, at the statewide

Republican Assembly, Tea Partier Maes defeated Blue Chip Republican McInnis for the top spot on the ballot. The victory was a narrow one—Maes received 49.35 percent of the delegate vote to McInnis's 48.89 percent—it was evidence of the schism within the state party.

Meanwhile, along came Tom Tancredo, a former Colorado state representative, a former six-term United States congressman, and a 2008 presidential candidate. Primarily railing against immigration, Tancredo had established himself as pretty much a one-issue extremist.

As Tancredo often does, he stepped into the spotlight. He declared that neither Dan Maes nor Scott McInnis was an electable Republican gubernatorial candidate. He said that they should both step aside and make room for a candidate who could win. Tancredo went so far as to issue an ultimatum: if they did not, he said, he would enter the race himself. This was not an empty threat. Tancredo had a considerable and devoted—bordering on cult—following, almost exclusively among Republicans.

Maes and McInnis did not do as Tancredo wished. Sure enough, in July 2009 Tancredo jumped into the fray as a gubernatorial candidate representing the Constitution Party.

The three candidates on the right spent a good deal of time and energy criticizing and attacking one another. What was unfolding in this election was a microcosm of what was happening within the Republican Party throughout the country. Major blocs of traditionally Republican voters, and therefore their candidates, were moving further and further to the right, and they were heading there for different reasons. Some went far right on immigration, others for taxes or guns or to defend their view of marriage. In short, there was no longer a united Republican Party in Colorado, no one Republican candidate to rally the party faithful. Suffice it to say, I felt like the luckiest guy in the world. It was like when I was kid playing electric football with Henry Baird and the vibrations were shaking the pieces away from me and clearing a lane.

And I only got luckier.

Maes and McInnis found themselves embroiled in scandals. The media unearthed the fact that McInnis had plagiarized a paper he wrote for a foundation that hired him after his time in Congress. Reporters looked into certain claims Maes had made about his careers in law enforcement and the telecommunications business and determined that they were untrue. Come the big Republican primary that August, Maes narrowly defeated McInnis. Then Tancredo turned on Maes.

My campaign remained focused on jobs and the economy. During one of the debates, in a lightning round of yes-or-no questions, I was asked if I supported the death penalty and I answered, "Yes." Soon, I would be giving more than a one-word answer to this question.

Just as we had in my mayoral elections, our campaign stayed positive. We ran what to this day remains one of my favorite campaign ads. In the thirty-second spot, I get in and out of the shower several times, fully dressed. In the voiceover, I say attack ads and dirty politics make me feel like I need to take a shower. This ad would pass any media "truth test," except for the part about my showering with my clothes on.

By 9:30 a.m. on election day, November 2, 2010, I led with 50.5 percent, Tancredo was at 36.8 percent, and Maes was in third with 11.2 percent. Those percentages barely changed throughout the day. Within two hours of the polls closing, I was declared the forty-second governor of Colorado.

During my victory address, inside a Denver hotel, I noted that it was a bittersweet moment for me. Only three days earlier, my cousin George Hickenlooper had died in his sleep in Denver, likely from sleep apnea. George and I met at the Wynkoop and discovered we were related—how could we not be with that name?—in 1991, during the Denver International Film Festival. He was telling a story about his great aunt, Olga Samaroff, when I blurted out: "Lucy Hickenlooper!" We talked about her husband Leopold Stokowski, whom she lost to "that bitch" Greta Garbo. George was a filmmaker, and loved a good story.

George was also the only son of an only son. Outside of his father, he'd never met another Hickenlooper. And I loved film as much as I liked music. We became immediate fast friends. He was at the Denver festival premiering his award-winning documentary *Hearts of Darkness*, but soon he was making features. He would put me into brief cameos in several of his movies, almost as a good-luck talisman. I ended up a member of the Screen Actors Guild, and still am. George directed movies like *The Big Brass Ring*, *The Man from Elysian Fields*, and his last film, *Casino Jack*, which was premiering at that same Denver International Film Festival, two days after my inauguration.

Casino Jack starred Kevin Spacey as Jack Abramoff, the D.C. lobbyist whose criminal trial and conviction seemed to confirm the most cynical view of Washington politics: that K Street was the tail that wagged the Capitol Hill dogs. During my one day on the set, Spacey, a truly amazing actor, came over to ask me endless details about local government every moment he had a break. Little did I know he was gathering background for his unforgettable role as Frank Underwood in *House of Cards*. When George passed away, he was making a documentary about my run for governor. He died sometime early Saturday, and I worked straight through the Tuesday election, but when I introduced *Casino Jack* Thursday night, I started to weep. The grief, and the stress relief, pierced a lifetime of genetics and family training, and I couldn't help but wonder if my mother had ever felt the powerful release that came with those tears. I hope so, but none of us kids ever saw it.

Thanks in large part to the media's coverage of the tumult on the

Republican side throughout the campaign, even casual political observers were aware that Colorado was a politically atomized state, with registered voters almost equally divided among Republicans, Democrats, and independents. So that I won with 50.1 percent against two opponents was not a surprise. If anything, considering these circumstances, I felt all the more fortunate and grateful that over half of such a diverse electorate invested their votes of confidence and the future of our state in me.

And regardless of single-issue differences of opinion and party affiliation—Tea Party, Constitution Party, Republican, Democrat, independent, whatever—we were all Coloradans. We all shared a desire to see the economy and job market in our state improve. During the campaign, I visited every one of Colorado's sixty-four counties, and time and time again, what I heard people tell me was a version of what James Carville had said when he was the lead strategist of Bill Clinton's first presidential campaign: "It's the economy, stupid." As far as I was concerned *that* was my mandate, and it could not have been clearer.

Only now, newly elected and having been thoroughly briefed on the circumstances I would be inheriting as governor, it was clear that another issue required more immediate attention: the state's $20 billion budget had a billion-dollar hole in it, all the more critical given that the general fund, that portion of the budget that we can directly manage, had dropped to $7.1 billion.

Unlike at the city, where the mayor crafts the budget, the Colorado State Constitution gives the legislature the primary responsibility of drawing up the budget, and the "line-item veto" authority delegated to the governor is in such broad categories as to be almost unusable.

The state legislature of my first session was a split chamber. Republicans had the House, Democrats controlled the Senate. A billion-dollar shortfall represented a full 15 percent of the state's operating costs. Massive cuts would be required. With thirty-five state senators and sixty-five state representatives, from a wide range of rural and urban communities, massive disagreements over what those cuts ought to be were likely.

On January 11, 2011 (yes, 1/11/11), exactly one year to the day after I announced my run for governor, Helen and I arrived early to the City and County Building. We enjoyed a most wonderful brunch with my senior staff in the mayor's office. They had managed to maintain the city's momentum and focus during the turbulence of my campaign. No issues, no embarrassing headlines. I thanked them all profusely, and then signed my formal resignation from the office of mayor of Denver.

Helen and I then walked across Civic Center Park and arrived at the capitol's west-side steps. This time, for my swearing in. On the walk over the day before, I had counted every step—663 to be exact. In my formal Inaugural Address that day, and the very next day, in my first State of the State before the General Assembly kicked off the legislative session, I pointed out that I had counted every step from the City and County Building to the capitol.

I wasn't trying to show off my ability to walk and count at the same time. I promised that our administration would measure our steps, our progress, in everything we did, so that the people of Colorado would know we were conscious of our obligations to them and to their tax dollars, and so that they could judge our performance and hold us accountable.

Not once in my Inaugural Address did I utter the words "Democrat" or "Republican," or even "party." I spoke about "partners." Specifically mentioning Senate President Brandon Shaffer and House Speaker Frank McNulty, I said I looked forward to "working together in the best tradition of the West." In my State of the State, I asked the General Assembly for bipartisan cooperation in all of the issues we would take on, especially the budget.

If you're getting the impression that I was obsessed with the budget, I was. I believed getting the budget done with true bipartisan support was critical. By true bipartisan support, I mean a majority of both Republicans and Democrats in both chambers. I believed such a collaborative success would be significant for three reasons.

One: If we created a collegial spirit now inside the capitol, it would lay the foundation for our administration's next three years, and possibly next seven years. If, on the other hand, this process imploded in tension and animosity, well, that would inhibit getting things done.

Two: Poll after poll showed that Americans had little faith in government. A truly bipartisan budget would give Coloradans reason to believe, in our state's democracy, at least, and to see that not all elected officials are petty bums.

Three: It was an essential step toward fostering a probusiness environment that would preserve and create jobs in our state. I had learned firsthand as an entrepreneur and a small businessman that the private sector is volatile enough. The business community feels less anxious and is more likely to grow when their government is stable. We all have seen the stock market get conservative during a presidential election, or when the nation flirts with war. No CEO or business owner wants to move to a state or gamble on starting or expanding a business in a state where the government is feuding with itself and dysfunctional, and where who knows what regulations and taxes may pop up. On my very first day in office, I signed an executive order compelling every state agency to scour its rules and look for redundant or flat-out nonsensical rules to trim or cut entirely.

During the four months of that first session, from January into May, our administration and the legislative leadership worked hard to finally get to a budget that no one completely loved or entirely hated. Along the way, everyone had to holster their egos, hold their noses, and make compromises, but we got to a budget that was useful. According to our informal vote count we had true bipartisan support. But the process certainly reminded me of hacking away at that crap in those vintage toilets all those years ago.

Fortunately, I had Alan Salazar leading our legislative strategy. Alan was my chief strategy officer and by far the most experienced member of our team when it came to politics. For years, he was deputy chief of staff and policy director for Colorado governor Roy Romer, and then for more than a decade was chief of staff to U.S. representative Mark Udall, which is where Alan was when I lured him away to come work in the governor's office. Everyone in the Dome knew of Alan's hard-earned reputation for being a man of his word. Just as Russell Schehrer had been the linchpin of the Wynkoop, with his tried-and-true recipes for masterfully brewing beer, Alan, with his recipes for deftly whipping policy into shape, was the linchpin of our legislative outreach.

Virtually every department took a hit in the budget. The toughest bit of negotiating was cutting $229 million from the state K–12 budget. I didn't like making such a harsh cut to education. Public education was important to me. It's why at the city, one of the very first things I did was push for the Denver Scholarship Foundation. My own son was in a Denver public school. The public education system is important to business leaders who are considering either to stay in a state or move to a new one. I've never met a CEO who didn't tell me that good public schools were a factor in his or her relocation algebra. But the cut had to be done.

For a while, some Democratic legislators balked at the idea that we were increasing the state's reserve fund from $140 million to $280 million, while slashing education, but 2 percent was unacceptable. As my mother, and probably just about any mother, would say, $20 million was not nearly enough of an emergency fund for a state the size of Colorado, with 5.3 million people, and moreover a state prone to natural disasters like wildfires. Largely thanks to Alan, Rox, and the remarkable work of our budget director, Henry Sobanet, we got to a budget.

But in the final days of the session, in early May 2011, our collaborative vibe began to unravel. Too often, good politics gets undone because someone somewhere in the process wants something and won't let it go; the quest for a quick political score for a few undermines the long-term win for the many. That's what was happening here.

All that was left to get the budget deal done was to get the Rules Bill done. The Rules Bill establishes the administrative guidelines for the operation of all state agencies.

House Speaker Frank McNulty wanted a law passed that would allow check-cashing businesses to charge more for their services. Senate President Brandon Shaffer was against it, and had refused to let the bill come to a vote in his chamber. So what does McNulty do? When the House gets the Rules Bill already passed by the Senate, he slips in an amendment for the check-cashing industry and sends it back to the Senate for final approval. I liked McNulty and Shaffer.

The Senate rejected the amendment and sent the Rules Bill back to the House for approval. McNulty and Shaffer were playing a game of chicken, not only with each other, but also with fundamental state operations. If the Rules Bill didn't pass, it would undermine the hard-earned spirit of collaboration that had gone into the budget.

Late one afternoon, I went up to the third floor of the capitol to visit Speaker McNulty. He poured two glasses of whiskey and I said, "So how do we fix this?" I've often been faulted for being overly optimistic and trusting; so be it. But more often than not, my faith in people proves correct. I believed Frank cared about doing the right thing for good government. I appealed to his better angels by saying as much. When I left Frank, he seemed inclined to relent, remove the amendment, and approve the Rules Bill.

Of course, Frank may also have changed his position thanks to an external nudge. The morning after I met with him, *The Denver Post* published a story about the holdup and McNulty's role in it. The *Post*'s editorial page editor, Dan Haley, a rather influential fellow, tweeted: "@RepMcNulty, do you really want to waste your political capital helping payday lenders? It's a no-win."

Suddenly, the capitol buzzed with tweets and chatter about the standoff, many of the sentiments echoing Haley's opinion. Alan Salazar may or may not have encouraged the *Post*'s reporter to do that story, and Alan may or may not have exchanged text messages with Dan Haley before Haley sent out that tweet. Who's to say? I choose to believe that Speaker McNulty made a magnanimous concession and let his bill die. The Rules Bill passed; and our first budget passed with 80 out of 100 votes—truly bipartisan.

The evening the session ended, in keeping with a long-standing legislative tradition, my staff and I joined many of the legislators at a local tavern. There was more about that session that gave me cheer. For one thing, our General Assembly had established a law to implement the Affordable Care Act in Colorado. Although we did so with the support of only one Republican, considering the fact that many states around the nation were engaged in political civil wars over Obamacare and getting nowhere, I'll count that as bipartisan enough. The legislation created our Colorado Health Exchange; rather than leave it up to the federal government to administer and manage the Affordable Care Act in our state, our exchange gave our state agencies local control over managing it and assisting Coloradans in navigating the myriad health plans. When the federal government's ACA Web site went down, ours stayed up.

As pleased as I was with that first session, I was just as encouraged by what we accomplished outside of the capitol. I had heard that Mike Long, the CEO of Arrow Electronics, one of the nation's largest distributors of electronic parts, a Fortune 200 company, might be looking to move his company's headquarters out of New York. Working with our Department of Economic Development, I made a case that Arrow would be a much bigger fish in a smaller pond like Colorado, and that I would do everything in my power to help them be the best in their industry. We were in the center of the country, had a very competitive tax structure, and perhaps most important for an innovative, growing company like Arrow, had become the primary destination for educated young people in the country, the so-called Millennials.

We emphasized what Mike already knew: that Colorado is the second-largest hub of the aerospace industry (and innovation) in the United States, and one of the very top states in terms of technology start-ups and entrepreneurs. These are the essential components of a healthy ecosystem that allows a company like Arrow to flourish.

One conversation led to another, which led to another, and in October Arrow announced it was moving its global headquarters to Arapahoe County, Colorado, beginning that November. Arrow was now Colorado's largest company in terms of revenues—$18.7 billion the previous year. Within five years, Arrow planned to add 1,250 positions to the already 1,000 people it employed in the state. Our Colorado Economic Development Commission approved $11.4 million in "Job Growth Incentive Tax Credits" for Arrow, which is really just the "ante" in these kinds of decisions, and a small sum compared with all the benefits a company like Arrow brings to the state, especially to the hundreds of smaller companies already here. When a Fortune 200 cutting-edge corporation like Arrow relocates to your state, other companies usually follow. And they did.

WHILE WE HAD BEEN courting Mike, I was drinking fracking fluid. It went down like this.

One day in the spring of 2011, I met with Dave Lesar, CEO for Halliburton, as well as Jim Brown, his CEO for the Americas, who was based in Denver. We sat at a long conference table in my office inside the capitol. Alan and one of his legislative aides were at the table with us.

I told Lesar I'd heard or maybe read somewhere that at a conference recently he drank an experimental prototype of a new fracking fluid to demonstrate how safe it was. Lesar confirmed the story was true. In fact, he said he had a jar of the stuff with him, said it was called CleanStim. A clear plastic jar came out of somebody's briefcase, filled with clear liquid, and Lesar slid it across the conference table.

I lifted the jar of CleanStim to eye level. Lesar explained it was made of all-natural FDA-approved ingredients, and, yes, safe enough to drink. I unscrewed the lid and took a swig. The room fell silent. I gulped it, wiped my hand across my mouth—classy, I know—and set the jar back on the table. It made me wish I had a Rail Yard Ale from the Wynkoop as a chaser. Across the table, Alan looked like he had just seen a ghost, or rather, looked like he had just seen his boss, the governor, drink fracking fluid. I turned to Lesar and said, "Well, it doesn't taste very good." Lesar quipped back, "I said it was safe to drink. I didn't say it was Gatorade."

When word that I imbibed a bit of fracking fluid found its way into the media, in some circles it was portrayed as if I drank the oil and gas industry's Kool-Aid; that the old oil and gas geologist was a patsy for the industry. Truth was, I was attempting to facilitate a partnership between representatives of the industry and the environmental community. My ulterior motive was to foster trust and cooperation between the two sides in the hope that we might get the parties involved to agree to the toughest fracking fluid disclosure rules in the country.

Early critics of mine were right about this much: my background as an oil and gas geologist did influence my perspective. I understood the evolution of hydraulic fracking. I knew that the innovations in technology, everything from the hydraulic fracking systems to the fluid, had become so advanced that it was a remarkably safe extraction method. The way fracking works is this: fracking fluid is pumped down a well under high pressure to "fracture" rock and release oil and gas. About 90 percent of the oil and natural gas wells in the United States have been fracked, and the fluids and the process have generated controversy because of concerns the process threatens groundwater.

As a guy who lived through the oil-fueled geopolitical crises of the 1970s, 1980s, and 1990s, I witnessed why our country needs to become 100 percent energy independent. I was a strong advocate for renewables. I was on the record often emphasizing the need to transition from coal. Based on experience and science, I recognized fracking was one of our very best and safest extraction techniques. Fracking is good for the country's energy supply, our national security, our economy, and our environment.

Fracking gets a terrible rap, mainly because the industry is terrible at public relations. One of the major arguments environmentalists and antifracking groups make is that the industry attempts to hide what's "really" going on. I had been telling industry representatives, like Lesar, that by relentlessly protecting the secret formula of each company's fracking fluid they were fanning the rumors and conspiracy theories. When there's a lack of information, people fill the gap with assumptions of the worst. The more forthright and transparent the industry could be, as I told Lesar, all the better for them. I asked him, "Why not make public all of the ingredients that go into the fracking fluid?"

Companies regarded that information as proprietary and were worried competitors could reverse engineer their secret formula. Which is what Lesar said to me. I pointed out that Coke puts the ingredients of that soft drink on the can, but does not list exact amounts of each ingredient—it keeps its recipe confidential. Coke was still the one and only Coke, and doing quite well. What about something like that? I asked.

Lesar said that just might be a concept worth further discussion, and there seemed to be a workable solution in it. Actually, what Lesar said was, "There's got to be a pony in there somewhere," and we spent a good ten minutes speculating on the origin of that phrase and what the heck it meant.

We convened a group of representatives from the industry and from environmental advocacy groups to collaborate on crafting possible disclosure rules. Industry voices included Jim Brown, the CEO for the Americas for Halliburton, and Noble Energy's senior vice president for the company's northern region Ted Brown (not related to Jim), along with Fred Krupp, president of the Environmental Defense Fund, and his national director, Dan Grossman, and Pete Maysmith of Colorado Conservation Voters. Let me be clear: these and others who met with us deserve a great deal of credit simply for getting together and giving this a try. Each of them had to deal with some degree of criticism for meeting with the enemy.

In early December, it seemed that one day we had consensus from all parties involved, and the next, the deal was falling apart. It was right about this time that my office got the call from a White House aide extending the invitation to Helen and me to attend the Kennedy Center Honors with President Barack Obama. After that joyous event, I returned to Colorado and more holiday cheer. We secured a final agreement on the fracking fluid disclosure rules.

All parties involved accepted rules that, among other things, required the industry to disclose descriptions of the products in the fracking fluid; they would be posted on a Web site. The exact chemical concentrations, however, would be kept confidential with our Colorado Oil and Gas Conservation Commission and released only to necessary officials in the event of an emergency.

Earlier in the year, I had bet Alan that we could get environmental and oil and gas leaders to stand shoulder-to-shoulder and tell the people of Colorado they had worked together to come up with the most transparent fracking fluid disclosure rules in the nation. Around mid-December, after Dan Grossman and Pete Maysmith stood shoulder-to-shoulder with representatives from Halliburton and Noble and other oil and gas companies, Alan paid me a buck. These fracking fluid disclosure rules would demonstrate that you can create a business environment where businesses could thrive, while also abiding by the highest environmental standards. Mike Paque, executive director of the Groundwater Protection Council, an association of state water agencies, told the *Post* that with this new agreement, "Colorado is cutting edge."

It seemed to me at the time that the way some media and activists were going after fracking was reminiscent of the early twentieth century, when the media skewered the oil and gas industry, personified by John D. Rockefeller. Only in our era, it was often bloggers wedded to a particular agenda who led the charge, cherry-picking some shreds of truth, or untruths, to make popular but inaccurate stories.

Of course, there were journalists of that period and ours who did their homework and got it right. The best-known investigative journalist of her day dogging Rockefeller was Ida Tarbell. She was the quintessential muckraker. In fact, in discussing our fracking fluid disclosure rules, more than a few times I quoted Teddy Roosevelt's famous speech "The Man with the Muckrake," which he gave in 1906 at a time when the oil and gas business was often unfairly vilified. A bit of it goes like this:

> The first requisite in the public servants who are to deal in this shape with corporations, whether as legislators or as executives, is honesty. This honesty can be no respecter of persons. There can be no such thing as unilateral honesty. The danger is not really from corrupt corporations; it springs from the corruption itself, whether exercised for or against corporations. . . .

The only public servant who can be trusted honestly to protect the rights of the public against the misdeeds of a corporation is that public man who will just as surely protect the corporation itself from wrongful aggression.

It's worth noting, I think, that no president has done more to protect the environment than Teddy. Among his enduring achievements as president, he doubled the number of national parks by designating and thereby protecting five more. He created four national game refuges, and set aside more than 100 million acres' worth of national forests. What's more, his openness with the media was unwavering. There's a famous story of Teddy welcoming a journalist to investigate his administration by writing him a note in which the president more or less said, "Give this man whatever he needs." Teddy Roosevelt was part of our inspiration when Helen and I chose the name for our son.

I don't think we will ever be able to allay all the concerns some people have about fracking, but I do believe providing this level of transparency goes a long way toward making people feel safer, and also takes unwarranted heat off the industry.

Having ended my first legislative session with a budget that passed with such strong bipartisan support, I felt we had begun to demonstrate to Coloradans that politically divided chambers at the capitol do not mean a divided Colorado; here in our state, hopefully, we were showing that the Colorado way of governing was collaboration.

And having ended the year by welcoming Mike Long and Arrow Electronics to our state, and by bringing together such historically opposed constituencies as the Environmental Defense Fund and Halliburton on the fracking-fluid disclosure rules, I thought we had begun to demonstrate that ours was a government that could facilitate a culture wherein a healthy business sector and a healthy environment were not mutually exclusive. In finding a harmony between the environment and business there was an alignment of self-interest that benefited all Coloradans.

I was also encouraged by an important metric in the public's eyes: the unemployment rate. Governor Roy Romer used to say in the 1990s that quality of life begins with a good job. At the beginning of 2011, the unemployment rate was at 8.6 percent; by December, that rate had dropped to 8.1 percent. I felt like we were heading in the right direction, but we were only just beginning and there was much left to do.

Thirteen

THE TIME OF MY LIFE

The many, *many* hours I spend with my senior staff crafting each year's State of the State speech are devoted to crystallizing our agenda for that legislative session and for the year ahead.

Among the top priorities we highlighted in the 2012 speech were our obsessive work to make Colorado the most probusiness state in the nation and our efforts to eliminate the fundamental nonsense of government. Since I signed the executive order on day one of my term as governor, every state agency had reviewed its rules and regulations and trimmed or entirely cut hundreds of them. The Colorado Department of Transportation (CDOT) found rules that were decades out of date. The Department of Human Services repealed 850 rules that were absolutely unnecessary.

In the speech, we also wanted to make sure we promoted a new state-sponsored cycling event, "Pedal the Plains." Whether mountain biking or road biking, Colorado is a cyclist's paradise. The previous year, we hosted the first USA Pro Cycling Challenge, which reached a worldwide audience of more than 20 million people and generated more than $80 million in economic activity in the state. The Pro Challenge was now an annual Colorado event.

We conceived Pedal the Plains in the hope that it would entice amateur cyclists to ride and tour our Eastern Plains. We envisioned that the event would not only be great for the sport of cycling, but would also give Coloradans, and of course any out-of-state visitors, an opportunity to see the rural farming communities that supply our food. Colorado's agriculture communities and the industries dependent on them were then leading the state out of the recession. In the last year, our agriculture exports had grown more than 20 percent.

Recognizing how important entrepreneurs were to our economy and a probusiness culture, we asked the General Assembly to financially support our Colorado Innovation Network (COIN) conference. We had launched the days-long COIN event—seminars and panels—the previous year with corporate sponsorships. I guess you could say I "borrowed," with their help, the idea from Northwestern University's Kellogg School of Management, which does a similar annual event. For us, the goal was to foster collaboration and idea sharing across private, public, and academic sectors, including Colorado's twenty-nine research laboratories, and ultimately infuse the Colorado business sector with energy and innovative ideas, and jobs.

In the speech, we eased into our policy agenda, ever so delicately hinting at what I suspected might be one of the more challenging items for us to get through the legislature. The previous year, we had created the Colorado Health Insurance Marketplace; now, with Congress utterly gridlocked in a feud over Obamacare, we needed funding for it. The legislators had an idea this was coming, and I conveyed as much when I said that making Colorado the best place for entrepreneurship also meant we must have "health care that is both affordable and accessible."

Near as I could tell, when I presented those ideas and a few other "asks" to the General Assembly in the 2012 State of the State, they were well received, with varying degrees of bipartisan applause.

Next up was our major policy agenda item for that session. I presented it just as we had decided I would in speech prep, which is to say, briefly and matter-of-factly. In between providing a firm end date for a major highway project that was under way in the state and calling on Colorado employers to first consider the résumés from our returning veterans, I said:

"We believe in equal rights for all regardless of race, creed, gender, or sexual orientation. We don't believe we should legislate what happens inside a church or place of worship, but government should treat all people equally."

I said: "It's time to pass civil unions."

Mostly everyone on the floor of the chamber rose from their seats and applauded. Each legislator who stood and clapped was an exclamation point on the statement. Many Republicans remained notably seated and stoic. One of them was our old friend Speaker of the House Frank McNulty.

We had considered making this ask in my first State of the State. But with the budget and all that went along with it—which was *everything*—in the mess it was in, we feared if we "asked for too much too soon," politically speaking, we might polarize the legislature from the start. If that happened, we might not only undermine the chances of passing a civil unions bill, but self-sabotage our entire four-year agenda before we had even begun.

Even during the speech prep for that 2012 State of the State, we debated whether we ought to include it. Some of the thinking went that it still might be "too divisive," "too toxic," "too off-brand." The latter concern was a reference to my reputation as a "middleman" who facilitated consensus rather than forcing a potential controversy. Alan touched upon this. He now believed we'd made a mistake by not putting civil unions in our first State of the State. He suggested that it was the right thing to do now, adding that the press was often criticizing me for not being bold enough. Indeed, during my first year on the job, the press had said as much about me at times. Whatever. I cared more about effective strategy than about garnering media kudos for being bold. I'm not sure there's much value in boldly promoting a policy that fails to make it through the General Assembly.

Of all the members of our senior team, Alan had given the most thought to our administration's strategy for civil unions, and it wasn't only because he ran our policy shop. For Alan, it was personal. Born and raised in Denver, Alan attended Catholic school, and for a time wanted to be a priest. He married his high-school sweetheart. Two years after the couple's son was born, Alan realized he could no longer suppress who he really was: he was gay.

Having a child, and holding the idea of raising his son to be true to himself . . . well, Alan felt that if he couldn't be honest with himself and those he loved most dearly, what would he be teaching his son? He came out to his wife, then gradually to his family, friends, and colleagues. He submitted a resignation letter to his boss at the time, Governor Roy Romer, who refused to accept it and was nothing but loving and supportive.

Alan's professionalism, his commitment to putting the larger political agenda of the administration above any one issue, was part of why he had not made more of a push to have it included in the first State of the State. Personally, he wanted to champion the bill yesterday, but professionally, the strategist in him knew that waiting for the right time was critical. Going into our first legislative session, Alan was the one who pointed out that pushing a civil unions bill would have amounted to dropping Alka-Seltzer in the fish tank. Alan felt, we all felt, like 2012 was the right time.

One of Alan's most effective legislative team members, Christine Scanlan, suggested I say it was time for "gay marriage." The rest of us thought that was "too loaded." It was Rox who first proposed the lines about civil unions that I said in the speech. We all agreed that it struck just the right note of politics and compassion.

It was time to pass civil unions.

Really, it was long past time.

After that State of the State speech, Alan and his team wasted no time going to work trying to muster enough votes in both chambers to get the bill passed. Every morning, I met separately with Alan and Rox for daily briefings on the issues each of them handled. Although Rox was unmistakably my second-in-command, as she put it, she and Alan were peers who swam in different lanes. More or less the way it broke down was Alan's lane was policy and communications, Rox's lane was the ocean-wide everything else. In my meetings with Alan early on in that second session, it became evident that we might have a tough time securing Speaker of the House McNulty's support for funding the health exchange and passing civil unions. The tension in the building was palpable.

While we were engaged in this policy work, about midway through the session, on March 26, we received reports of a fire scorching a large swath of rural southwest Jefferson County, just outside the town of Conifer.

As more information came in, we would learn that the fire started with a prescribed burn. The Colorado State Forest Service ignited the burn within a fire control line on March 21, and extinguished the fire on March 23. Or so the Forest Service thought. For about a day and a half, officials checked on the embers, and then they stopped. Shortly thereafter, high winds kicked up, somewhere in the range of 55 to 65 miles per hour, and blew embers beyond the fire control line into the dense woods. The fire was reborn, and over a period of a week the flames of what became known as the Lower North Fork Fire spread through 4,140 acres, required massive evacuation efforts, and in the end charred about 1,400 acres, destroyed twenty-seven homes, and killed three people.

While the fire burned I traveled to the site. It was the first disaster to occur during my administration, and I wanted to be there to unobtrusively learn and provide what help I could. You hear about the bravery of first responders all the time, though not often enough, and as I began to witness that day, whatever you hear fails to do them justice. Seeing the men and women going toward and into those flames while everyone else was moving away from them was a reminder of what real selflessness and public service looks like.

Along with Rox, I visited emergency shelters established by the Red Cross. People and pets who had fled their homes at a moment's notice looked shell-shocked. People flocked to us. Lines formed. It became a town hall of angry, frustrated Coloradans. They were outraged that a prescribed burn, which is supposed to be a controlled burn, was the cause. They were furious because, as they said, officials had waited so long to call for evacuations. A number of people told us they had called to report the fire early, but were dismissively informed that it was a prescribed burn, so there was nothing to fear.

On the scene, we learned that we had to get our state Department of Human Services coordinated with the insurance commission, and with the county, to ensure that the Red Cross had all of what it needed. We spent hours talking to victims and responders. Rox wrote down the concerns, and together we hustled to make sure all available resources were marshaled to address what was the obvious first priority: getting the blaze under control and putting out the fire.

Considering all that I had heard from the victims, I wanted to see the damage and get perspective on the site. The National Guard had a space helicopter and they flew Rox and me over the flames. The devastation was overwhelming. We could see houses where people were still refusing to leave and trucks on the ground with authorities trying to warn people and get them out.

The three who died in the fire were Sam and Linda Lucas and Ann Appel. In the aftermath of the fire I got to know Ann's husband, Scott. They had two sons, one in his late teens and the other in his early twenties. The boys were not home the day of the fire, and that afternoon, Scott left his ailing wife, Ann, in order to run some errands. By the time Scott returned, the fire made it impossible to reach his home and his wife, and Ann was unable to escape. Scott lost his land, his home, his business, and his wife. He shared with me the anger and frustration I had heard from others at the shelter. I assured him, and many others I talked with, that we would review all that had and had not been done. If there were procedures that needed to be improved, we would improve them.

The more we learned about the Lower North Fork Fire, the more we saw that mistakes had been made, largely due to poor organization and poor communication within and among those organizations and with the residents affected. In response to a study we commissioned on the fire, our administration consolidated fire and emergency management functions into a single state department to streamline the chain of command and expedite decision making. In time, we would do more. We could never undo this damage, but we could be sure it served to goad us to reduce the chance such a tragedy would happen again.

Back at the capitol, our second budget passed with a larger majority than the first. This time 94 out of the 100 legislators voted in favor of it. We also secured funding for the health exchange. But civil unions didn't make it.

Alan and his team did a masterful job of ushering the civil unions bill through three committees. Brandon Shaffer's Democratic-controlled Senate quickly voted in favor of the bill and sent it to McNulty's House. The bill had the votes to pass in the House. McNulty knew it. But for weeks, he refused to allow it to come up for a vote.

My reaction? To paraphrase *The Big Lebowski*, I was of the mind that this aggression would not stand. While I don't see any margin in making enemies, and admittedly, I've never been one to go looking for a political fight, this wasn't about politics, this was about civil rights, humanity, doing the right thing. McNulty had blocked the vote because he said his caucus didn't have ample time to consider the civil unions bill. So I gave him more time.

One of the powers a Colorado governor has is the ability to call a special session of the General Assembly. It's rarely done. It's considered the legislative version of the nuclear option. On May 9, 2012, the last day of the legislative session, I called a press conference and announced that I was ordering a special session.

"Last night," I said, "we had a moment of historical significance in the state of Colorado, when the bill legalizing civil unions died in the House. And there were a lot of questions about how that happened: was there enough time, was there not enough time? Along with that bill, thirty other bills died. . . . So we've decided without question, we intend tomorrow to call for a special session."

In a special session, which according to the state constitution would last three days, the governor and his staff, not the legislature, set the agenda. Of those thirty bills that the Senate had signed and which then died in McNulty's House, we were going to make sure civil unions would be among the issues considered and, we hoped, voted upon.

I continued: "I spent a long time in the restaurant business, and a lot of people who helped us create that business didn't have the same rights as everybody else." My voice cracked. "I'm a little bit sleep deprived so emotions come a little bit too quick to the surface. I had a call yesterday from one of them who just asked, 'If not now, when?'"

As you all know by now, like my mother I guess, I'm not easily given over to emotions, but in this moment, I teared up. I wrapped up with, "So our goal is to make sure we do everything we can to make sure there is a fair, open debate on the floor of the House and Senate and the issue gets discussed, that we allow people the chance to vote on it, and we move forward, we move this entire state forward to make sure, as Martin Luther King Jr. said, 'The arc of the moral universe is long, but it bends toward justice,' and we want to make sure that arc continues moving forward."

In the special session, Frank again saw to it that the civil unions bill did not come up for a vote. He ensured that the bill never made it out of committee hearings. The Speaker told the media he believed Coloradans were more concerned about jobs and the economy. I was disappointed both politically and personally.

There was no doubt Coloradans cared about jobs and the economy. There was also no doubt that was a top concern of my administration. At the beginning of 2012, the unemployment rate in Colorado was 8.1 percent; at the end of that year it was 7.2 percent.

In the forthcoming November 2012 elections, we would find out just how important civil unions were to the people of Colorado.

NOW, TWO YEARS into the job, one of the questions I was most frequently asked was, "How do you like being governor?" A close second was, "Did you really drink fracking fluid?" In response to the first, I had gotten into the habit of saying, "I'm having the time of my life." It was true. I loved the job. I felt I was exactly where I belonged, doing exactly what I was supposed to be doing. The job was far more challenging than I had ever imagined, and I loved that, too. I didn't run for governor expecting it to be easy, and I got more than I bargained for. As far as I was concerned, it was a good deal.

A friend of mine once told me I have "constructive attention deficit disorder," meaning I have a knack for thinking in myriad different directions at once. I think that's accurate. I'd go so far as to say I have a *need* to think in many different directions at once. Seems to me that's common to entrepreneurs. Indeed, I loved working with a team of big hearts and brilliant minds to find solutions to an ever-changing variety of concrete problems. Government, politics, has lots of moving parts. My dad was an engineer. I am my father's son.

More and more, I felt I understood the enthusiasm I saw in the faces of those mayors and their senior staffers I had met with more than a decade ago. I understood why David L. Cohen couldn't stop talking about his time in government, even if it meant he might miss yet another vacation. I didn't want a vacation, either.

Rox's question: Did I feel called?

Yes, I felt called.

Yes, I was having the time of my life.

Then came the summer of 2012.

The tragedy that was the Lower North Fork Fire was without question the lowest point in my time as governor thus far. That fire destroyed so much so quickly: twenty-seven homes, twenty-seven families who lost virtually everything they owned. Three people killed. It was hard to imagine anything worse. But it got worse. Much worse.

And once it started, it didn't stop for the next two years.

One of the chief causes of the Lower North Fork Fire was the ground conditions. The previous winter had been extremely dry. The state received only about 15 percent of its average annual precipitation. About 90 percent of Colorado was under severe or worse drought conditions.

And it was hot. That summer, temperatures across the state were often near or above 100°F. And there's very little humidity in our semiarid state: throughout Colorado, our relative humidity was in the single digits, maybe occasionally in the teens. And it was windy. On many days that summer, winds were recorded blowing between 50 and 70 miles per hour. Dry, hot, and windy. The Lower North Fork Fire was only the beginning.

On June 9, lightning struck a forest in the mountains west of Fort Collins in Larimer County. This High Park Fire burned for more than two months, scorching more than 87,000 acres. It destroyed more than 250 homes and killed a sixty-two-year-old woman. In terms of the number of houses burned, the High Park Fire was the most destructive fire in Colorado history—at the time.

On June 23, another wildfire erupted just northwest of Colorado Springs. The Waldo Canyon Fire forced the evacuation of more than 30,000 residents of Colorado Springs, Manitou Springs, Woodland Park, and several mountain communities, and even a partial evacuation of the United States Air Force Academy. On June 26, just when it appeared firefighters had held the fire and were maybe on the verge of beginning to contain it, a nearby dry thunderstorm—alas, no rain—generated 70-mile-per-hour winds that invigorated the flames, and the fire took seventeen days to contain. In the end, that fire claimed 350 homes in a matter of hours. The Waldo Canyon Fire damage surpassed that of the High Park Fire, making it the new most destructive fire in Colorado history.

In the wake of these back-to-back devastating wildfires, our administration requested a federal emergency disaster declaration from the White House. Federal emergency disaster declarations provide federal funding to state and local governments, private nonprofit organizations, and home owners. On June 29, President Obama came to Colorado and toured the communities damaged by the Waldo Canyon Fire.

That afternoon, he issued the declarations for both the High Park and

Waldo Canyon fires. The federal dollars would provide desperately needed assistance to tens of thousands of residents who needed to secure temporary housing, repair their homes, or build new ones. The White House also made federal funding available for crisis counseling and disaster unemployment assistance for all of the Coloradans affected by the two fires.

If you believe that natural disasters are acts of God, what happened on Friday, July 20, 2012, was an act of the devil.

That night, I was at the Broadmoor Hotel in Colorado Springs. I'd been invited to celebrate a friend's birthday party. Sometime before one a.m. I was reading in my room when there was a thumping on my door. I opened it and our state treasurer, Walker Stapleton, informed me there had been a shooting at a movie theater in Aurora. "It looks bad," he said. "Turn on the TV."

At that point, the news did not have many facts to report about what appeared to be a mass shooting in Aurora at the Century 16 movie theater. The shooter had been apprehended. No one was sure yet how many people had been killed or wounded. The news footage was of police cars, ambulances, lots of flashing emergency lights and confusion. As I watched the news, Rox called my mobile phone. She added a few more details. A man had walked into a midnight premiere of the film *The Dark Knight Rises* dressed in tactical clothing; he then set off tear gas grenades and fired into the audience with multiple firearms.

I arrived at the scene at eight a.m. There weren't very many people there. The Aurora police had set up a mobile command center. Rox and I went inside and joined Aurora mayor Steve Hogan for a briefing from Aurora police chief Dan Oates. An FBI agent and another police officer or two were present. They were going to show us footage of a video an officer had recorded of the crime scene for evidence. The crime, the chief said, was appalling. Chief Oates told us the shooter's name, but said that when they spoke to the public, they were not going to refer to him by name. They implored Mayor Hogan and me to do the same. I couldn't have agreed more. Just as on 9/11, when I thought the media unintentionally promoted the power of Osama bin Laden, I believed we should not give mass murderers the attention many of them, if not all of them, crave.

Chief Oates informed us that there was reason to believe the shooter's apartment was booby-trapped. Aurora PD had a cherry picker with a camera cranked to the window of the shooter's apartment. Sure enough, they looked inside and saw a cat's cradle of wires and explosives. Police evacuated the building, and bomb squads spent hours defusing the nest of explosive devices.

Chief Oates showed us the video. It had been taken on a handheld camera. The footage began with a walk through the front doors, past the concessions down the halls and into the screening room, where the officer went through the aisles and scanned the rows. Since the victims had been removed, nothing had been touched. It was the most chilling and macabre spectacle I have ever seen. The screening room was dark; the light on the camera eerily illuminated what we saw. As the camera recorded the rows, it showed popcorn everywhere, and random articles of clothing strewn about, all of it mingled with the blood on the floor.

There was so much blood on the floor, on the seats. As the camera panned over row after row, the chief gave what descriptions he could. Here's where someone had tried to hide. Here's where someone had lain on top of their loved one hoping to save them. There were no guns or bodies in the video, but you sensed the magnitude of the slaughter. In the stillness of the scene, you felt the absence of life and the presence of death and evil. With every passing minute of that twenty-minute video, I felt as if my heart folded in half and then into quarters, and then onto itself, smaller and smaller until there was just this intense focused ache in my chest.

That day we started visiting the hospitals. Over the next two and a half days, we visited everyone who was wounded. Peyton Manning, who had just been signed to the Broncos, called many of the surviving victims and never told the press. As we toured the hospitals, we learned that several of the victims survived because police first responders disregarded protocol. There weren't enough ambulances for the number of wounded, so rather than wait for additional or returning ambulances, police transported victims to the hospitals themselves. The cops were going not by the book, but by what their heart-driven instincts told them to do.

According to the now legally established facts, the shooter bought a ticket and sat in the front row, joining an audience of about four hundred people. Not long after the film started, he ducked out through an emergency exit by the screen, which he propped open.

He went to his car, parked near the exit door, changed into protective clothing, and armed himself: with a couple of canisters filled with a smoky gas, a twelve-gauge Remington 870 Express Tactical shotgun, a Smith & Wesson M&P15 semiautomatic rifle with a 100-round drum magazine, a Glock 22 .40-caliber. All of the weapons were purchased legally.

A half hour into *The Dark Knight Rises*, he reentered the theater through the exit door, dressed in black, wearing a gas mask, a load-bearing vest, a ballistic helmet, bullet-resistant leggings, a bullet-resistant throat protector, a groin protector, and tactical gloves. At first, the audience thought this was some kind of promotional stunt; after all, it was the local premiere of the film.

He threw two of the gas canisters, which released a gas that obscured the audience members' vision, burned their throats and eyes, and caused their skin to itch. He fired the twelve-gauge at the ceiling, then fired it at the audience. Then he went through his arsenal. He got off several rounds of the Smith & Wesson M&P15 semiautomatic rifle with a 100-round drum magazine, which malfunctioned. If it had not, there's no telling how many more people would have been killed or wounded. He also used the Glock 22 .40-caliber handgun. In total, he fired seventy-six shots in the theater: six with the shotgun, sixty-five from the semiautomatic rifle, and five from the Glock.

The shooter was a twenty-five-year-old from Oak Hills, California. He graduated from the University of California with a degree in neuroscience in 2010. The following year, he enrolled in the University of Colorado's neuroscience Ph.D. program. In 2012, his grades plummeted and he dropped out. He lived in a one-bedroom apartment in Aurora.

He physically wounded seventy people who went out that night to see a movie. He murdered twelve people. In the stories of all of those who were wounded and murdered are profound examples of love, life, heroic sacrifice, and unfathomable loss and heartache.

The twelve people killed:

Jonathan "Jon" Blunk, age twenty-six, pushed his girlfriend, twenty-one-year-old Jansen Young, to the floor and was fatally shot while shielding her body with his own. Young survived and has said, "I guess I didn't really know he had passed, up until I started shaking him and saying, 'Jon, Jon, we have to go. . . . It's time for us to get out of here.'"

In memory of eighteen-year-old Alexander "AJ" Boik, more than a thousand people helped create a black-and-purple patchwork quilt: black to represent the traditional color of mourning, purple because it was AJ's favorite color. His high school classmates had voted him "most likely to become the next Pablo Picasso." Boik was to begin classes at the Rocky Mountain College of Art and Design in the fall.

Twenty-nine-year-old Air Force Reserve staff sergeant Jesse Childress went to the movie that night with two friends. His father, Shannon Childress, has said there aren't words to describe his grief. He told *The*

Denver Post he is unsure how to respond to people when they ask how he is doing. "What am I supposed to say?"

The family of Gordon Cowden, age fifty-one, issued a statement that said he would be "remembered for his devotion to his children and for always trying his best to do the right thing, no matter the obstacle." Cowden's two teenage children were with him that night at the theater. News reports said they "escaped unharmed." That phrase seems off to me, as these children left that night with the pain of having lost their father.

Jessica Ghawi, twenty-four, was at the movie with her friend Brent Lowak. Jordan Ghawi, Jessica's brother, wrote in a blog that the two friends dropped to the floor to take cover from the spray of bullets. "Brent then heard Jessica scream and noticed that she was struck by a round in the leg. Brent began holding pressure on the wound and attempted to calm Jessica. It was at this time that Brent took a round to his lower extremities. While still administering first aid, Brent noticed that Jessica was no longer screaming."

According to a statement from Kelley Vojtsek, the girlfriend of Navy Petty Officer 3rd Class John Larimer, twenty-seven, "John and I were seated in the middle area. When the violence occurred, John immediately and instinctively covered me and brought me to the ground in order to protect me from any danger."

Matt McQuinn, twenty-seven, pushed his girlfriend, Samantha Yowler, also twenty-seven, to the floor, and protected her body with his. Samantha was shot in the knee.

Friends of Micayla Medek, twenty-three, who were there with her that night quickly informed her family that she had been wounded, but it took nearly twenty hours for her family to learn that she had been killed.

Alex Sullivan had gone to see *The Dark Knight Rises* on his twenty-seventh birthday. That day also marked his first wedding anniversary.

In a statement, his family described Alex as "a gentle giant, known and loved by so many. He always had a glowing smile on his face and he made friends with everyone."

Alexander Teves, twenty-four, had recently graduated from the University of Denver with a master's degree in counseling psychology. He was killed while protecting his girlfriend, Amanda Lindgren, who has said, "I wouldn't be here without him."

Rebecca Wingo, thirty-two, went to the movie on a date. Fluent in Mandarin, she worked as a translator for the U.S. Air Force. She was raising two daughters, ages nine and five, while putting herself through school. She hoped to become a social worker to help teens transition out of the foster-care system.

Veronica Moser-Sullivan was the youngest victim, only six years old. Shortly after arriving on the scene, Aurora police sergeant Michael Hawkins found the child with a critical wound in her abdomen. He has said that as he rushed her to an ambulance the small girl was "bleeding all over" him and that when he laid her on the stretcher, "I realized at that point that she had probably died."

Veronica's mother, twenty-five-year-old Ashley Moser, and her boyfriend took Veronica to the movie that night. It was a night out to celebrate the fact that Ashley had just learned she was pregnant. Ashley was shot three times. One of the bullets that remained lodged in her spine left her paralyzed. During surgery, she suffered a miscarriage. A day later, the Sunday after the Friday shooting, Ashley learned that her daughter Veronica was dead.

The shooter was charged with 165 counts, including first-degree murder and first-degree murder with extreme indifference, attempted murder and attempted murder with extreme indifference, and explosives and weapons charges. The trial would begin in April 2015.

What do you say to someone who has just lost her home and all that was in it? What do you say to someone who has lost his home and his wife, as Scott Appel did in the Lower North Fork Fire? What do you say to a husband, a wife, a mother, a father, a daughter, a son, whose loved one has been critically wounded in a mass shooting and is undergoing surgery and may or may not ever fully recover, may or may not ever walk again?

I'm sorry?

Sorry didn't begin to cover how I felt. And yet whatever I felt paled in comparison with what they felt. Each of their agonies was uniquely their own. Fact was, I felt I didn't have the right to feel anything. I had no idea what to say. I did say I was sorry. I said, "Please let us know if there is anything we can do." I said, "Coloradans are thinking and praying for you." I said those things because I didn't know what else to say. Because that's what you're supposed to say. And because they were true.

President Obama returned to Colorado to meet with victims of the shooting and their families. He had experience in the role of consoler in chief. Not all that long ago, he had visited Tucson for a memorial service to recognize the victims of the shooting rampage there that left Congresswoman Gabrielle Giffords badly injured. He spoke at a memorial service for the more than two dozen miners killed in a West Virginia mine explosion the previous year. Most recently, he had gone to Joplin, Missouri, to mark the one-year anniversary of the deadly tornado that ripped through the city.

He told me that all I could do in moments like this was just be there.

I tried to be there.

In the days, even hours, immediately following the Aurora shooting, there was much talk of guns. The debate over gun control was inevitable—especially in our state, scene of the 1999 Columbine High School mass shooting. It was a necessary and good debate to have—only, in my opinion, not right now.

The Sunday after the Friday massacre in Aurora, I appeared on CNN's *State of the Union* and NBC's *Meet the Press*. I was asked whether I thought there was a need for stricter gun control laws. While the families were still in shock and grieving, while some of them had yet to bury the loved ones they had lost, I believed it was too soon to turn the discussion to the politics of gun control. I also was convinced that mental health issues were part of the discussion. On *Meet the Press* I said:

> I think that [gun control] debate's going to happen. It has already started. But you look at this person, again, almost a creature, if he couldn't have gotten access to guns, what kind of bomb he would have manufactured? We're at a time, an information age, where there's access to all kinds of information. . . . I think he was almost a terrorist that wanted to take away not just from the people here, but from the country, our ability to enjoy life, to go to a movie theater. Which for most of us is a refuge where we can get away from the pressures of life. It's a human issue. How are we not able to identify someone like this who is so deeply, deeply disturbed?

IN THE BACKGROUND throughout this long, terrible summer, Helen and I had reached a shared realization that we would separate. On July 31, we issued a statement:

> After years of marriage that have added tremendous love and depth to both of our lives, we have decided to separate. This decision is mutual and amicable. We continue to have the utmost respect for each other, and we remain close friends. We intend to continue functioning as a family that spends a great deal of time together. In fact, we will embark on our annual family vacation together this

week, share meals often, and plan to spend holidays together. You can continue to expect to see both of us out in the community—sometimes together, sometimes solo. Please feel free to include both of us in social gatherings as we will not find it awkward.

Our chief concern right now is the well-being of our son, so we ask everyone to respect our privacy as we make this transition. While public office made this announcement necessary, it will be the only statement we make on this private matter. We want to thank our friends, family, and community for all of the support you have shown us as a couple and as individuals, and for the support we know you will provide as we move forward.

Obviously, before this release went out, Helen and I talked with Teddy about our separation. The day we gave him the news—suffice it to say, that was a hard day. In my personal life, it was as hard a day as I can remember. Teddy's ten-year-old freckled face was knotted in pain and disbelief. But unlike many of the families I had been visiting with over the last two months, Helen and Teddy and I still had one another. Although Helen and I would be apart, we were and always would be a family. Helen and I and Teddy were alive. Helen and I could still hold our son, watch him grow. We were fortunate.

Fourteen

GUNS

During November and December 2012, major events unfolded that would dramatically shape the remainder of my first term, which it seemed went by in a flash.

That November, President Obama won his second term. He carried Colorado with 51 percent of the vote, while Mitt Romney got 46 percent. During that election Coloradans also voted to pass Amendment 64—making Colorado the first state in the country to legalize recreational marijuana. And our friend Frank McNulty learned just how strongly Coloradans felt about his decision to block civil unions. He and his Republicans lost control of the House. Going into the next session, the Democrats controlled both chambers of the state legislature.

On December 14, 2012, a twenty-year-old man dressed in black clothing and armed with a Bushmaster XM15-E2S semiautomatic rifle and several magazines shot his way through the locked plate-glass front doors of the Sandy Hook Elementary School in Newtown, Connecticut. Inside, he fatally shot twenty children—all between the ages of six and seven years old—and six adult staff members. Before he went to Sandy

Hook Elementary and slaughtered those children, the shooter killed his mother at their Newtown home. When first responders arrived at the school, the shooter committed suicide.

In the immediate aftermath of the Aurora massacre I had said that this was not the time to talk about gun policy. As we embarked on the 2013 legislative session where we would spend the next four months shaping our state policy and laws, I was of the mind that now was precisely the right time. I made that as clear as I possibly could as we kicked off the session with our State of the State speech.

I began by taking stock, reminding the General Assembly where we had been and where we were, so that we could be that much more thoughtful as we charted where we were going. The year 2012 was, I said, a hard year. At one point the previous summer there were ten wildfires raging across Colorado—388,000 acres burned, 648 homes destroyed, and six people killed. Then the Aurora shootings in a dark theater. Dozens wounded, twelve lives lost. I asked for a moment of silence to honor those who had died the previous year, and so that we could remember all of those who were still recovering.

I noted the dedication and sacrifice of our first responders to those tragedies, the ones who put their lives on the line. Some firefighters in Rist Canyon watched their own homes burn as they fought to save a historic schoolhouse. There were so many heroes, we couldn't possibly mention all of them by name. But we thanked Specialist Duran Cornelius. He and the members of his Colorado National Guard firefighter unit were activated to fight the High Park Fire. Colorado Springs fire chief Rich Brown and the men and women in his department had what must have been one of the most arduous summers of their lives, battling the Waldo Canyon Fire. Colorado Springs mayor Steve Bach did everything he could to hold that community together.

At the Aurora shooting, less than ninety seconds after the first dispatch, officers were on the scene. Standard response protocols gave way to gut instincts. Police cruisers became makeshift ambulances. We thanked Aurora mayor Steve Hogan, police chief Dan Oates, and fire chief Mike Garcia, and all of the men and women who served under them.

In that speech, we noted that we had met survivors who helped strangers escape the theater, teenagers who rushed their friends to emergency rooms. We remembered the family members whose loved ones died while shielding someone else. There were so many stories of courage and resilience. I mentioned that one victim in an Aurora hospital told me: "The outpouring of light and love is so much more powerful than any darkness."

Indeed.

Now, I said, "We have an obligation to prevent similar tragedies, to do good, to bring light to darkness. We have an obligation to represent the best that is Colorado. This isn't a Democratic or Republican agenda. It's a Colorado agenda. It's our common mission."

I acknowledged our new Senate President, John Morse, House Speaker Mark Ferrandino, Minority Leader Bill Cadman, and Minority Leader Mark Waller.

I noted that our history of addressing difficult problems together made it possible to discuss gun violence and mental health. Not one or the other. Both.

"There are no easy solutions," I said, but "we shouldn't be restrained from discussing any of these issues. Our democracy demands this type of debate."

Then we got to it.

"Let me prime the pump: Why not have universal background checks for all gun sales? . . . Surely, Second Amendment advocates and gun control supporters can find common ground in support of this proposition:

let's examine our laws and make the changes needed to keep guns out of the hands of dangerous people.

"It's not enough to prevent dangerous people from getting weapons. We have to do a better job of identifying and helping people who are a threat to themselves and others. That is why we are requesting your support for a comprehensive overhaul of our state's mental health system. . . . Issues related to guns, mental health, and child welfare have added challenges to the agenda we began two years ago. The urgency behind our original agenda, however, continues. . . ."

Chief among those other issues was still the economy. We had made great strides. Unemployment was down. *Forbes* magazine had recently listed Colorado among the five best states for business. We were now in a position with the budget where we could begin to restore funding for education. Admittedly it was not enough to make up for the cuts that had been made in response to our $1 billion shortfall. We still had much left to do, but we were getting there.

Then there was Amendment 64. Although marijuana was illegal according to federal law and some Coloradans might have been against legalizing it, the majority had won the day. We now had to develop, from scratch, the framework to regulate and monitor the production, sale, and distribution of a federally banned substance. We already had a task force at work considering the legal and policy implications of Amendment 64. This was, quite literally, uncharted territory, a historic democratic experiment. We were determined to implement this new law, the will of the people, in a way that promoted the health and safety of all Coloradans. We were especially mindful of the impact on our children. We needed to do all we could to keep marijuana out of the reach of kids.

In just about any other legislative session our efforts to implement Amendment 64 would have been the dominant issue in the capitol. But the 2013 session was about guns. Legislators knew there was public support for background checks. According to a *Denver Post* poll conducted that January, 80 percent of those surveyed supported background checks for all gun sales. That same poll also showed that more than 60 percent of those surveyed supported limits to ammunition magazines. Of course, if that same survey were conducted in any of the heavily Republican districts that many of our legislators represented, the results likely would have been very different.

On February 2, the legislative leadership—Senate President Morse and Speaker Ferrandino—asked me if they would have my support for a bill that would limit high-capacity magazines. I said if the bill made sense and the votes were there, I would sign it—which is pretty much what I say when discussing any potential piece of legislation. I had already clearly stated that I wanted to pass a bill for universal background checks. Morse, a former Colorado law enforcement officer, wanted to propose a bill that would have held the manufacturer and the retailer civilly liable for any gun used in a crime. We had heard through the capitol grapevine that he had such a bill in mind. By then, we knew federal courts had already ruled that such laws were unconstitutional. Morse asked me if I'd support such a bill and I told him no for that very reason.

About a week later, Speaker Mark Ferrandino's House introduced three gun bills: One would make high-capacity magazines with more than ten rounds illegal, albeit with certain grandfather exceptions: if you already owned magazines with more than ten rounds, you wouldn't be breaking the law. Another would make background checks mandatory for *any* gun sale or transfer. The third would require the customer to pay a fee for the background check. There were zero Republican legislators in support of the bills. To be fair, even some Democrats didn't support them, at least as they were currently written.

During those days, and in particular, the day they were introduced, there were countless hearings and meetings going on surrounding the gun bills. There were many passionate Coloradans on both sides testifying at hearings and protesting around the capitol. A large number of the sheriffs of Colorado's sixty-four counties came to protest the bills.

Generally speaking, these sheriffs, all of them elected in Republican counties, objected for the same reasons the Republican legislators objected. One of their arguments was that a high-capacity bill didn't make sense and was unenforceable. They didn't think it was practical or useful to arrest people with guns having magazines of more than ten rounds. They correctly pointed out that these magazines were still legal in other states and that anyone could order them for home delivery. As far as the background checks went, their main argument against it was that only law-abiding citizens would get the background checks; the bad guys wouldn't bother. In other words, some sheriffs argued, the background checks wouldn't do much, if anything, to prevent guns from getting into the hands of bad guys involved with gun-related crimes.

That same day, planes flew over the capitol with banners that said: "HICK DON'T TAKE OUR GUNS." From around eight a.m. until late in the afternoon, a caravan of cars circled the capitol, honking horns and covered in signs protesting the bills.

That afternoon, in my office, I met with David Keene, the president of the National Rifle Association. As you might guess, Keene was not too keen on the proposed legislation. With all the racket going on outside we had a hard time hearing each other, but as we talked, I tried to find middle ground. Keene agreed that mental health needed to be addressed. I guess you could say we agreed on the need to address mental health and agreed to disagree on the rest.

On February 12, about a week after the bills were first introduced, the House amended the high-capacity-magazine bill. Now the proposed ban was on magazines with more than fifteen rounds. The original ban on magazines with more than ten rounds was based on a federal law that had long since sunsetted. Drafters of this new amendment to the House bill made the change because many guns are manufactured with magazines holding ten to fifteen rounds. The thinking behind the change was that the bill might get more buy-in, or at least less resistance, if it didn't attempt to make some of the most popular guns illegal.

The background check bill was also amended to include a provision that allowed a licensed gun owner to loan his or her gun to anyone at any time for a seventy-two-hour period without needing a background check. In other words, if someone wanted to lend his friend a gun to go hunting, he could do so without needing to put his friend through a background check. The bill was also amended to allow family members to transfer their guns to extended family members, such as nieces, cousins, et cetera, without needing a background check.

As the session progressed and the debates over the bills became more intense, I thought about the objection to background checks raised by the sheriffs and Republican legislators. Maybe they were right; maybe background checks don't snag bad guys.

I came home one night, tired and cranky, and made the mistake of complaining to eleven-year-old Teddy. Sarcasm dripping, Teddy asked, "Daddy, what do you do all day at work that's *sooo* hard? Make decisions? Dad, get the facts, make a decision, check, next." He paused for effect, and repeated it: "Get the facts, make a decision, check, next. Every day I have to go into school and learn something that I didn't even know existed the day before, and if I don't get it completely right, my next day is misery, 'cause everything is based on the day before." And he went on. After ten minutes, I had to agree that sixth grade was harder than being governor.

But when I woke up the next morning, I realized that he was right: we hadn't gotten the facts. Republican legislators were united in saying that crooks weren't stupid, they weren't going to sign up for a background check, so why were we wasting the time and money of law-abiding citizens in a frivolous exercise? We had the national data, but we hadn't asked for our local facts. We had been doing background checks on half the gun purchases, and we were arguing that we should expand that to all gun purchases. But we didn't have results on those purchases that we did check.

So when I got to work, I called our office of public safety. What did we find in the previous year? Was it worth our time and the ten-buck fee we charged? Looking at the numbers from the previous year, 2012, when we were running background checks on roughly half of the gun purchases, here is what we found: In a state with a little more than 5 million people, we stopped 38 people who had been convicted of homicide from buying a gun. We stopped 133 people convicted of sexual assault, 680 burglars, and 1,100 people convicted of felony assault (where someone usually goes to the hospital) from buying a gun. And just in case you really don't believe that crooks are stupid, we arrested 420 people, when they came back to pick up their new gun, on an outstanding warrant for a violent crime.

I told this "Teddy story" on Colorado Public Radio, because it was cute, and the numbers were compelling, but it cost me. One of Teddy's chums came into school the next week with a link to the recording of the show that he'd gotten through his parents. Teddy came home in a huff and asked what I was doing, stealing his idea. I apologized, of course, and said I hadn't stolen anything, and had he listened all the way through, he would have heard that I gave him complete credit. "What more do you want?" I asked. He gave me his thinnest smile, and said, "Sure, Dad, whatever. Do you even know what the word 'royalty' means?"

And they say our public schools aren't getting better.

As far as the arguments I'd heard against banning high-capacity magazines, I could not ignore the connection between guns with high-capacity magazines and mass shootings.

One study charted forty-four mass shootings between May 1981 and the December 2012 Sandy Hook tragedy—mass shootings meaning three or more people were killed—where the shooter used high-capacity magazines of thirteen rounds or more. In these mass shootings, 423 people were murdered, including two police officers, and 422 people were wounded.

It seemed to me there was ample evidence that background checks were worth the small fee and the ten-minute wait to do the check, and to support the high-capacity-magazine bill.

In early March, I received a call from Michael Bloomberg. He was irritated with us. Mayor Bloomberg was a staunch supporter of strict gun laws. With the fortune he had made in the news business, he was financing a national campaign to toughen gun laws. On the phone, he told me he felt that the House bills weren't tough enough. He was concerned about the provision that allowed a gun owner seventy-two hours to share his gun with a family member or an extended family member without needing to undergo a background check. Once again, I guess you could say, we agreed to disagree.

Thus far, I had the sheriffs from Republican counties, the NRA, Mayor Bloomberg, Republican legislators, and even some Democratic ones upset with me. I figured we must be doing something right. Truth was, of course, there was a great deal of support for these bills. Mark Kelly, United States Navy captain, astronaut, and husband of Gabby Giffords, came to Colorado to testify in support of the bills.

All three of the bills moved from the House, where we picked up one Republican supporter, and through the Senate, where they passed, but without unanimous Democratic support.

I was scheduled to sign the bills on March 20, 2013. I fully expected that was going to be a difficult day for me politically. Then something happened that reminded me that a difficult political day really isn't a difficult day at all.

The night before I was to sign the gun bills, a Tuesday night, I was at a dinner with a friend and local businessman, Rick Sapkin. Rox called. We had a rule that whenever we called each other, no matter what, we would always take it. It was just after 8:30 p.m. She had a terrible tone in her voice: the emotionlessness of someone who is overcome with emotion and can't let it get in the way. The first time Rox told me what had happened, I didn't hear her. Rick and I were in a noisy restaurant. "What?!" I said. The second time I heard her loud and clear.

"It's Tom. Tom Clements. He's been shot. He's dead."

It took a minute to sink in.

Tom Clements headed our state's Department of Corrections. Shortly after I was elected governor, I hired Tom to come from his home state of Missouri, where he had run that state's DOC. Tom had a reputation for being a progressive corrections director, who cared deeply about the mental health of his prisoners. He believed it was critical not to simply lock up criminals and then let them loose. For their own sake and for society's sake, Tom's guiding principle was to prepare prisoners for their ultimate transition back into society, which meant treating them as human beings.

One of the topics I discussed with Tom during the job interview was solitary confinement. Colorado then had more than 1,500 inmates in solitary, which our DOC called Administrative Segregation, or Ad Seg. These were criminals convicted of serious crimes, had discipline problems, or were dangerous in the general prison population, but in Ad Seg, they were locked up in a cell for twenty-three hours a day.

Many of these inmates had some form of mental illness; there was ample research showing that locking them up in Ad Seg only made their mental states worse. On average, inmates who were sent to solitary in Colorado spent twenty-three months there. Considering that 97 percent of inmates are ultimately returned to their communities, and some of them were discharged right from Ad Seg into society, this seemed to me like a bad idea all the way around.

I started researching Ad Seg long before I was elected. I first heard about it from my old friend from Buckhorn Petroleum, Jack Ebel, the guy everyone loved, the guy who took up collections for employees in need, the guy who did his best to allay his colleagues' anxieties during the transition, the guy who got Russell to brew the carbonated lighter beer at the Wynkoop, and also persuaded our chef, Mark, to put the Pojoaque vegetarian green chili on the menu.

Well, Jack's son, Evan, was locked up. He had an extensive record. He'd experienced blinding rages since childhood. Evan had severe mental health issues that no one could diagnose or deal with. None of his meds from the age of ten ever worked. He was in and out of trouble throughout school, and Jack and his wife at the time, Jody, tried literally everything. Beginning when he was nineteen years old, Evan pleaded guilty to a number of crimes: a couple of cases of robbery and felony menacing; robbing people in their homes at gunpoint. He pleaded guilty to assault charges and leaving the scene of an accident after he carjacked a man and then crashed the car. Jack understood that his son deserved to be in prison, but, as Jack explained to me, Evan had spent the last six years in Ad Seg, and Jack could see with every biweekly visit that this was making Evan worse, not better.

When I brought this up with Tom, without ever mentioning Evan Ebel, he knew all the statistics. He knew the overuse and abuse of Ad Seg was a very bad and very dangerous practice. He was already of the mind that it needed to be addressed. In the two years that Tom was on the job as our head of DOC, he and his staff cut the number of inmates in Ad Seg by more than half: from 1,505 inmates (among the highest rates in the country) to 726. Tom believed that Colorado should be the worst place to commit a crime and the best place to get a second chance.

Only a couple of days before Rox called and gave me the news that

Tom had been killed, he and I had been in a meeting together. Even when Tom was talking about the most difficult things, like cutting back Ad Seg, even though many of his management team didn't agree, he'd always make jokes and have a lighthearted tone. It's been said that when someone dies, all the tears we shed are selfish tears because we feel bad about what we have lost from our lives. Tom changed the dynamic of our administration's whole cabinet. Tom was someone who worked in a cold, hard world with a remarkably warm and tender heart.

When Rox first called me, she didn't have any information. All she knew was that Tom had been shot in the doorway of his house. I went numb. Shut down. It was like when my stepfather, Bill, called me and said Mom had died. I asked Rox, What do we need to do? How was Tom's wife? It was the only time I recall Rox not knowing what to do. She was devastated. She adored Tom. We all did. Asking how Tom's wife, Lisa, was doing was a stupid question.

Over the course of the next twelve hours or so we learned that sometime around 8:30 p.m. the doorbell rang at the Clementses' home in the town of Monument. Tom answered it, and a guy in a pizza delivery uniform fatally shot him in the chest. Within minutes, Lisa called police. Deputies arrived and found Tom and Lisa inside the home on a set of stairs. Medical crews performed CPR on Tom. He died on the scene, in his home, in front of Lisa. Tom was fifty-eight years old, and left behind his "three girls": Lisa and their daughters Rachel and Sara.

A massive investigation was then under way, involving sheriff's deputies and investigators from state, local, and federal agencies. The state troopers insisted on beefing up security for Rox and me. In the hours after the shooting, there was no suspect. The only clue linked to the killer was a car, a Cadillac sedan with mismatched plates that a neighbor spotted near the Clements home around the time of the shooting.

The next day, Wednesday, March 20, I signed the three gun bills.

Among the supporters who gathered with me were Mark Kelly, Sandy and Lonnie Phillips, and Megan Sullivan. Sandy and Lonnie Phillips's twenty-four-year-old daughter, Jessica Ghawi, had been killed in the Aurora theater shooting. They traveled from San Antonio for the signing. "It's a good day," Sandy told *The Denver Post*. "The state of Colorado is making great strides to save lives. Hopefully, other states will follow in this state's footsteps." Megan Sullivan's older brother, Alex, was also murdered in the theater. "My brother was killed by a person with a hundred-round magazine," she said. "He didn't have a chance."

My mind was on my murdered friend, Tom, and his wife and their two daughters. After signing the gun bills, I left the capitol and went to the home of my deputy legal counsel, Stephanie Donner, who had just had her second child, a boy. Stephanie had been essential in shaping the gun legislation. She was the one who informed me that Morse's original idea had been unconstitutional. Stephanie is Jewish, and was hosting a bris for her son. Many members of my cabinet were in attendance, as was most of our senior staff. We gathered there to celebrate Stephanie and her family, while we were mourning the very recent news of Tom's murder. In Judaism, the ceremony is a reminder that our spiritual, emotional, moral, and ethical perfection requires human effort. Jews believe that God cannot do this. Asked to speak, I talked about how precious the human life is and said that along with mourning the passing of a wonderful human being and friend, Tom, we were welcoming a beautiful baby boy, and in all death there is a life.

Two days later, in the late afternoon, the state patrol's chief investigator came to my office to give me a briefing. Authorities were fairly certain that the man who had killed Tom Clements had been killed the day before, after a high-speed car chase and a shoot-out in Texas.

In the briefing I learned that a sheriff's deputy in Montague County, Texas, pulled over the suspect on a routine stop, unaware of the search in

Colorado. The suspect shot Deputy James Boyd and then fled. Boyd, who was wearing a protective vest, radioed to report the direction the car was heading. After a chase during which speeds reached up to 100 miles an hour, an eighteen-wheeler smashed into the suspect's car, which caught fire. The suspect jumped out and shot at the officers. They returned fire and killed him.

I was told the casings from the suspect's 9mm Smith & Wesson were the same brand and caliber as those used by the gunman who'd killed Tom. Law enforcement was confident that the suspect had killed Nathan Leon, whose side job was delivering pizzas for Domino's, then taken his uniform and his black 1991 Cadillac, dumped Leon's body, driven to Tom's home, killed him, and then made his way to Texas.

I received the briefing in my office. The investigator had set up a big projection screen, and as he talked, he was moving through a lot of slides, showing the scene at Tom's house, the crashed car and other images from the shoot-out in Texas, then a mug shot of the suspect, then a shot of the Domino's uniform. . . . "Wait," I said. I interrupted because I thought I saw the word "Ebel" at the bottom of the previous screen of the mug shot, and there he was. It was the son of my longtime friend Jack Ebel. I had a wave of nausea.

Up until that point, the people who had come into my life as if cosmically preordained—my *karass*, to borrow the Kurt Vonnegut term I had come to admire and believe in—all amounted to an extended community that created joy and made life more wonderful. Here, now, were Jack Ebel and Tom Clements, two of my friends, intersecting in this horror.

Making the tragedy worse, the Colorado Department of Corrections mistakenly released Evan Ebel before he had completed his full sentence. While he had been serving an eight-year prison term, he pleaded guilty to punching a prison correctional officer in November 2006 and was to serve a consecutive prison term of an additional four years. The reason for the release, according to the DOC, was a judicial "clerical error." The way the forms in his file were written, it was not clear that his sentences were to be consecutive.

Evan Ebel's motive for killing Tom Clements remains the subject of an ongoing investigation. However, there is no doubt that three families have been enduring an indescribable pain: the Ebel family, the Clements family, and the family of Nathan Leon.

Nathan was twenty-seven years old when Ebel fatally shot him on March 17, 2013. He and his wife, Katie, were raising three daughters— twins, age five; and a seven-year-old. Nathan—"Nate" to those who knew him best—had delivered pizzas on the side. He was a junior library assistant at IBM in Boulder. He was working the extra job because he wanted more for his wife and three little girls. According to what his family told *The Denver Post*, Nathan was an excellent guitarist. Like his father, John, he loved computers and gadgetry, and roller coasters.

Nathan had aspirations of going to college to become a psychologist or a crime-scene analyst. When he returned home from work, his girls would run to him, squealing with joy. "He was my role model. He was a different kind of a man," his father, John Leon, told the *Post*. "He would always see good in people. He never raised his voice. Never." His widow, Katie, told the newspaper that she regularly visits the spot where Nathan's body was found. Sometimes she takes her daughters, and she tells them they are visiting the location where "Daddy became an angel."

THE ANGEL IN *It's a Wonderful Life*, Clarence Oddbody, really did put it best: "Each man's life touches so many other lives. When he isn't around he leaves an awful hole, doesn't he?"

Tom Clements's death left an awful hole in our administration, in each one of us. Staffers would see one another in the halls, exchange a look, and begin to weep. To say that no one felt much like working would be an understatement. But the state must go on. Tom himself would have said as much. Until we found someone to take over the Department of Corrections, Rox, as if she didn't have enough to do, became the interim director of the DOC, along with her chief of staff duties.

Alan and his team worked with the House and the Senate, and when the 2013 legislative session was complete, there were reasons to smile, at least for a while.

We became the first state in the nation to pass laws to regulate the legal sale of marijuana. Every other regulated industry has benefited from years of trial and error, and could look to other states or even other countries for models of what has worked and what has not. That was not an option here. Our chief legal counsel, Jack Finlaw, and Barb Brohl, executive director of the Department of Revenue, facilitated months of collaboration between legislators, marijuana legalization advocates, opponents, industry leaders, policy experts, and law enforcement, and we established regulations for marijuana legalization and recreational pot shops.

The General Assembly agreed to a 15 percent excise tax and an initial 10 percent sales tax for recreational marijuana. For the sake of public safety, we set a legal limit of active THC, the psychoactive chemical in marijuana, that drivers can have in their blood so that juries have a benchmark to judge whether someone was too high to drive. The Colorado Department of Revenue created an innovative seed-to-sale tracking system. The rules were written. Recreational sales of marijuana would begin on January 1, 2014.

One of the challenges to being the first in the world to create a brand-new industry is that the regulatory structure we started with was bound to have profound effects on which businesses would prosper, and which businesses would perish, or never exist. In 2013, one of the major questions was whether we would require that our marijuana businesses be "vertically integrated."

Vertical integration meant that licensed marijuana dispensaries would have to grow their own marijuana. In the medical marijuana world, there was already vertical integration. A medical marijuana patient would come to a dispensary with his doctor-recommended plant count, and the dispensary would agree to grow those plants for him, and the patient would buy from that store. But for the recreational system, marijuana plants would not be tied to doctor recommendations, so there was no logistical reason the industry had to be vertically integrated.

Many argued that vertical integration would help with enforcement and regulation. It would be much easier to ensure fidelity to the system if there was one owner as we tracked marijuana plants from seed to sale. Furthermore, they argued, there would be fewer licensees in the system, which meant that the Marijuana Enforcement Division would have to perform fewer background checks, as well as fewer changes of ownership, and would be able to spend more time enforcing public health and public safety regulations. The Department of Revenue saw some merit to the argument that having fewer licensees, at least initially, would help create a smooth rollout. It was no surprise that the major supporters of vertical integration were the medical marijuana industry. They had the knowledge, capital, and infrastructure to capitalize on that structure. And for everybody else it would be a huge barrier to entry.

On the other side, people argued that vertical integration would make a few actors far too powerful. Growers become more economically efficient the larger they get. Under a vertically integrated system, a few growers would get larger and larger, allowing their prices to fall, and they would open more and more stores, selling marijuana at a much lower price than their smaller competitors. At some point, these few actors would then have all the economic and political power to be able to change the regulatory environment to whatever suited them best. Some argued that this was a reason to ban vertical integration.

The Amendment 64 task force attempted to split the baby. They would require vertical integration, but there would be a cap on marijuana grower sizes and the number of licenses an owner could hold. It was a bit of a clunky solution, and one that clever lawyers could probably work around. Over the year, the legislature, industry, the Department of Revenue, and the governor's staff came up with a better solution. For the first ten months of legalized recreational marijuana, we would require vertical integration. We wanted to be able to know our actors, and know that our systems were working, before we opened up the structure too much. (In October 2014, we would end our vertical integration rule, removing one barrier to entry that could potentially have concentrated the industry into a few actors.)

We passed two laws addressing undocumented residents. One law enabled students without legal immigration status in our state who have graduated from Colorado high schools to attend our state colleges and universities at the in-state tuition rate. The more educated our state's residents are, the more each and every one of us has a chance to fulfill his or her potential, the better off our state is. Another law enabled undocumented people to get driver's licenses. If undocumented residents are driving, and they are, let's at least do what we can to ensure they are properly trained and have insurance. Because no tax dollars can go to supporting programs for undocumented residents, we made this a user-fee-supported service. With agreement from community leaders—stakeholders, in political-speak—we set the rate for these services at three times the typical fee in order to get these Department of Motor Vehicles programs up and running.

Because of budgetary pressures, state employees had gone four years without a raise. They were made to take furloughs and their pension contributions went up. Now that our budget was stabilized, we were able to finally award them a raise, albeit a modest one.

We passed legislation that granted income and child tax credits to lower-income working families.

Along with passing the gun legislation, we took steps to improve Colorado's mental health services. We approved spending $20 million to overhaul the state's mental health crisis response system. The legislation established a request-for-proposals process to launch a statewide twenty-four-hour hotline, twenty-four-hour walk-in stabilization centers, and respite care, among other services.

Last but certainly not least, a bill to legally recognize same-sex civil unions was signed into law in Colorado. Less than a year after Speaker McNulty condemned the bill to a "kill committee," and along with it, his party's majority in the House, State Representative Carole Murray, a Republican from conservative Castle Rock, voted in favor of the civil unions legislation. She said she did so because of her "Republican belief in personal liberty, equality, and individual responsibility for each and every one of our citizens."

One of the bills that did *not* make it out of that legislative session was an attempt to abolish the death penalty in Colorado. My senior staff helped keep that bill from passing.

Make no mistake, I wanted to see the death penalty abolished. I am against the death penalty.

Well, first I was for it.

But now I am against it.

Some of my detractors have criticized me for saying what I wrote right there; they've made a joke out of my changing my position on the death penalty, as if changing your position on an issue as profound and irrevocable as taking a human life, and in the name of justice, is a character flaw. If it is, add that to the list of my flaws.

My views on capital punishment changed as that third legislative session was drawing to a close, when I had to decide whether or not I was going to allow the state to carry out a mass murderer's death sentence. My reasons for not wanting that bill to abolish the death penalty to pass were tied to my thinking about what I would do with that order. Rather than use the mass murderer's name, I'll go with his DOC "Offender Number": 89148.

On May 1, 2013, the District Court in Arapahoe County issued a warrant for 89148's execution, setting the date to fall between August 18 and August 24, 2013. Five days later, on May 6, legal counsel for 89148 submitted a petition for executive clemency, meaning I had to decide whether I would grant this mass murderer a reprieve, a commutation, or a pardon.

Pardon, meaning I would set 89148 free. Commutation, meaning I would unilaterally lessen the sentence. Reprieve, meaning I would postpone the execution.

As I reviewed the materials submitted to me along with the request for executive clemency, Teddy's good counsel was in my head. "Get the facts, make a decision, check, next."

Here were the facts: At ten p.m. on a Tuesday night in December 1993, a nineteen-year-old who had recently been fired from an Aurora Chuck E. Cheese killed four former coworkers and seriously wounded another in the restaurant, after hours. With a .25-caliber semiautomatic, at close range, 89148 killed Sylvia Crowell, nineteen years old, shot in the head; Colleen O'Connor, seventeen, fell to her knees and begged for her life and 89148 shot her through the top of her head; 89148 fatally shot nineteen-year-old Ben Grant in his left eye as he vacuumed; 89148 forced fifty-year-old Marge Kohlberg, the store manager, to open the safe, grabbed about $1,500, and shot her twice in the head. Offender 89148 shot twenty-year-old Bobby Stephens through the jaw, but he played dead and lived. A few hours later, police tracked down 89148 in a girlfriend's apartment.

On May 22, 2013, I decided to grant 89148 a reprieve from execution. I presented my reasons in my executive order. My decision had nothing to do with the specifics of this or any other case. I was not "retrying" 89148's case. The jury in the original trial had done that and in the fifteen years since the shooting, the mass murderer's counsel had gone through appeals. In my executive order, I addressed why I could not and would not support the death penalty system as a form of justice.

First, practically speaking, I presented the fact that the state simply was not prepared to carry out an execution. We did not have the drugs to carry out a death sentence. There had been only one legal execution in Colorado since 1967. That one was more than fifteen years earlier, in 1997. The drugs required to make the fatal concoction for lethal injection were difficult or impossible to obtain. Because of restrictions the Food and Drug Administration had imposed, pharmaceutical companies faced obstacles in distributing the drugs.

Legally speaking, I presented many facts. Among them were: If the state of Colorado is going to undertake the responsibility of executing a human being, the system must operate flawlessly. Colorado's system for capital punishment is not flawless. A recent study coauthored by several law professors showed that under Colorado's capital sentencing system, death sentences are not handed down fairly. Many defendants are eligible for capital punishment but almost none are actually sentenced to death. The three inmates who were currently on death row committed heinous crimes, but so have many others who are serving mandatory life sentences.

I cited what one former Colorado judge said to us: "The death penalty is simply the result of happenstance, the district attorney's choice, the jurisdiction in which the case is filed, perhaps the race or economic circumstances of the defendant."

I pointed out that eighteen states did not have the death penalty, and seven of the states that did had not carried out an execution in a decade. The United States was one of only a handful of developed countries that still used the death penalty as a form of punishment. Not to mention, estimates for the cost of the judicial process for 89148 ran north of $18 million.

I stated that the challenge of implementing a death sentence is compounded by the fact that the people of Colorado, and their elected representatives, are divided on the question of whether punishment of death or punishment of life in prison without the possibility of parole should be the maximum penalty for criminals in our state.

This debate, I pointed out, was evident during the 2013 legislative session when a bill was introduced to repeal the death penalty. In the executive order, I wrote that I opposed the passage of that legislation because repeal of the death penalty ought to be raised with the people of Colorado and not just their elected representatives. I added that it is likely that my decision in this case would continue the intense conversation Coloradans were having about the death penalty.

I concluded by stating that I once believed the death penalty had value as a deterrent. There was zero evidence to support the idea that the death penalty was a deterrent or that it did *anything* to make our world a safer or better place. Ordering the death of another human being would weigh heavily on any person's conscience. Some victims' families have said that only an execution will bring closure and a sense of justice. Other victims' families say they seek a different kind of closure—one that does not involve an execution. I wrote that there was nothing we could do that would ever bring their loved ones back. Some grief is so deep that it never completely disappears. I expressed how grateful my staff and I were for these families' willingness to share their stories.

My executive order for reprieve, in short, meant that as long as I was governor, 89148 would not be executed. My hope was that in the wake of my decision, Coloradans who supported the death penalty would reconsider their views on capital punishment, take a fresh look at some of the facts I presented in the executive order, or perhaps review the full scope of those facts as I had and, like me, change their minds. There were worse things one could do, such as, in my opinion, take another human life.

Although I did not submit them as a basis for my executive order, there were also troubling facts about 89148's case. Since the trial and sentencing, the mass murderer had been diagnosed as bipolar. In 2006, Department of Corrections mental health staff agreed that 89148 suffers from bipolar disorder. This information was not available to the jurors at trial. In addition, neuroimaging confirmed that 89148 had brain damage.

A jury must be unanimous in their decision to deliver a sentence of death. Three of the original jurors in this case had stated in affidavits that they might not have voted to execute 89148 if they had been informed he was bipolar.

"If I had heard evidence that [89148] has bipolar disorder, this may have made a difference in my sentencing verdict. Learning that [89148] suffers from this serious mental illness could have convinced me to take the death penalty off the table." (Affidavit of Juror U, October 2012.)

"If I had known that 89148 had this serious mental illness, it may have changed my decision about whether to sentence him to death or life without parole. Knowing about his bipolar disorder could have mitigated my impression of him as cold and remorseless, and it would have made my decision at the sentencing stage much harder." (Affidavit of Juror C, October 2012.)

"I think the jury should have been told about 89148's mental illness. I would have wanted to know about this in making my sentencing decision, and would have carefully considered any evidence of mental illness that was presented. If I had known that 89148 was mentally ill, it might have changed my decision about what punishment to impose." (Affidavit of Juror T, October 2012.)

Get the facts, make a decision, check, next.

NEXT. MY GOD.

Next: In the summer, groups dissatisfied with the gun legislation invested millions of dollars and probably millions of hours and mounted a campaign for special recall elections in the two districts where Democrats were the most politically vulnerable. Both of the state legislators in those districts—who had, of course, supported the laws—Angela Giron and the most passionate champion for the legislation, Senate President John Morse, lost their seats.

Next: In the early fall, Colorado endured another natural disaster. We had been through the fires; this time it was a flood. The media, which can sometimes be hyperbolic in their descriptions, described the flood as "biblical." In this case, they were accurate. The rains began in Boulder on September 9, 2013, and spread over more than a dozen eastern counties, mostly rural farming communities. After the hard drought and all the fires, rain was welcome. I remember waking in the middle of the night and hearing the steady patter on the roof, smiling—finally nature was delivering something good.

But after a couple of days of steady rain, it started raining hard, and once it started, the rain didn't stop for five days. When the downpours finally ended, rain totals for that five-day period neared the average amount of precipitation for an *entire* year.

In total, twenty-four counties were affected; *18,000* people required evacuation; more than 28,000 dwellings were either damaged or totally destroyed; more than seventeen inches of rain fell in Boulder County alone. The surging St. Vrain Creek cut off access to the town of Lyons, and large portions of the communities of Estes Park, Jamestown, Loveland, Drake, Longmont, Glen Haven, Greeley, and Evans were underwater, devastated. At least thirty state highway bridges had been destroyed, and another twenty were seriously damaged, with repairs to damaged bridges and roads expected to cost many millions of dollars. Miles of freight and passenger rail lines were washed out or submerged. Our assessment of total flood-related damage would exceed *$3 billion.*

As soon as possible, Rox and I climbed into a National Guard chopper to see how bad it was. Of course, as fate would have it, I had endured major hip surgery less than a week before (think getting your car's brakes relined), and so was on crutches, and even the normal scramble into the chopper was clumsy and painful. We lifted off from just south of Denver. We flew east and then due north. In no time, the city gave way to the clusters of suburban residential neighborhoods, and soon those were behind us and we were over fields and plains and farms. A hard bank left, to the north, over and along the Big Thompson River, up and over the foothills, into the mountains, over our towns like Boulder and Nederland and Jamestown and Lyons. The first thing I couldn't help but feel was how vast Colorado is. How spread out we are. How much distance and terrain—and life—there is between Coloradans.

And then we came upon the devastation.

It really did take my breath away.

The bridges and roads—so many bridges and roads—crumbled and gone. Houses and trailers and businesses and cars and bikes and children's swing sets—twisted, scattered, washed away. As if they meant nothing to anyone. Lives. So many lives upended, awash. I could see our residents. Young families, whose lives together were just beginning. Older people, who thought they had seen just about everything life was ever going to throw at them, in disbelief. Everything I saw at first had me thinking that everything and anything good had been shredded and scattered and broken.

From our bird's-eye view in the chopper, I started to see something else: I saw that the truth of what was really happening was the opposite of what I first thought. The good was not broken.

I saw people moving toward one another. Climbing over, walking through, getting across. I saw people finding ways to reach one another, to check on one another, to help one another, to support and at times literally carry one another. I saw people gathered on porches and in driveways. Some of these people no doubt had been neighbors for years. I saw them digging out, lending a hand. I saw them smiling and hugging. Many of them, when they looked up and saw the chopper, waved and smiled as if to convey, *We're fine.*

I watched our National Guard helicopters swoop down and land on islands in the middle of communities that otherwise were almost entirely underwater. But really, everywhere I looked I saw the heroics of first responders, of Coloradans. I saw community. I saw kindness. I saw love.

While we flew over the areas ravaged by the flood, I asked myself the question I'd been asking myself over and over during the last however many months: Why?

I guess everyone has to come up with his or her own sense of it all. But seeing all of this—seeing my own speck of a shadow in it—I've had a couple of takeaways: There really isn't anything at all between us except what we choose to put there. And we are connected to the very best of ourselves, to the very best of what we can and should be, when we are connected to one another.

I see plenty of broken roads and broken bridges but I don't see a single broken spirit.

What I see is the opposite of woe.

What I see is giddy-up.

THERE WERE two hundred lane miles of state highway either completely washed away or damaged. Fifty bridges were gone or rendered structurally unsound. Farmers on the Eastern Plains needed to harvest what was left of the crops or stood to lose that profit. People needed to get to work, perhaps now more than ever. Kids needed to return to school. The sooner the roads and bridges were repaired, the sooner Coloradans could begin getting back to their lives. Winter was looming. Once the snow season started, it would be virtually impossible for the Colorado Department of Transportation to do the work that needed to be done.

The day after the rain stopped, we called a press conference. I gave the director of CDOT, Don Hunt, a near heart attack when I promised the people of Colorado that all of the roads and bridges would be repaired by December 1, 2013. In fairness, I did discuss this with Don beforehand, and while his team's preliminary guess was mid-January 2014, he said they could do what needed to be done. Or at least that's what I heard him say. Our goal was to at least have all roads and bridges temporarily repaired such that they would be safe and serviceable to drive until we repaired all of it better than it was before. Even before we wrapped that press conference, we could hear the scoffs. The sentiment that we'd never get it done was palpable in the air. In many places, not just the asphalt, but whole ledges on the sides of canyons had been completely washed away.

My administration, all senior staff and cabinet members (myself included), made a point of traveling and visiting every one of the communities affected by the flood. We wanted to see and hear what we could do to help. On October 9, 2013, I visited Estes Park around 3:30 p.m. Estes Park sits at the entrance of Rocky Mountain National Park and serves as the gateway into the park. The main economic driver is tourism. Estes had suffered a one-two punch to its economy. There was the flood, and then, on October 1, the federal government closed down Rocky Mountain National.

As you may recall, that's when Congress had been fighting over ways to avert the federal budgetary crisis that was dubbed the "Fiscal Cliff." They couldn't agree on a plan forward, so instead, they closed down the entire federal government. Which meant all federal parks were closed.

Tourists from inside and outside Colorado could not come to Estes to enjoy the famous elk bugling season and the changing leaves in the weeks before the park would close for winter. I met with the mayor of Estes, Bill Pinkham, in the middle of Main Street. As we talked, the store owners were still pushing water out of their storefronts, without any hope of tourists coming back before they closed the park for the winter.

I asked Mayor Pinkham if there was anything we could do to help the struggling town. The mayor said, "Open Rocky Mountain National Park." As we drove back to Denver, I made two calls: one to the White House to David Agnew, the president's director of intergovernmental affairs, and another call to Sally Jewell, the new head at the U.S. Department of the Interior. Both said they needed a little time, but by the time I got to Denver an hour later, while they didn't have the details finished, they said if we'd honor our side of the bargain, they would get the park open.

Traveling with me that day was our deputy chief legal counsel, Stephanie Donner, back from maternity leave. Actually, Stephanie had cut her maternity leave short to assist with my execution-reprieve executive order. I'm not super fond of lawyers. It has always seemed to me they point out a million reasons why you can't get something done, and almost never help you figure out how you *can*. I liked Stephanie because she would cut to the chase and help me figure out how to get it done. I turned to her and said, get it done. Forty-eight hours later we had negotiated and executed an agreement with the Department of the Interior, and before Saturday morning, the park was open. Over the next two weeks the park saw more than ten thousand visitors who entered through Estes.

On November 26, much of our senior team and cabinet traveled to the town of Lyons for a ribbon cutting to celebrate the opening of a roughly fifteen-mile stretch of Colorado 7. It was the last of the twenty-seven state and federal highways damaged or destroyed by the September flood to reopen with temporary repairs. Don Hunt and his team at CDOT were remarkable. Several supervisors, salaried—meaning they did not receive overtime—worked more than ninety hours per week for seven straight weeks. CDOT completed the job five days ahead of our self-imposed December 1 deadline. "I know you heard from people across the country," I said that day. "No one believed this would be open before spring, but people at CDOT said we would."

The Denver Post was on hand that day and talked to a few of the locals. Ron Cheyney, who lived nearby in a cabin just off Colorado 7, told the *Post* that when he heard our December 1 deadline, "I didn't believe them." Mark Milburn and his wife, Sharon, who lived nearby, walked down Colorado 7 that Tuesday morning to reunite with the neighbors down the road. Milburn told the *Post*, "This feels like we are back to civilization." That was the goal.

Fifteen

SLIM CHANCE

One night in the winter of 2014, I was startled from my sleep. I shot up in my bed and listened to make sure I had heard what I thought I had heard. For a few long seconds there was nothing, only the pronounced quiet of the snow falling outside the windows of my home. I lay back down. I figured maybe I was hearing things. Sure enough, there it was again: the doorbell, followed by a pounding on the front door. I looked at the clock on the nightstand: 2:30 a.m. I thought, *What in the hell?* I swung my feet onto the floor.

At that point in 2014, I was well into my the fourth and final year of my first term, and shin-deep into my campaign for a second term. There was no way I wasn't going to run for reelection. I was having the time of my life. Maybe not every minute of every day, but every day I could not wait to get to work. Thing was, it wasn't looking so good for me. My opponent was Bob Beauprez, a former United States congressman who had served in Washington, D.C., from 2003 to 2007. Bob, as he would tell everyone who asked, was a Colorado native who had unsuccessfully run against Bill Ritter in the 2006 gubernatorial race. Bob's campaign made a few mistakes back then. Now he was making far fewer mistakes. Depending on which poll you looked at, either we were neck and neck or he was ahead. Pundits predicted a mean, even sleazy, campaign.

At the time, according to every poll, Americans were unhappy with President Obama. "Obamacare" was polling as a failed-policy dirty word—a political liability for Democrats around the country, including Colorado, where we'd created our Colorado Health Insurance Marketplace to implement it, and where experts were predicting a Republican landslide. Pollsters were saying it could go either way for me.

As I got out of bed, shuffled my way across the wooden floors, and headed downstairs, I heard a third round of doorbell-ringing-banging. I reached the front door and peered through the frosted-glass window. It was one of the plainclothes Colorado state troopers assigned to my security detail.

In the wake of Tom's assassination, the security detail remained on heightened alert, and I assumed that if a trooper was banging on my door in the wee hours of the morning there must be one helluva good reason. Naturally, my mind went to the safety of Helen and Teddy, who was now eleven years old. Since Helen and I separated, we now lived just a block and a half away from each other, and on this night Teddy was with his mother.

"What is it?" I asked the trooper.

"Governor, have you heard or seen anything suspicious around the house tonight?"

I said I had not and asked why. The trooper explained that during a routine nightly patrol of the grounds around my private residence, he had found footprints in the otherwise undisturbed snow. The tracks led from the fence near the alley behind the home to the back door.

The color drained from my face. "Show me," I said.

In the backyard, the trooper traced the footprints that started, just as he said, at the back fence, which separated the yard from the alley. The trooper said it looked as though someone had pushed through the gate and walked to one of the home's two rear doors.

In the glow of the trooper's flashlight, I stood with him in silence for a few moments, looking at the prints. I looked at him, then back to the prints, then back to him again. I was collecting my thoughts. After eighteen years in the tavern business, I'm never too sharp in the morning, let alone in the middle of the night. I knew who had made the prints, but there was no way I was telling anyone, not yet, not even my security detail. And so, I chose my word carefully.

I said the footprints were mine. I said I had walked out to the back gate after dinner to take the trash out to the bin in the alley. It had stopped snowing shortly before dark, as my neighbors were just coming home from work. There were so many prints, not even Sherlock Holmes would have been able to tell who had or hadn't walked that way that night. Indeed some of the footprints were mine, but not all of them. The trooper shrugged acceptance of my explanation and returned to his unmarked car parked in front, and I returned to my bedroom.

As I slid back under the covers, in the tone of a tired, mischievous schoolboy, I told the woman in the bed next to me, "They're on to us."

For a few minutes, I discussed with this lovely lady, who had in the previous months so completely captured my heart, the fact that after I left with the troopers in the morning bound for the state capitol, she would need to be especially careful not to draw attention to herself as she exited the back door and made her way through the rear fence and up the alley to her car. We guarded our privacy for two reasons. One: I had not yet told Teddy that I had begun dating, and two: I was deep into my reelection campaign.

In the words of political consultants, I knew that if my relationship with Robin Pringle was made public, that would likely subject her to political attacks. Me being attacked was one thing; this woman I had come to love was another.

In October 2013, I arrived late to the annual gala at the Denver Museum of Contemporary Art. It had been two long years of the worst droughts, wildfires, floods, and shootings in Colorado history. Not to mention my own marital droughts and wildfires, which had led to Helen's and my separation the year before. My pal Greg Maffei, CEO of Liberty Media, a $45 billion media holding company, had saved me a seat at their company table. It had been a long day. We were just putting together my reelection campaign. I might have been a little glazed as Greg introduced me around the table.

The woman on my right was Robin, his vice president of corporate development, part of the team that identified and then worked to improve the performance of Liberty's acquisitions. We had met several times before, even sat next to each other at a private dinner, but hadn't really noticed each other. She was twenty-some years younger than I was, and maybe I had been unconsciously tuning her out. This night was different.

She made some crack right off the bat, I did a double take, made my own zinger right back, and we were off and running. We talked about everything under the sun, from why Colorado was so special and unique, to how the disruptions of tech were decimating whole careers. She knew all the words of all the old show tunes that my mother had loved so well, and as we dissected the romance of the West, we sang verses of Cole Porter's "Don't Fence Me In" back and forth to each other, laughing as we both tortured the melody. At one point, Greg looked across the table and teased us, saying, "Hello, you know there *are* other people at the table!" Everyone laughed, and we went back into our bubble.

I had to leave right after dinner and I thought that was pretty much that. But I did think about her. She had what we used to call Bette Davis eyes, large and luminous, and she had been wearing a bright pink skirt with a black blouse, loud but elegant. She wasn't exactly my style, but I liked her. And to be fair, despite the ages-old *Esquire* photo spread, I had zero style.

Then she sent me an e-mail the next day, and I responded, and we started a correspondence that picked up right where dinner had ended. She was funny and smart, loved food and people and restaurants. She had curated a galaxy of friends—her own *karass*—that defied easy description. She would hang with gardeners or tycoons, chefs or musicians, bellhops or ballerinas. She had five godchildren with five different old friends, and more in the offing. And she liked politics.

Our schedules were both crazed, she traveled almost every week, and I was in early reelection mode. But we got together for coffee after a bit, then more correspondence, then finally a glass of wine before going to our separate evening engagements. I think we were both kind of hooked on each other, but we didn't really get to dating until into 2014.

We would see each other only once or twice a week, given our schedules, and, again, neither of us wanted to create fodder for political attacks, so we got together privately for the better part of eight months, until after the election in November. Neither of us talked to friends or coworkers. I did tell my security detail shortly after that night of footprints in the snow. It is a unique and wonderful thing to get to know someone without any input from friends or family. All you know is what you hear and see firsthand, and you don't get to bounce your impressions off or practice responses with even your closest friends. My sense was that we got to know each other faster and more deeply than any other relationship in my life.

One of the first times we got together, after it became clear that she was exploring more than just a friendship, I had mentioned one of my all-time favorite movies, Howard Hawks's 1944 classic *To Have and*

Have Not, during the filming of which Humphrey Bogart met and fell in love with the nineteen-year-old and twenty-five-years-younger model Lauren Bacall. I had jokingly called Robin "Slim," as in Bogart's nickname for Bacall in the movie and after, and Robin smiled and said, no, you mean as in Slim Keith, Howard Hawks's wife at the time, a stylish L.A. socialite whom Robin admired. Such an interesting coincidence of random bits of information. Despite their age difference, the marriage between Bacall and Bogart was largely a happy one until Bogie died in 1957.

Anyhow. The campaign heated up all on its own. The congressman—that's what I called Bob Beauprez, because Coloradans had never felt much love toward Washington politicians, especially in the wake of the federal government shutdown—came at me pretty hard for the decision I'd made on the death sentence reprieve. He came at me pretty hard, too, on the economy. Generally, near as I could figure, his campaign was predicated in large part on showing how I wasn't a leader. He didn't like that I was so collaborative despite praising my collaborative efforts when I was mayor.

Traveling the state during that fourth year of my first term, I visited all sixty-four counties, just as I'd done the first time, and told people what I thought was the story of our administration:

We'd had more than our fair share of trying times. In the wake of the Waldo Canyon Fire and the Aurora massacre in 2012, most of us probably thought we would never again experience a year like that, but we were wrong. Every season of 2013 presented another unthinkable test. During the spring, Tom Clements was assassinated. Throughout the summer, there was yet another run of wildfires: the Black Forest, Royal Gorge, West Fork, and Red Canyon. In the fall, we got the flood—against the backdrop of the politicians in D.C. who couldn't get along well enough to keep the federal government's doors open. In the winter, another shooting. A student at Arapahoe High School in Centennial fatally shot a seventeen-year-old classmate, Claire Davis.

I talked about how, although Colorado had been burned, flooded, and once again endured senseless, inexplicable violence, we did not let that define us. That was not our story. Our story, what we showed the world, was that Colorado does not shut down. Colorado does not quit. Colorado does not break.

What we showed the world was that Colorado is the opposite of woe. Colorado is where we come together and giddy-up. On the campaign trail, we met folks out there who were still grieving, still recovering. We talked with people still feeling the impact of the national economy's downturns. But I asked them to consider our record and judge for themselves.

Colorado's unemployment rate had not gone up. It had gone down—to the lowest levels since 2008. The year 2014 was our fourth consecutive year of economic growth. I cited a study from the University of Colorado's Leeds School of Business that showed that Colorado could expect robust job growth in virtually every sector of the economy in 2014. I touted the fact that Colorado was ranked among the top five states in the entire country for business, careers, and job growth; that four of the top ten (and five of the top twenty) communities in the country for start-ups were right here in Colorado: Boulder, Fort Collins, Denver, Colorado Springs, and Grand Junction. We were also one of the very best environments in the country for small business. According to the Kauffman Foundation, which knows a thing or two about small businesses, when it comes to creating a small-business climate, in 2014, Colorado earned a grade of "A." That's up from a "B+" in 2012.

Colorado hosted a record number of tourists in 2014. We gratefully welcomed even more hunters than in the previous year. Agriculture was employing 173,000 people and in the previous year had contributed $41 billion to the state economy.

On the campaign trail, I would say things like, "In Colorado, we work for our luck." I would submit for the voters' consideration that while the public sector is not a job creator, it does have an obligation to help promote private-sector growth. That had been our priority since day one. In fact, one of the first things I did when elected to office three years before was launch a strategy to be a thoughtful and supportive partner with the business community. We reached out and built relationships with people in fourteen regions from around the state, and based on what we heard, we designed a Colorado Blueprint that focused on six core objectives: build a business-friendly environment; increase access to capital; educate and train the workforce of tomorrow; retain and recruit companies; cultivate innovation and technology; and create a stronger Colorado brand.

I wasn't so naive as to think that there weren't Coloradans out there who rolled their eyes when we launched the Pedal the Plains cycling tour to promote all of the beauty and opportunity of some of Colorado's most gorgeous rural communities. But, hey, while we were out there doing the pedaling thing, we got to talking with Darrell Hanavan, of the Colorado Wheat Growers Association. Darrell told us that two of the nation's leading flour milling companies—ConAgra Mills and Horizon Milling—were forming a joint venture, Ardent Mills. They were six months into a search for a new headquarters, and Colorado hadn't made the final cut.

Darrell wanted to try a Hail Mary: he requested that I call the executives of this new company. In roughly a month, Darrell and his team helped us persuade Ardent Mills to locate its headquarters here in Colorado. We pointed out that Colorado is a place defined more by its future than by its past, which was clearly also the case with Ardent Mills. In 2016, Colorado celebrated our Broncos' winning the Super Bowl; for our rural communities, landing Ardent Mills, a billion-dollar headquarters, was a Super Bowl–caliber victory, or maybe a Flour Bowl victory. It all began with the Colorado Blueprint relationships we forged across the state, and then we pedaled closer to success on our bikes out on the plains.

The thing we talked most about on the campaign trail—meaning, we didn't shut up about it—was the fact that in 2010, when it came to job growth, this state was ranked fortieth in the nation. Now, four years later, in that same ranking, Colorado was ranked fourth-best job growth state. Over and over again I would say, "We went from fortieth to fourth."

Since January 2010, we had added 170,000 jobs. In the wake of the gun legislation, we lost a gun manufacturer, but three Fortune 500 companies moved to Colorado, along with twenty-six other companies. I'd point out during the campaign that the unemployment rate in Colorado had dropped from 9 percent in 2010 to 6.5 percent, which outpaced the national rate. Unemployment in the rural towns, such as Grand Junction, lagged behind urban employment rates but was improving.

My pitch for reelection was that we had more left to do. The unemployment rate was still not low enough. We wanted to do more to help facilitate job growth throughout the state.

Of course, I told my story. After all, my story was still the only one I had. I talked about my life in beer and politics, my unconventional path to running for office. Starting as a rock-head geologist. Getting laid off . . . well, at this point, you know the rest.

Moving forward, I said, I wanted to do more to improve our infrastructure. In the wake of the floods, we proved our ability and commitment to rebuild bridges and roads. We've seen what can happen when we lose that infrastructure.

We wanted to do more to support and improve education.

Regardless of what part of the state I was in, I would almost always talk about Colorado's oil and gas industry. I'd point out that it contributes $29 billion to our economy. But mindful of Teddy Roosevelt, I'd also point out that it is critical that industry operators recognize their moral and legal obligation to protect our air and water. We'd had some luck with that, brokered the nation's strongest fracking fluid disclosure rule, and shortly thereafter implemented the nation's first-ever methane capture rule, making Colorado the leader in the nation in controlling these emissions.

And regardless of where we were campaigning, I'd talk about water. Roughly 80 percent of the state's water supply falls west of the Continental Divide, in the Western Slope, rural communities where about 20 percent of the state's population resides. Yet the majority of water consumption occurs east of the Divide, in the Front Range urban areas, home to about 80 percent of the state's residents. Every conversation about water begins with conservation. But that's not enough. For decades, Western Slope and Front Range communities had been at odds over water usage and tunnel diversions and the like. For the first time ever, our administration was in the midst of brokering a comprehensive statewide water plan, in which all of the stakeholders were collaborating and agreeing to a unified strategy to move forward. Constituencies that once had been arguing in courts were now talking with one another and working together. Together was the only way forward.

And then there were the guns. My opponent liked to get on me about the guns, too. We were out to take everyone's guns. Nonsense. When you look at the massacres at Columbine High School and the Aurora movie theater, and at other shooting tragedies, guns are only a piece of the puzzle.

It was clear we had to focus on mental health: trying to identify and assist those who are feeling isolated, bullied, and the mentally ill in general and, trite as this may sound, to give attention to those who are feeling abandoned and unloved. Already we had invested more than $34 million to create and bolster programs such as school-based mental health services, and behavioral health community centers, and round-the-clock mental health crisis centers.

Bob talked about maybe trying to undo Amendment 64. Bad idea. We had implemented the voters' wishes on marijuana. We were committed to making sure that children and parents understood brain development and the risks of underage use. We were committed to securing safe neighboorhoods and diminishing the number and influence of drug dealers in them. It has been one of the great social experiments of this century, and while not all of us chose it, being first meant we all shared a responsibility to do it properly.

During that campaign, we knew that regardless of political leanings, the typical American, and the average Coloradan, doesn't think much of politics or politicians. Shutdowns. Debt ceiling duels. Parties locked down, unwilling to compromise. Who could blame the voters? There was so much negativity.

The public sees politicians as operators who put their own self-interest or their party's agenda above the people; who are obsessed with petty pursuits and who ignore the public service part of being a public servant. The widely held perception today is that politicians divide and selfishly scheme in the moment, whereas public servants unite and plan for the greater good.

As far as I was concerned, whether we live in a mountain community or in a city, whether we are surrounded by cows or concrete, we all want the same things: the chance to earn a good wage, give our children a decent education, enjoy clean air and clean water. Vigorous debate is our ally. Partisanship is not. Skepticism is productive. Corrosive cynicism is not.

Election night, November 3, 2014, was a nail-biter. That night, our campaign holed up in a few rooms at the newly renovated Union Station in LoDo. When I first moved to town in summer 1981—heck, even when we opened the Wynkoop in October 1988—Union Station was a massive run-down station without much of anything coming or going. Now it was a magnificent hub, home to a fantastic hotel, bars, restaurants, coffee shops, a breakfast place, a burger joint. It had it all. It was in a LoDo that had it all. And it connected to world-class rail lines, just a short walk from Mile High Stadium and Coors Field.

As the numbers came in, it was closer. But our agile pollster Chris Keating kept reminding us that our strongholds in Denver and Boulder had not yet reported. Our campaign manager, Brad Komar, a twenty-seven-year-old wunderkind, was calm and confident. Although he was insanely young, Brad had been working on campaigns since he was a kid. He started in 2007 as a field organizer for Hillary Clinton's first presidential run when he was barely twenty. By 2012, after a couple more campaigns, he ran a congressional campaign in Pennsylvania and lost. In February 2013, he ran the lieutenant governor campaign for Ralph Northam in Virginia and won.

I say this with love and as a guy who himself has spent a life dressing terribly: Brad's sense of style is somewhere between a depressed insurance salesman and a depressed insurance salesman. Interestingly, he is about as risk averse as a depressed insurance salesman, too. But that's what makes him so darn good. Brad is all about the numbers. As he sat in our hotel room that night with his laptop in hand, based on his read of where the votes had come from and where they still would come from, Brad—as well as Chris Keating—sometime around 9:30 p.m. predicted we would win, still without the media calling the election. When the sun came up, however, we had won, 49.1 percent to 46.2 percent.

As I finish this story of my life in beer and politics, I'm barely into my second term, but we've staked out the next three years. We're moving Colorado from being the thinnest state to being the healthiest state—healthy in every sense of the word.

We want every Colorado resident to be within a ten-minute walk of a green space. We are expanding biking by providing safe routes to schools all across the state, and expanding and conneting both biking and hiking trails statewide.

We've begun an ambitious effort around experiential learning, whereby kids spend some portion of each week working at local businesses. We have partnered with the Markle Foundation and LinkedIn to create a platform where students can, if they choose, build an online résumé that registers every badge or certificate the student receives, whether from a community college, a workforce training center, or a private employer.

We are going to push ourselves even further to reduce red tape, expand access to capital for entrepreneurs, and continue to make Colorado the most pro-business state, but also the one with the highest environmental and ethical standards. We already have over a hundred cyber-security companies in Colorado, and intend to establish a national center for cyber intelligence in Colorado Springs. We will reduce teenage pregnancy by 60 percent from the 2009 levels. And that's just for starters.

And just as I'm barely into my second term, I'm only a few weeks into my marriage to Slim. Robin and I were married on January 16, 2016. In case any of you were wondering, no, Robin was not pregnant. Our wedding ceremony was in a small Denver church; we were surrounded by a close group of friends and loved ones—our new, shared *karass*.

We were especially grateful that Helen was among those who joined us on that day. And Teddy, thirteen years old, dressed in his jacket and tie, my son poised to be a man, who was and always will be my best man, did one of the readings. My heart swelled as I watched him walk to the podium near the altar, clear his throat, and read from the First Letter to the Corinthians:

Love is patient; love is kind; love is not envious or boastful or arrogant or rude. It does not insist on its own way; it is not irritable or resentful; it does not rejoice in wrongdoing, but rejoices in the truth. It bears all things, believes all things, hopes all things, endures all things.

Love never ends. But as for prophecies, they will come to an end; as for tongues, they will cease; as for knowledge, it will come to an end. For we know only in part, and we prophesy only in part; but when the complete comes, the partial will come to an end. When I was a child, I spoke like a child, I thought like a child, I reasoned like a child; when I became an adult, I put an end to childish ways. For now we see in a mirror, dimly, but then we will see face to face. Now, I know only in part; then I will know fully, even as I have been fully known. And now faith, hope, and love abide, these three; and the greatest of these is love.

That reading could not have been more perfect for that day, and really, as far as I'm concerned, any day. It resonated with me. When I was a child, indeed, I thought like a child. I'd go so far as to say, when I was a young man, too often, I still thought like a child. But in time I put away my childish ways little by little; I suppose if you had to put a date on it, it was the day I held Teddy in my arms for the first time. In short order, I became a father, then a mayor, then a governor. Each one a gift, filled with immense responsibilities, challenges, heartaches, and joys. Each one requiring me to have faith and to hope; each one reminding me that the greatest of these is love. And now I was fortunate to have Robin in my life and a second term as governor and years more to spend with Teddy. While this is where my story thus far ends, it is also where the rest of my life begins. Where we go from here, who knows? You know me, I've got more than a few ideas in my head.

Giddy-up.

ACKNOWLEDGMENTS

Where to start?

I want to thank my wife, Robin, and my son, Teddy, for their genial forbearance in the face of many, many nights, especially these past few months during the crunch, when I would spend so many of my home hours away from them. Teddy, your spirit and love infuses pretty much every page. I know that my long stretches of writing and editing were a sacrifice for you, so I do hope you someday think it was worth it.

And Robin, it would never have happened without you, the true old soul in this family circus. You have been my North Star through the thinking and writing of this from beginning to end, and your enthusiasm for life around you helped make the process more of a joy, less of a hill to be climbed. There is a sweet irony that you helped me write hundreds of pages about the opposite of woe and in the process revealed that it is you yourself; you are the opposite of woe.

My co-conspirator, Max Potter, was masterful in giving me enough rope to hang myself, but loosening the knot just enough for me to inhale sufficient oxygen to continue. The fault for clumsy or inarticulate parts of the book, and there are more than a few, lies directly at my feet. There was a reason I was "called" away from a career in writing. Thank you, Max. And I think if he were writing this he would certainly thank his wife, Lori, who picked up all the considerable slack in the family, as he left her a book widow. For the last seven months, to be sure, she worked full time as a first grade teacher. He would want to at least try to express all the additional things she did that he did not because he was in the "shed" writing. Likewise for his sons, True and Jack. He spent no time with them. No skiing. No hikes. No trips. They would come and visit him in the shed every day after school and were so understanding. Max would want to proclaim to the world how remarkable they are. And indeed they are!

Max would also want to thank Michael Hainey, Kristen O'Neill, Chris Outcalt, Josh Hanfling, and Luc Hatlestad, who read so many drafts and, along with Ellen Golombek, throughout the process kept him relatively sane. Also, Rich Rys, for his eyes on the page. Rick Sapkin: he knows why. Frank Bruni for being such a supportive friend throughout.

My former wife, Helen Thorpe, who is as good a writer as I know (and whose book *Soldier Girls* could be a textbook in narrative), not only indulged my intention to write about parts of our lives that were painful for both of us, she even shared detailed notes she had taken at the time of several events. Thank you.

There is literally no way I would have been able to pull off this book without my literary agent, Larry Weissman, and the team at Penguin. Thank you, Larry. And a big shout-out to my editor, Scott Moyers—you da man(!)—and his team of Christopher Richards, Meghan White, Kate Griggs, Bill Peabody, Nicole LaRoche, Darren Haggar, Juli Kiyan, and Matt Boyd. Thank you for your patience. And, of course, I am grateful to Penguin Press president, the legendary Ann Godoff.

J. R. Moehringer gave invaluable advice and permission to use his pig story. Rick Reilly was on a sailboat in the South Pacific when I caught him on his mobile and he granted permission to use his column. And the Vonnegut estate was instantaneous in letting us use words and phrases that Kurt had shared with me, and what a gift that was.

I owe so much to Roxane White and Alan Salazar and Lindy Eichenbaum Lent, not just for all the help in trying to get the book right, and reading drafts, but for all the help trying to get government right. Roxane especially: we worked as partners for almost a dozen years, and your integrity, humor, and grit infused every day.

Henry Sobanet provided real insight in early drafts, as did Scott Wasserman and Stephanie Donner.

Zoe Knight, our ace library researcher, needs a medal.

I have been blessed as an elected official to have great "wranglers," who have to please as many outside people as possible and at the same time stay on schedule. Tony Young set the bar in our first campaign and through most of my City years, and the sequence of Alexander Price, Will Shafroth, Derrick Dash, and Conor Hall has immersed me in quality.

In a similar way, the Denver Police officers and Colorado State Patrol officers who have been part of my security details these past twelve years each deserve citations for meritorious conduct. I have always loved to drive, and the deprivation of that privilege has made me evolve into a frequent backseat driver, for which I try to apologize constantly. I appreciate all your efforts.

My friend Nick Browning suggested that when a boy loses his father, in many ways he has to learn to raise himself. Fortunately, I had a family and over the years an extended family of friends that helped with much of the heavy lifting.

I would especially want to recognize my sisters, Betsy and Tad, who helped with the book in remembering all manner of family lore and legend, and my brother, Sydney, who read a draft of "the whole damn thing." But especially for all the times they took time out of their lives to help fill mine. And my wonderful stepfather, William Macdonald, who in a just world would have two chapters devoted only to him.

All my cousins, both on the Hickenlooper side but especially on the Morris side, merit their own books. Stewart and Ellenor and Rick and Bunny Alcorn and all their progeny are a vast reservoir of childhood "Johnny Hick" stories. (Luckily, I managed to protect our readers from most of them.) Growing up, the Alcorns, along with the Cantrells, especially Sam and Charlie, would spend one or two weekends a month banging around one another's houses. In so many ways my salvation. The Blackwoods and the Stevensons we saw less frequently but still love dearly. On the Hick side, Skip and Susan Hickenlooper have been a reliable source of old family stories, and Bill and Laurie Hickenlooper helped welcome me to Colorado.

I had wonderful friends growing up, in addition to the Bairds, such as Bobby Littlewood, Bob Latshaw, and Fred Ditmann, to help keep me out of too much trouble. Not to mention all the Rulon-Millers up the hill. John Baird was catcher/friend extraordinaire, and Bruce Conrad, Brock Dethier, and Haig Brown have remained lifetime friends, as have Ben Ginsberg, David Groverman, Tom Bentley, John Horan, Perry Hamilton, and so many others from Haverford.

Bill Burton introduced me to the joys of geology before I could see them, let alone understand them. Wendy Starr, Marcie Henry, Lloyd Komesar, Bill Pearson, Dean Richelin, Debbye Addis, Athan Billias, and Genevieve Kerr were part of the Buoyancy Network in college, not to mention the dogs Kazak and Hilda. Ellen Driscoll, you are as graceful in life as you are in your sculpture, and that is a high standard few can match. Becky Ramsay and her husband, Nick Browning, have been an integral part of the journey for forty some years, as have Tracy Killam and her husband, Michael DiLeo. Tracy, you are one of the most insightful people I have known. Mark Masselli and Jen Alexander, with Tenzin, Maggie, Karma, and Kobi, have been, in various combinations, trusted advisers and allies for those same forty-some years.

Jim Gutmann was not only an extraordinary professor, but also really did teach writing as well as he did mineralogy. Jelle DeBoer, master of techtonics, knew that sending me to Costa Rica to do field geology in the Tilaran mountains would change my life, and he was right. Peter Patton was more than a professor, he was a true friend (and a helluva card player). Tom Metcalf and David Mauldin were masters of their respective crafts, Tom with complex geology and David with oil paint. David, what a field assistant you were in the Beartooths, and what pictures you painted. Tom, that trip to Honduras, with our resident genius Larry Kennedy, the Middletown Tegucigalpa 10-Day Road Race and All-Night Boogie, was once in a lifetime. (Thank goodness.) Fred Snider and Geoff O'Bara were elder statesmen among the grad students.

Colleen Feely, Mark Stevens, and Jody Chapel were an able welcome committee to Colorado, as were Ellen Spangler, Bob and Sue Clough, and Ned and Margot Timble. Lawson and Vandy Stiff, as well as Jack and Cathy Ebel, have covered my back for a long, long time. Judy Goebel was a wonderful friend and ally at Buckhorn, Laura Welch was a true friend when I needed one, and Judith King is a wonderful force of nature to all around her. The late Karen Harris was taken from us way before her time.

Charlie Papazian not only helped create the craft brewing industry, but with Bob Pease and Daniel Bradford, driven by the facilitation and relational skills of New Belgium's Kim Jordan, was able to welcome a merged, single association to support all craft brewers.

Jerry and Martha and Brooke and Casey and Joe Williams left their fingerprints all over the Wynkoop, as did Mark Schiffler, Russ Schehrer, Tom Dargin, and Barbara Macfarlane. Matt McAleer and later Marty Jones created and burnished with me the brand that became Wynkoop. So many customers became friends and then supporters, but all the Hirschfelds, both the Robinson clans, and all the Garts really stand out (especially Sydney!). Lee and Katey Driscoll, Tony and DeLisa Mayer, and Fred Taylor and Claudia Garza all came into my life as a package via my sister in Rhode Island, and interestingly all three fathers of the men played significant roles in mentoring me at one time or another. The late Fred Mayer especially invested a lot of good Silver Oak helping me sort out some complicated situations, and his wife, Jan, was a patient sounding board.

Sam Arnold, Ed Novak, and even Danny Meyer in New York provided models of how restaurants can work best, and each provided valuable advice at opportune times. Danny even agreed to come down to D.C. and spend a morning explaining to thirty of America's governors how customer service is a crucial part of any enterprise. Rich Grant and later Sid Wilson (Teddy's godfather) helped explain to me the basics of public relations with travel writers, a wonderful community. They laid the foundation for how to use communications strategies in campaigns as well as in governing. Kat Jones, of Milkshake Media in Austin, did a "brand evaluation" of me, as if I were a box of breakfast cereal, before I ran for mayor in 2003, and Alexis and often Steve Kaufmann have many times reinforced that early media political training. While a historian and not a media sharpie, Patty Limerick has helped write important speeches and organize complex trains of thought with a clarity and focus that is almost magical.

Joyce Meskis was the best partner and friend a young entrepreneur could have had. Charlie Woolley (and Dana Crawford) shared the vision of using historic buildings to reinvigorate abandoned neighborhoods, and Jack Barton (and Shirley and their late daughter, Leslie) were other early partners and mentors. Scott and Jane Smith, Chuck and Mary Lou Murphy, and Brian and Cathy Magee in Omaha are more of that virtuous circle of great partners who became great friends.

Patty Calhoun, Dick Kreck, Lynn Bartels, Bill Husted, and the late Penny Parker (along with so many others) provided a valuable interface to the two great newspapers Denver enjoyed back then, and that invaluable "round peg," the alternative weekly *Westword*. More recently, Dean Singleton has shared his life and political observations, which have been a significant influence. Greg Moore, the late Donald Seawell, the late Gil Spencer, John Temple, and Vince Carroll have invested their lives with making media the essential partner that good government requires.

Tina Poe, Kate Paul, and Vicki Aybar-Sterling introduced me to the joys of cultural nonprofits, and Denise Montgomery helped sharpen the connection between the arts and business. Lisa Ireland lobbied the "powers that be" to take a chance on me. Lewis and Susan Sharp welcomed me to the Denver Art Museum, and Fred Hamilton made sure I kept my focus. He and his wife, Jane, have been loyal friends, and I have reached out to Fred (and our barber, Jerry Middleton) many times for their wise counsel. Likewise, Jim Kelly and Amie Knox and the Greenbergs, Millers, Stricklands, Barons, and Katiches have been savvy advisers and good friends for some twenty years now. Chris and Sarah Hunt as well as Lanny and Sharon Martin moved mountains to create the Clyfford Still Museum. Adam Lerner and Elissa Auther have been great friends even as they breathed life into the Denver Museum of Contemporary Art. Chuck and Becky Morris, as well as Michael Goldberg, Chris Tetzeli, Libby Anschutz Brown, Pat Stryker, Christy and Walter Isenberg, and more recently Ben and Lucy Ana Walton are all enhancing Colorado as a center for music and musicians. Colorado has a number of amazing musicians who have patiently indulged my admiration of their art, including Ryan Tedder, Todd Park Mohr, Isaac Slade, Joe King, Wes Schultz, Jeremiah Fraites, Nathaniel Rateliff, Joe Pope, and Billy Nershi, not to mention bands like Old Crow Medicine Show and the Avett Brothers, who *should* be based in Colorado. On the natural science side, Kirk Johnson (Teddy's other godfather) and Chase DeForest, as well as George and Shandra Sparks, helped build my nonprofit network. Cathy Finlon has integrated her faith in art, history, and scholarships into a remarkable civic record.

Chris Gates and Andrew Hudson and Chris Romer should all share blame for my turn to public service. Chris's father, Governor Roy Romer, was a quiet adviser for all my early political life. Ken Salazar helped me bridge into the world of politics, and with his brothers, especially John, was always ready to help. That first campaign in 2003 was a joy, and Paul Llevine, Lindy Eichenbaum Lent, Sarah Hughes, and all the team left indelible memories of how to change momentum through a good plan and hard work. Adam and Katie Agron (who I claim proudly to have introduced) were friends before, during, and ever after the campaign, as were Ian and Karen Wolfe, who I *should* have introduced.

ACKNOWLEDGMENTS

Mark Udall, Diana Degette, Gary Hart, Tim Wirth, and David Skaggs were all gracious to an outsider who must have at first seemed more than naive. Bill Owens, governor when I first became mayor, showed me the traps and pitfalls of politics despite our differing politics. Bill Ritter, my predecessor as governor, was remarkably candid about the personal toll the office can take, and the differences between city and state politics, always with absolute integrity. Jane Harman gives the best advice, political or otherwise, of anyone.

Few mayors could be as lucky as I was to have followed leaders like Federico Peña and Wellington Webb. Leadership does make a difference, and Michael Hancock, with Janice Sinden, Scott Martinez, and the mayor's team continue that tradition. Elbra Wedgeworth, then City Council president, guided my first years as mayor. Michael Bennet, Cole Finegan, Kelly Brough, Roxane White, and most recently Doug Friednash have been a procession of extraordinary chiefs of staff. John Huggins, who directed our transition, consolidated all the agencies that touched economic development into one office. Lisa Flores and Mike Roque both helped me stay connected to the most challenged communities, while Beth Conover created the City's first sustainability effort, parts of which became a national model. Aurora mayors Ed and Paul Tauer, as well as Steve Hogan, like all the metro mayors, have been great partners. Chris Henderson and David Roberts provided the city private sector expertise.

Norm Brownstein, Larry Mizel, Steve Farber, and Doug Sesserman, among others, helped facilitate my political education in so many ways. Christy Ferer helped expand the territory to New York City. Willy and Sheila Walker introduced me to Washington, D.C., and Ray and Kathy LaHood, along with Shaun and Liza Donovan, helped make government business truly a pleasure. David Agnew, and his successor in the White House, Jerry Abramson, always went above and beyond any possible calls of duty.

One of the challenging aspects of writing this memoir was not being able to include so many of the people who, ironically, have been so important to our success. Among them: Mike Melanson, Ben Davis, Chris Keating, and Laura Warren, who oversaw my first gubernatorial campaign, working without rest or recognition, and to this day provide reliable advice. Juanita Chacon was a godsend as treasurer for both mayoral campaigns, as was Patricia Cortez (whose husband, Manuel Martinez, helped us get our Wynkoop liquor license), treasurer for both campaigns for governor. In the reelection, Pam Alexander generously shared her network and marketing savvy.

In the State Capitol I had the pleasure of working with a number of principled but pragmatic leaders. Speaker of the House Dickey Lee Hullinghorst, just like her immediate predecessors, Frank McNulty and Mark Ferrandino, has deep convictions but is always willing to listen to both sides. Similarly, Senate President Bill Cadman, like his predecessors, Morgan Carroll, Brandon Shaffer, and John Morse, has become a master at balancing the competing desires of a diverse party. Senator Mark Scheffel and Representative Crisanta Duran, the majority leaders in both houses, are no less skilled.

At the State, John Huggins again managed the transition process. In addition to Roxane White, Kevin Patterson, Don Hunt, and Jack Finlaw came with me from the City, providing crucial continuity. Blair Richardson, who volunteered his help both before and after the transition, suggested we work with Geoff Smart in hiring our cabinet and senior staff, which was a gift. He helped attract people like Kristin Russell, our secretary of technology when we first came into office at the State; Suma Nallapati, who took her place when Kristin returned to the private sector after four years; and

ACKNOWLEDGMENTS

Aaron Kennedy, who after creating and running Noodles and Company spent two years as Colorado's first chief marketing officer. I met Ellen Golombek as a flight attendant in 1994, not realizing she would someday be our secretary of labor.

Andrew Freedman, along with Barb Brohl and the rest of their team, orchestrated that collaborative effort that created the nation's first set of regulations for recreational marijuana—no one could have done a better job.

Ken Lund joined us as chief counsel, but in six months was willing to move over and really transform economic development at the State. Jim Crowe and Al Yates have been treasured lunch and dinner companions, sharing their thoughtful interpretations of contemporary politics. Throughout all my public service, Grady Durham, Fred Taylor, Ken Gart, and Gary Ceriani generously have kept watch over my finances.

Many good friends, like Ken Gart (our "bike czar"), Donna Lynne (rec centers), Ryan Hechman (civic leadership), Erik Mitisek (cyber), and Noel Ginsburg (experiential learning), have stepped in to bring private muscle to help expand the public good. Scott and Virginia Reiman, Greg Stevenson, Christine Bennaro, Ray Baker, and David McReynolds are somehow involved in a variety of everything. Mike (and now Michelle) Fries agreed to chair Denver's Biennial of the Americas six years ago, and has pulled together a team, led by Erin Trapp, that is creating an event of genuine hemispheric importance. Ann and Hal Logan (Reach Out and Read) and Gloria and Rick Higgins (Denver Preschool Program) have likewise been significant contributors to the local civic ecosystem.

In terms of generosity and building a great state, Dan Ritchie deserves his own line.

Kent Thiry (DaVita) and Mike Long (Arrow Electronics) agreed to move their global headquarters to Denver, and I cannot overstate the impact that they as individuals and with their leadership teams have on the civic life of the entire state. They join other leaders of large enterprises, such as John Hayes at Ball Corp, David Eves at Xcel Energy, Hikmet Ersek at Western Union, and Leo Kiley while he was at Coors, in demonstrating that good leaders and their successful businesses are generally closely connected to their home community. Many entrepreneurs and executives have become friends through their philanthropic efforts, families such as the Sies, Anschutzes, Morgridges, Ergens, Malones, Schadens, Marsicos, Jornayvazes, Strykers, Waltons, Merages, Martins, and so many others, usually with the expert facilitation provided by Jamie Van Leeuwen and his team at Community Partnerships. Anne Warhover, Linda Childers, Tim Schultz, and others have equally been partners while directing the foundations established by previous generations. A number of out-of-state property owners, notably Louis Bacon and Paul Jones, have worked with the state to make significant contributions to Colorado's open space and the improvement of wildlife habitat.

Greg Maffei, who is drawn to politics as much as he is to business, has been a reliable sounding board, and with his wife, Sharon, has provided much good advice. Peter and Cathy Dea are the best of friends, and along with Roger and Meredith Hutson, Ted Brown, Brad Holly, and Scott Moore have kept me connected to the world of geology. Rick and Shelly Sapkin, Mark Falcone and Ellen Bruss, Michael Bennet and Susan Dagget, Willy Mathews and Laura Barton, John Hereford and Andrea Dukakis, Ken and Deborah Tuchman, Chris Osborne, and John and Maureen Kechriotis are all friends whose loyalty and affection surpass reasonable expectation. Bill Carver has been such a good friend for such a long time, he deserves the last word. Thank you to all.

INDEX

INDEX